Poverty and Problem-Solving under Military Rule:
The Urban Poor in Lima, Peru

T0385980

Latin American Monographs, No. 51
Institute of Latin American Studies
The University of Texas at Austin

Poverty and Problem-Solving under Military Rule

The Urban Poor in Lima, Peru

by Henry A. Dietz

University of Texas Press, Austin

ISBN: 978-1-4773-0766-3
Library of Congress Catalog Card Number 79-620013

Requests for permission to reproduce material from
this work should be sent to:
    Permissions
    University of Texas Press
    P.O. Box 7819
    Austin, Texas 78712
utpress.utexas.edu/index.php/rp-form
First paperback printing, 2014

For Anne
and for my parents

Contents

Tables

Plates

Figures

Map

Chart

Acknowledgements

As innumerable scholars working overseas have discovered, the success or failure of field work frequently depends on the skilled and patient assistance of sympathetic hosts. Professionally, socially, and personally, an investigator from the United States leans on friends and associates heavily—far more, indeed, than he may care to admit. An acknowledgment seems quite inadequate repayment; nevertheless, it is one of a very few ways of publicly expressing appreciation.

During 1970-1971 and again in 1975, the Pontifical Catholic University in Lima and its social science research center, CISEPA, provided me with a base of operations that was consistently supportive and helpful throughout the research. Its then director, Dr. Jorge Capriata, extended himself and his Center in every way, as did Dr. Rolando Ames. My thanks also go to Francisco Codina, Mickey Markquardt, and Pepe Aspiazu at the Centro de Investigaciones Sociales por Muestreo in the Ministry of Work, all of whose assistance helped to create, type, and print the questionnaire. Abe Lowenthal, Richard Dye, and others at the Ford Foundation office in Lima were a constant source of support.

The individuals in Lima who assisted in and facilitated field research include Srta. Olga Paredes and Srta. Consuela Fuertes of the Ministry of Housing's Dirección de Pueblos Jóvenes, both of whom gave inordinate attention and sympathy to the study. Their assistance was fundamental and critical to its success. In the same office, Soc. Crisólogo Padilla and Soc. Oswaldo Rocha, along with Srta. Rosa Bustamante, all gave freely of their time and knowledge. At Acción Comunitaria del Perú, Arq. Ernesto Paredes, Soc. Fernando Llosa, Sra. Alicia de Boluarte, and Srta. Julia Flores all provided time, data and assistance, as did Soc. Jaime Gianella and Soc. Gustavo Riofrio of DESCO. Soc. Orlando Llontop, a friend and *hermano* of some ten years, gave endless friendship and advice, as did all of the members of the family of don Federico and doña Enriqueta Sánchez G. Others who provided criticism, support, and suggestions include Scott Palmer, Janet Ballantyne, Steve Stein, Lucho Millones, Julio Cotler,

Marcia Koth de Paredes, and Padre Humberto Cauwe. Many of the interviewers in Lima came from the School of Social Work at the Universidad Ricardo Palma, whose aid was essential in carrying out the data collection. Above all, of course, are the several hundred pobladores who consented to the interview, and the many dozens who became acquaintances and close friends. All showed enormous patience in answering questions and filling in gaps that kept appearing.

On my return to the United States, first to Palo Alto and then to Austin, several people helped in analysis and writing. Sue Hull and then Linda Fields at Stanford helped with both the usual and the bizarre computer problems I encountered; Professor John J. Johnson, Janet Dubbs, and Margaret Herlin graciously provided a setting for work. Richard Fagen can never be repaid for his time, patience, and sheer inability to be satisfied with first and second drafts; his impact on the entire study was extraordinarily beneficial.

In Austin, I have profited from many exchanges with colleagues, primarily Rick Moore; his dogged persistence with computer-related snarls, along with his remarkably thorough involvement in the entire project, have been of enormous assistance. Sam Popkin provided encouragement, perhaps more than he realizes. Support from Bill Glade at the Institute of Latin American Studies, The University of Texas, has been consistent and generous. From the beginning, Wayne Cornelius has been a close friend and constant source of stimulation.

This study has been financed through a Social Science Research Council Foreign Area Fellowship Program grant for 1970-1971, supplemented by funds from the Stanford University Center for Research in International Studies. Later, grants from the Ford-Rockefeller Foundations' Program of Social Science and Legal Research on Population Policy (Grant RF-73070), from the Institute of Latin American Studies and the University Research Institute, both at the University of Texas, and the American Philosophical Society in Philadelphia, all assisted in completing the work. The *Journal of Political and Military Sociology, Social Science Quarterly, Urban Anthropology,* Sage Publications, and the University of Pittsburgh Press have all graciously permitted me to use data or excerpts from previously published material.

An author's family inevitably enters at this point; mine is no exception. Gillian and later Allison both in their own ways provided assistance and relief when life became too tense. Anne's contribution was immense. The field work, the coding of the questionnaires, the writing of the dissertation—indeed, the entire undertaking—would never have gotten off the ground without her support. The project has always been a collaborative effort, and simply would not be here except for her ability to encourage, criticize, and assist in every possible way.

Poverty and Problem-Solving under Military Rule:
The Urban Poor in Lima, Peru

Part I. Urbanization, Participation, and Poverty

1. Participation and Authoritarian Rule: The Urban Poor and the Military in Peru

In virtually all of Latin America, two major tendencies—one demographic, the other political—have come increasingly to the fore since World War II. The first of these, urbanization, has been rapid, large-scale, and unprecedented in its scope and impact; the second, institutionalized military rule, has affected well over half the countries of the region. Neither of these represents an entirely new or unknown phenomenon, of course; Latin America has had a few cities, such as Buenos Aires and Rio de Janeiro, that have been among the world's major metropoli for many decades. Furthermore, the military has been a constant political presence in nearly every Latin American country since the 1820s, when independence swept the region.

Nevertheless, it can be persuasively argued that both phenomena have, during the past two or three decades, taken on fundamentally new aspects. Once considered a region of rural, peasant populations, Latin America has experienced an abrupt decline in rural growth: from 1960 to 1975, the estimated rural population increased by only 14.2 percent. However, the urban (20,000 or more) population increased by 89.4 percent during the same period, and urbanites now outnumber rural dwellers, 190 million to 120 million (Fox, 1975). The reason for such extraordinary growth lies only partly in a decline in the urban mortality rates; the major impetus has clearly come from a redistribution of people through massive rural-urban migration. Most capital cities in Latin America have more than a million people; at least three cities—Buenos Aires, Mexico City, and São Paulo—now exceed 10 million each; and others, such as Bogotá, Caracas, Lima, and Santiago, all have over 2 million. The influx of migrants into capital cities has not only transformed Latin America into an urban region but has also brought millions of poor if not destitute people into cities, thereby creating extraordinary demands on urban services, labor markets, and housing facilities.

These demands are, during the 1970s, being faced increasingly by governments headed by military men. As already noted, military involvement has
been a part of Latin American political life for a hundred and fifty years; what
makes the past fifteen years or so qualitatively different is the way in which the
military has become involved. Horowitz's statement of 1966—that the military
"has enough power to prevent governments unfavorable to itself from exercis-
ing authority, but not enough to rule for any length of time" (Horowitz, 1966:
150)—simply no longer holds true. Brazil since 1964, Peru since 1968, and
Bolivia, Ecuador, Chile, and Argentina for somewhat less time, are (or have recently been) under some form of institutionalized military rule. In every case,
the most important characteristic has been the expressed, conscious determination by the leaders not only to exclude civilian electoral politics but to govern
on a long-term basis. The rationales for such a step vary across regimes, but
most military men apparently believe strongly that they are more capable than
the civilian sector of handling the developmental problems and tasks that confront their nations.

Although the literatures dealing with both of these phenomena—urbanization and military rule—are now impressive, little detailed work exists on the
political repercussions that occur when the two meet head on. Greater numbers of migrants moving into increasingly larger cities signifies that more people than ever may be in a position to confront, as well as to be confronted by,
governments determined to bring about substantial changes in the political
relationships between citizen and state. The ways in which these changes are
being carried out vary greatly, from the repressive Chilean instance, through
the politically and economically conservative Brazilian case, to the reformist,
experimental Peruvian example. But despite innovations designed to restructure citizen-state relationships, all militaries have been forced to grapple with
the fact that the majority of urban dwellers (especially migrants) are poor.
Just how poor urbanites behave politically under military rule, however, and
how they respond to populist authoritarian non-electoral rule, remain unex-
plored questions.

This investigation explores the political relationships between mass (the
urban poor) and elite (the national government) in Peru. It assumes that
actions taken by one affect the other, and thus stresses the reciprocity of
elite-mass interaction. Although the political behavior of the poor and the
government are analytically isolatable, in reality they influence one another
continually, and it is this reality that this study hopes to describe. The study
does not fall within the local community power structure tradition associated
with Hunter (1963), Miller (1968), and many others, since it does not treat the
urban poor in isolation from such larger, macro-social concerns as the

distribution of power in the political system. On the other hand, it does not view the urban poor as a passive receptor of government policies made exclusively by elites who operate free from external pressures. Instead, the poor are here seen not only as vitally affected by the nature and structure of power at the nation-state level but also as capable of influencing policy in both its formative and implemental stages.

The book examines a single country and a single city—Peru and its capital, Lima—and a specific regime as well, the administration of General Juan Velasco Alvarado (1968-1975). And although such limitations may in some ways inhibit wide generalizations, they also present the opportunity for a thorough look at political participation under conditions of populist authoritarian rule. Velasco's regime showed much concern with encouraging and stimulating participation, especially in those sectors it considered to have previously been marginal to the political process, and with incorporating the poor of Peru into a "revolution of full social participation."

Under electoral conditions, the relationships between an individual citizen and his government are frequently mediated by intervening collectivities (parties, bureaucracies, unions, voluntary associations of all sorts) and activities (campaigns, elections, and the like). Given an authoritarian, non-electoral system, however, many such groups and activities disappear, and different rules both define and govern participation (Woy-Hazelton, 1979). Nevertheless, even under authoritarian conditions, citizen and leader alike realize that pressures can still be brought to bear and can still be felt, although *how* these pressures can be created and exercised will differ greatly among regimes (Runciman, 1969: 87-88). Although representation in the Western, electoral sense is absent, conditions that might be viewed as constraints from an electoral perspective can and frequently are turned to advantage under authoritarian conditions. Citizen-state interactions, therefore, must be examined in light of the type of regime that exists and the political context that a particular type of regime creates (McDonough, 1973).

Whatever the regime, citizen-state relationships are seldom direct. Rather, they are virtually always carried out through intermediate organizations such as political parties, neighborhood associations, unions, professional groups or a whole range of special interest groups. In some nations, groups may form at the grass roots level; in others, elites may control both the number of and the membership in these groups. Nevertheless, though specifics differ across regime types, the functions of the groups remain the same: to allow interest articulation and aggregation to take place and to facilitate as well as control demand-making aimed at the political system (see Almond and Powell, 1978: chapters 7 and 8).

Lima's urban poor under any type of regime have a fairly constricted number of such organizations. The majority are neither union members nor factory workers (cf. Inkeles, 1969; Inkeles and Smith, 1974); some are either nominal or enthusiastic political party members, but find such affiliation useless under military rule; and others belong to groups whose functions are purely social or recreational. But all are de facto members of a particular neighborhood, and even though many may not belong to a formal community organization, simply living in a neighborhood gives an individual some vested interest in his surroundings and their potential for improvement. As Hirschman (1970), Orbell and Uno (1972), and Huntington and Nelson (1976: 93-103) point out, a person in a specific setting has three basic options if he is unsatisfied with conditions: he can do nothing, he can complain, or he can leave. Regardless of the alternative, the individual's place of residence will affect his choice among these options.

Thus the specific neighborhood of residence exerts a strong, reciprocal, mediating influence on both Lima's poor and the political system. In the first place, as we shall see subsequently, the local community has a great deal to do with what sorts of problems a poor individual (or family) will confront, the intensity with which a need will be articulated, and the way or ways in which these needs will be presented to the authorities. Idiosyncratic events not only shape a neighborhood's creation and existence but also affect its inhabitants' perceptions and behaviors through a variety of contextual influences (Cornelius, 1975; Prysby, 1975; see also Valkonen, 1969). Secondly, political elites and their bureaucracies may draw distinctions between or among different juridical types of communities, thereby either directly or indirectly influencing an inhabitant's choice among Hirschman's options. For instance, and as discussed in detail in chapters 3 and 4, the Velasco government made certain resources available to the poor in one type of neighborhood but not in another. Those in the former might be therefore more inclined to stay than to move; those in the latter might react in opposite fashion. Thus, as Cornelius (1975) notes, the local community acts as an arena for political learning—and each community will offer a different lesson and experience.

For whatever reasons, therefore (and there are many), the local community becomes a buffer between its inhabitants and the political system, and mediates their interactions. For the individual, his needs and demands, his support for (or opposition to) the system, and his knowledge of politics may all be intimately affected by his local community. For the elites and the national political system in general, their policy preferences, outputs, and overall responsiveness may be colored by the context and structure of the local community.

Rokkan (1970: 23) summarizes the complex processes that produce individual political decisions, and identifies as crucially important "the *roles* the individual has in his life environments, the *collectivities* he identifies with, the *choices open to him* within his *immediate local community* and the choices open to him as a *subject of a national political system*" (emphasis in original).

For this particular study, the roles of the individual are influenced by poverty: the choices available to him within the local community are in turn determined by the community itself, and by constraints established by the national government, which is in its turn bound by external, supranational influences. How the individual, his community, and the national system interact, and the behavior patterns that result from and direct these interactions, constitute the major questions for investigation.[1]

Dependency and Clientelism: Internal and Micro

Before these matters are pursued further, however, an additional, closely related area needs to be introduced. National regime types clearly influence individual citizens, whether rich or poor; likewise, massive urban poverty is apt to provoke some sort of policy response from elites, whether passively by its sheer presence or actively by petitions, demands, or some other technique (Portes, 1975: 110). But it can well be argued that both rapid urban growth and military rule in Peru have been brought about in significant part by prevailing conditions of structural dependency and underdevelopment. The concept of structural dependency emerged as a reaction to the development and modernization literature of the early 1960s (Walton, 1977: chapter 1; Fagen, 1977). The dependency perspective basically claims that development and underdevelopment are inevitably and inextricably part of the same process. As development (sustained, relatively independent economic growth through industrialization and high technology utilization) takes place in one country, the same national and international forces that stimulate this positive growth will also perpetuate inequalities and retard development elsewhere. This development-underdevelopment parallelism maintains itself through external obstacles as well as internal barriers.[2]

Dependency as generally understood refers to a situation in which a country's economy "is conditioned by the development and expansion of another economy to which the former is subjected" (Dos Santos, 1970; cf. Bath and James, 1976: 5). Thus structural, dependent linkages between center (developed) and peripheral (underdeveloped) nations accelerate and sustain conditions of underdevelopment. As Walton (1977) notes, "The underdevelopment, or misdevelopment, of Third World nations is seen as being caused by structural relationships between them and the advanced nations. . . . These center-periphery relationships are characterized in terms of bilateral inequality" (11).

Underdevelopment, which derives from the dependent relationship, manifests itself in capital and material scarcities, in the domination of cities (or, more specifically, a primate city) over the countryside and over national life in general, in the investment of much domestic capital in urban land speculation to avoid chronic inflation, in excessive land subdivision, in inflated land prices, and in passive governmental controls (Portes, 1970: 7-79; Castells, 1977: 39-63; Gilbert and Ward, 1978). Cityward migration takes place in massive volume, in large part because of the concentration of resources in urban areas; however, poverty and restricted resources prevent the migrant poor (or native-born poor, for that matter) from entering the housing or land market. As a result, the effects of cityward migration are structural and collective, and force the poor to take illegal actions (land invasions, squatter settlements) to survive (Portes, 1976: 56; Leeds, 1969; Rodríguez et al., 1973; Guerrero de los Rios and Sánchez León, 1977; Riofrio, 1978).

Peru and Lima are perhaps archetypal for Latin America as a whole. When the Velasco-led coup occurred in 1968, its leaders found themselves heading a nation whose overall socio-economic conditions exemplified late-blooming, dependent, capitalistic underdevelopment. Very rapid urban growth without accompanying industrialization had over time channeled massive numbers of rural-origin poor migrants into the primate metropole of Lima. Peru's economy consisted of a primitive, stagnant, and overpopulated agricultural sector; a manufacturing sector comprising two unequal subsectors: a small, modern urban enclave dependent on high-level, imported, capital-intensive technology and a larger, traditional urban subsector consisting of self-employed individuals and a multitude of small-scale, low-technology artisans; and a burgeoning service sector, again with extraordinarily divergent modern and traditional counterparts, that is, industrial owners or managers and white-collar professionals in contrast to market laborers, unskilled service workers, and street vendors (see Webb, 1975, 1976; Webb and Figueroa, 1975; Quijano, 1970; Santos, 1975, among many). Exports consisted of primary products whose prices were established externally; imports were largely industrial, finished manufactured goods or foodstuffs.

Rural-urban migration, slums, squatter settlements, and the effects of these phenomena on Lima are all discussed in detail in chapters 2, 3, and 4. What is important to understand here is that Peru's underdevelopment influenced virtually every policy move of the government, conditioned the lives of the poor, and shaped the contours of elite-mass relationships.

The study assumed from its inception that the presence of a reformist but still authoritarian military government would affect the political behavior of the poor. As field work and analysis proceeded, however, this assumption, though supported by much evidence, appeared to be too simple. That is, on one level a military regime can negate certain kinds of political activity, and can likewise employ methods (repression, armed force, coercion) unacceptable to most electoral administrations or to their citizenries. The poor, moreover, will react to and at times confront an authoritarian regime in a somewhat different fashion than they will a civilian. Indeed, the poor demonstrate a considerable ability to adapt to authoritarian rule and to extract resources from such a regime. But on another, more abstract level, it became uncertain whether any type of regime (liberal democratic, reformist, regressive military, or whatever) other than a fundamentally revolutionary one could make any significant impact on the structural conditions that have produced Peru's cityward migrations and urban poverty and inequities in the first place (cf. Horowitz and Trimberger, 1976).

The study does not propose policies that might ameliorate basic socioeconomic conditions or causes of dependency. Instead, it agrees with Castells (1977: 43), who argues that,

> from an analytical point of view, the main thing is not the political subordination of the "underdeveloped" countries to the imperialist metropolises (which is no more than the consequence of a structural dependence), but *the expression of this dependence in the internal organization of the societies in question* [emphasis mine].

For example, if Lima represents a primate city whose economy and society are strongly conditioned by underdevelopment, how can or will a military bent on reform react to widespread urban poverty, especially as it becomes manifest in illegal land invasion? What sorts of coping mechanisms can the poor employ under such a regime and such societal constraints? Are there weaknesses peculiar to a reformist military that the poor might exploit? Answering these and similar questions requires concentrating on the political behavior of poor people in conjunction with an authoritarian reformist government, while assuming that this behavior is constantly conditioned by underdevelopment. Underdevelopment therefore acts as a backdrop against which both the poor and the authorities "make choices about their environment *within certain varied yet structurally determined alternatives*" (Walton, 1977: 144, emphasis in original; also Walton, 1979a:163). Although dependency and underdevelopment in general derive from external circumstances, conditions within a nation can parallel external relationships: "The development of the more advantaged sectors of the peripheral society occurs at the expense of the development and well-being of those sectors that are less advantaged" (Fagen, 1977: 9; also Cotler, 1970: 407-412). Thus Peru (peripheral) is related to the industrialized capitalist economies (center) as its own poor are related to its wealthy, as its rural areas are linked to its urban centers, and (most important for the present discussion) as Lima's poor are connected to the city's and nation's elites: inextricably, asymmetrically, and disadvantageously.

Internal conditions that maintain dependency and underdevelopment have not been fully examined. Flynn (1974) makes a helpful suggestion when he notes that the concept of clientelism "can greatly help to understand some of the mechanisms of . . . control which help to maintain dependency" (134). By usually accepted definitions, a clientelist relationship involves two actors of unequal status and power (the patron and the client) who engage in a mutually beneficial, reciprocal, but asymmetric and exploitative relationship (Powell, 1970; Kaufman, 1974; Poitras, 1974; Lemarchand and Legg, 1972). Clientelism generally applies to elite-mass interactions within the boundaries of a country, whether on a national, regional, local, or individual basis (Powell, 1974; Cotler, 1969; Foster, 1965; Whyte and Alberti, 1976; Schmidt, 1977). Therefore, dependency for the purposes of this study will refer to the macro, generally externally-derived structures that promote underdevelopment or dependent development (Cardoso, 1973). Clientelism, in contrast, will refer to parallel domestic power relationships, institutions, and structures that maintain the power asymmetry conducive to underdevelopment.

Both dependency and clientelism vigorously reject the notion that a nation's wealthy and poor are divorced from one another or that they operate in separate, discrete dual economies and socio-political systems (Dos Santos, 1970). On the contrary, both insist that elite and mass are necessarily intertwined. From this perspective, therefore, Lima's poor are an integral part of the city; they are, however, as Janice Perlman (1976) has argued, integrated under conditions that are inequitable and that are disadvantageous to themselves (Perlman, 1976; Weisslitz, 1973: 113-117; Montaño, 1976).

The notions of structural dependency and clientelism are useful concepts for several reasons. In the first place, they offer one way of moving beyond describing the particular characteristics associated with Latin American urbanization into explaining *why* such phenomena exist. Secondly, a dependency perspective demands a holistic, multi-level analysis. It links external and internal actors and structures; it connects rural and urban developments; it requires a historical as opposed to a static interpretation; and it argues convincingly for an inherent reciprocity between elites and masses, politically as well as economically.[3]

But in the case of Peru, dependency has much more than academic utility. Dependency, underdevelopment, and clientelism were thoroughly familiar concepts to the Velasco regime, and its spokesmen and planners incorporated both the language and the perspective of dependency into social as well as economic policies (see Velasco, 1973). Pronouncements of the period often refer to dependency and its consequences; the five-year plan and many working papers and other documents from the Instituto Nacional de Planificación (National Planning Institute) frequently employ dependency analysis when evaluating investment procedures, employment problems, capital formation, and other essential areas. On the other hand, government spokesmen and planners seldom used Marxist analyses based on the mode of production or the inevitability of class conflict (Philip, 1978: 76).

The point is that dependency and clientelism are not introduced here only as fashionable scholarly concerns. The national government of General Velasco used the concepts consistently for policy formulation as well as for rhetorical purposes. Dependent capitalism evolved into far more than an analytic concern; it became a reality to confront and combat. The Velasco regime was thus keenly aware of Peru's external dependency and its internal clientelist structures, and took upon itself the tasks of increasing its independence internationally and of eliminating traditional socio-economic clientelistic inequities internally. For the former, Peru consciously assumed a position of spokesman for Third World, non-aligned nations and pursued economic and diplomatic ties with socialist and communist nations. For the latter, the regime focused almost immediately on "the oligarchy" and undertook redistributive policies such as agrarian reform through land expropriation (with compensation), the creation of new forms of worker participation in ownership and management, and other reforms, all aimed at diminishing internal clientelistic inequalities and underdevelopment. The regime's experimentation with new forms of political participation thereby became an essential part of its program, and citizen-state relationships assumed a high priority throughout the seven years of the regime (Palmer, 1973; Lowenthal, 1975; Woy-Hazelton, 1978, 1979).

Political Participation and Authoritarianism: Citizen, Community, and Nation

Identifying the major actors and levels from which political behavior emerges raises (but does not answer) another key question: What constitutes a political act, and how can politics be best conceived in a context of urban poverty, military rule, and inequitable clientelistic structures? For both elites and masses during the Velasco period, *redistribution* aimed at reducing Peru's extraordinary inequities became a fundamental concern. Thus politics came to deal expressly with the "authoritative allocation of values" (Easton, 1965) and with who got what, when, and how. Values for the poor (although, as we shall see later, not necessarily for the regime) were largely material goods for communal benefit; in Pennock's (1966) terms, they were political goods in that they sought increased security and welfare (422-423). The way(s) in which the social, economic, and political systems and their elites condition the distribution of these goods or values, the extent to which the poor can and do utilize these goods, and the efforts of the poor to increase their availability all constitute politics in its essence.

Political participation in the most general sense refers to attempts by citizens to influence government and its activities or personnel or direction in some fashion (see Verba and Nie, 1972; Huntington and Domínguez, 1975; Huntington and Nelson, 1976; Ozbudun, 1976; Milbrath and Goel, 1977; Booth and Seligson, 1978: Introduction). Within the liberal democratic tradition, participation usually involves affecting "the decisional outcomes of government" or "influencing the selection of governmental personnel and/or the actions they take" (Verba and Nie, 1973: 2). Broadly speaking, most conceptualizations include giving the citizens the opportunity to have some direct or indirect voice in the selection of leaders as well as to influence both the formulation of policy and the distribution of outputs (see Weiner, 1971: 164-165).

Such definitions, however, are not useful in most countries in the world where democracy is not operative, and the Peruvian instance is no exception (Adelman and Morris, 1973: 107-108). The military after 1968 gathered together the reins of power and made macro-level decision-making a closed, internal affair. Power flowed from the top down, and the many experiments in worker participation and self-management were always guided by directives and policies from this power locus (Palmer, 1973; Lowenthal, 1975). Under such conditions, definitions of political participation designed to conform to liberal democratic expectations become irrelevant.

Little (1976), among others, has attempted to overcome such problems by pointing out that participation is, at heart, little more than an associational activity directed at the political system. Participation thus becomes analytically separable from other regime-related characteristics such as the distribution of power, and therefore is not to be equated with control over the rules of the game, or control over the consequences of becoming involved. Rather, participation comes to mean involvement by individuals in collective activities aimed at influencing some function(s) performed by the political system (Little, 1976: 454). From this perspective, political participation undeniably exists under extraordinarily varied regime types, and indeed is almost surely present in all polities. Cross-national differences do not emerge because one regime *permits* participation while another does not. Fundamental systemic characteristics such as the distribution of power or the types of participatory mechanisms and structures can of course drastically alter the frequency with which participation occurs, the effects it has on government, the forms under which it appears, and the decisions as to who has access to politics. But those same systemic characteristics have little effect on whether participation exists or not.[4]

This view of participation re-emphasizes the need to include both the individual and the political system *in relation to one another.* To know only that a citizen is involved—that is, that he is a member of a party, or that he campaigns, or that he takes part in neighborhood affairs—is to know little if anything about the nature of the macro-level political system. For instance, Little (1976) concluded that Soviet citizens "as a whole are involved more frequently and in greater numbers in collective, politically related activities than are the American people" (455). The crucial difference for contrasting the two citizenries lies not in whether participation exists but rather in the characteristics of the systems themselves. Thus individual-level data reporting how people become involved, though important, say nothing about whether such involvement influences who gets what.

In the same fashion, classifying a regime as democratic, authoritarian, or totalitarian, or describing power as centralized or dispersed, says nothing about how citizens actually participate or what participation means *to them.* Knowledge limited either to the individual or to the regime offers little leverage for understanding how citizen involvement occurs or what relevance participation has for both the citizen and the state.[5]

As noted earlier, the local neighborhood acts in a variety of important ways to influence both the poor and the government and the relationships between them (Cornelius, 1975:5-11; Huntington and Nelson, 1976:15). In the first place (and as discussed later in greater detail) the local community serves to differentiate among the poor. For example, the legal distinction drawn in Peru between slums and squatter settlements determines in part what sort of access a neighborhood will have to the national political system and what sorts of resources will be available to it. The slum dweller operates at a significant disadvantage vis-à-vis his squatter counterpart, despite equal poverty or similar objective communal needs. In like manner, but from the opposite end, a squatter may see a certain need as "politicized" (i.e., as ameliorative through political actions), whereas the slum dweller faced with the same need may see no recourse other than his own efforts. Thus, the type of neighborhood, juridically speaking, greatly influences the options available to its inhabitants. Anthony and Elizabeth Leeds (1976) have argued that in order to account for behavioral differences among urban squatters, one must examine the variations in the forms of the political systems that the squatters confront. Their perspective is clearly congenial with the one presented here; the major difference is that the Leedses compare cases based on three different political systems (Brazil, Chile, and Peru), whereas this study is confined to a single country and to one type of regime. The role of the political system for the Leedses is directly analogous to the impact of the local community within the single case of Peru. The political system here is a constant; the community of residence is the variable that affects individual and system, and which in turn is affected by both as well.

The study as a whole therefore extends beyond much of the existing literature in two ways: it explores "the interface between elites and popular groups [and] the manner in which the activity of either segment is structurally constrained by the other" (Walton, 1979a:163), and parallels Cornelius's (1975) contextual, holistic study of how community characteristics influence political activity. Extra-local phenomena, in other words, must frequently be called upon to explain local events. Moreover, as Levine (1979:178) cogently notes, any comprehension of urbanization requires a continuous dialectic between institutional and individual levels of data and analysis.

The study includes many instances of how the type of community, or the history and idiosyncracies of a specific neighborhood, affect the poor and the government. For the moment, it should be remembered that regardless of micro-level community differences, the urban poor have similar sorts of needs, whatever the regime type.[6] Their problems include employment instability, insufficient income, lack of decent housing and services, and structural barriers that block access to channels of mobility and to resources available through political involvement. But although the problems of the urban poor may be similar, the nature of dependent capitalism and underdevelopment makes economic resources (capital, jobs, employment options, socio-economic mobility) extremely scarce. In addition, the means made available to the poor by the political system, as well as the means the poor may themselves create for resolving these problems, vary greatly across neighborhoods as well as across regimes.

In an electoral democracy, the poor (potentially, at least) have strategies open to them—block voting, demonstrations, campaign support (Lipsky, 1968; Piven and Cloward, 1977)—which their counterparts in an authoritarian system either may not have or may feel will entail too great a risk to be employed. During the Velasco years, strategy predicated on electoral politics was clearly inappropriate. In addition, and as discussed in greater detail later, the regime established other constraints. For instance, it showed both its capacity and its willingness to clamp down hard on opposition; it was also careful through its own political structures (see below) to make resources available only if requests were for specified goods and only if these requests were expressed and articulated in certain ways and through designated channels.

Communal Needs and Political Behavior

Most of the stimuli that provoke the urban poor to political action in any system flow from the conditions of poverty and the consequences of being poor. Housing (inadequate, unavailable, too expensive, inappropriate), basic utilities (non-working, too expensive), social benefits (too bureaucratic, unavailable, degrading), employment (poor wages, seasonal, not enough openings), education (lack of opportunity to remain in or return to school), income (not enough, sporadic), and politics (too distant, too complex, unresponsive) are, as noted earlier, problem areas common to the urban poor everywhere. Any one or a combination of these factors can provoke political action by the poor, ranging from a visit to some agency or city hall all the way to city-wide rioting. The urban poor, in other words, have basic, fundamental needs, and the great majority of these are material or service-related. The variables include the intensity with which a need is felt, the priority ranking of needs, the likelihood that an objective need will be transformed into political action (will, in other words, become a "politicized" need), and the form that political action will take.

This study focuses on the attempts by the urban poor to obtain *communal* or public goods through primarily (though not exclusively) *non-disruptive* means. A poor citizen can obviously have a purely individual need: he may need a meal, or a job, or clothing, or any number of such goods. Such needs, though absolutely essential, are nevertheless individual in nature. In contrast, communal needs are those that, if supplied, would clearly benefit not only the individual but his neighbors as well. Such needs include basic amenities (potable water, electricity, sewerage), infrastructure (schools, markets, streets and sidewalks), services (police and fire protection, mail service, health facilities), regularization of land tenure, and the like.[7]

On the other hand, the study pays less attention to actions by the poor to protest systemic problems such as inflation or unemployment. Although these problems of course vitally affect the urban poor, who may complain bitterly over them and may even mount a protest or threat in some fashion (e.g., bread riots), such problems are not communal since they exist independent of local neighborhood conditions. And although communal and systemic problems may both exist because of underdevelopment, the urban poor at times seem not to blame the international or even the national economic systems per se, or the unequal distribution of resources, for local neighborhood needs (Portes, 1971, 1972).

A variety of conditions influence the means by which communal problems are articulated and the forms that political activity take. One variable that distinguishes among these means and forms is the presence of demonstrative protest strategies. Protest as a political tool exists within virtually any regime; Peru has had perhaps more than its share under civilian and military rule alike. Indeed, Payne (1967) characterized violence as an integral part of Peruvian democracy, especially for settling labor disputes. Mass-based urban (and rural) violence has occurred frequently since 1968 as well, both in Lima and elsewhere, generally as strikes or demonstrations in reaction to economic conditions (inflation, low wages, devaluation, price hikes). Most political activity by the urban poor aimed at neighborhood improvement is, however, not demonstrative or illegal.[8]

Although protests on a large scale were certainly not unknown during the Velasco years, only a few were caused directly by neighborhood frustrations. Thus the bulk of this study deals with non-disruptive, peaceful (if not mildly demonstrative) political behavior. The urban poor in Lima recognize that the government has a virtual monopoly on force; they also know that the government controls valuable resources such as legal recognition, land titles, and technical aid. Additionally, the squatters especially find themselves in a position where involvement in disruptive activities may contain more risk than benefit. Hence, political actions undertaken to ameliorate communal problems generally consist of nondisruptive, conventional activities such as collaborative community efforts, neighborhood organizational involvement, and petitioning directed at government bureaucracies.

Political Participation: A Contextual Definition

Political participation was defined earlier as involvement by individuals in collective activities aimed at influencing some function(s) performed by the political system. Now that a more explicit context has been supplied, however, this definition needs some modification and narrowing. Political participation for the urban poor of post-1968 Lima consisted of individual or collective efforts to supply neighborhoods with public goods, sometimes but not always through attempts to obtain a favorable distribution of governmental resources. Note that this definition is distinctly instrumental; it is neither just ceremonial nor just supportive, and it explicitly includes (but is not limited to) the notion of placing a demand or request at appropriate access points to the

political system. This definition implies that political involvement most frequently arises because of a desire to obtain an objective need. In other words,
psychological values, attitudes, and pre-dispositions toward participation,
though doubtless important in motivating involvement, may not be the prin-
ciple cause of involvement (Leeds and Leeds, 1976:200, 234). Of course, not
all individuals will become equally involved in politics because of common
needs or because of residence in the same community, nor will participation
take the same form for all those who do become active. Rather, political involvement as defined here will presumably take place when the poor perceive
that rational expenditures of time, money, energy, and other such resources
have a reasonable chance of being rewarded by a return of desired benefits
(Portes, 1972:273).[9]

At first glance, this definition has little distinctive about it. The Leedses
(1976), for instance, identify "political" as ". . . any action . . . by an actor
to maneuver public or private bodies which is aimed at extracting goods and
services from a given system by other than . . . money" (194; Cornelius, 1975:
74-75). And in a study done in the United States, Orbell and Uno (1972) describe participation as an "individual's response to a need he experiences in his
(neighborhood) environment . . . and as directed toward some agency, usually
governmental, that has the power to do something about it" (476). Clearly,
these two definitions and the one employed here have much in common.

The major theoretical distinction lies in the idea that political participation
relevant to communal problem-solving can include activities that are not directed toward external governmental actors or resources (see Booth and Seligson, 1978, 1979). In other words, intra-neighborhood actions employing
purely local resources (money, labor, or whatever) can be political if they involve the resolution of communal problems.

Methodology and Timing

Although this study stresses the reciprocal aspects of elite-mass interactions,
its basic perspective and bias assumes the point of view of the poor. Rather
than being concerned with elite selection, elite decision-making processes, or
elite reactions to the poor, I wanted to explore the ways in which the poor
perceived, coped, behaved, and survived under authoritarian rule. Peru under
Velasco was especially appropriate; by the time of initial field work (1970-
1971), the Revolutionary Government had started to define and to implement
its major policies, although major participatory structures such as SINAMOS
(see chapter 8) were still nascent. Their absence in 1970-1971 allowed me to

see how the poor either were able to or were forced to make do prior to any significant governmental planning and restructuring. Political interactions under these circumstances were presumably reduced to essentials.

When I returned in 1975 for follow-up research, SINAMOS was in full bloom. Although time exigencies forbade replication of the survey, I still obtained a detailed account of how SINAMOS and other such structural innovations had or had not altered the previous stituation.

The survey data used throughout the study are original and were collected in 1970 and 1971 (see Appendix A for a full account, and Appendix B for the formal questionnaire). The questionnaire itself and the research as a whole were developed in conjunction with Wayne Cornelius's study in Mexico City (Cornelius, 1975) while we were at Stanford together. Some five squatter-inhabited *pueblos jóvenes*[10] were selected purposively so as to include wide variation along several important dimensions (see chapter 2 and Appendix A); later, a central slum neighborhood was also included. Approximately 100 male heads of household were selected randomly and interviewed, for a total N of 522.

All of the quantitative data have been buttressed with a wide variety of ethnographic information. I spent many hours in each of the areas, attending meetings, fund-raising projects, fiestas, and other such activities. Trying to pin down the history of each settlement involved more hours of informal discussions with long-term residents and leaders. Despite the impression that I would hear a different story each time I asked a person about his neighborhood, I believe that I was able to put down as detailed an account as could be written. In addition, people who became especially close friends willingly spent much time telling me their own stories. All of this information of course added immeasurably to the empirical data generated by the survey.

I also came to know a number of lower-level employees (architects, engineers, social workers, and urban planners) in relevant governmental agencies. Through them I could obtain a perspective on the government's views of urban problems, and also had access to files, archives, records of meetings, and other documents. Although I met a fair number of higher-placed bureaucrats and agency directors, my interactions with the personnel who were responsible for putting policy into practice on a day-to-day basis were far more useful than formal discussions with ministry and agency leaders. Combining information on the individual poor as well as the structures that affect him will thus avoid some of the shortcomings Eckstein (1976) attributes to studies that do not take into account both aspects of poverty.

From all these various data emerged the present book. The following chapters present a brief discussion of the Velasco regime and its emphasis on redistribution and mobilization, the settings for the urban poor in Lima, and a description of the specific research communities. Part II then traces the movement of the rural poor to the city, offers an overall profile of the poor in their communities, and presents a detailed empirical analysis of the different types of political participation that develop among the poor. Part III examines the nature of elite-mass political interaction, first in the early days of Velasco and then during the years when the regime was most intensively involved in control and mobilization.

2. The Velasco Administration

When General Juan Velasco Alvarado assumed office as President in 1968, Peru as a nation faced a variety of serious, seemingly intractable problems. The man he overthrew, Fernando Belaúnde Terry, had been elected in 1963 with considerable optimism but had proven to be a visionary rather than a pragmatist, and an inept administrator as well. His efforts at agrarian reform had been mild at best, and had been diluted through congressional majority opposition; his tendencies to spend large amounts of capital on non-essential projects produced inflation and, in 1967, devaluation; and his handling of the 1965 guerrilla uprising in Ayacucho allowed the military to gain confidence in itself and to lose patience with civilian political processes and politicians.[1]

This last point deserves some further discussion. Belaúnde's Acción Popular (Popular Action) party operated as a distinct minority in Congress, despite an alliance with the Christian Democrats. APRA (Alianza Popular Revolucionaria Americana, or Popular American Revolutionary Alliance) and Unión Nacional Odriista (UNO, or National Union of Odría) members controlled a clear majority. Belaúnde's effort at reforms often paralleled APRA's own goals; however, APRA's unwillingness to allow Belaúnde to take credit kept legislation bottled up or watered down. Compromises and stalemates became, over the years, increasingly irritating to the military, who had become more and more reformist (as discussed below) and saw electoral politics as hopelessly inefficient and corrupt.

Belaúnde's frustrations and the opposition's intransigence kept many of Peru's most pressing, fundamental problems from being seriously addressed, let alone resolved. Throughout the 1960s, Peru maintained its unenviable record of having one of Latin America's least equitable income distributions. By 1970, with a per capita GNP of $480, the lowest 40 percent of its population received (pre-tax) 7 percent of the income, the next 40 percent received 34 percent, and the top 20 percent gathered in 60 percent (Chenery, 1974: 8-9). Regional imbalances were drastic; income differences between the highest and lowest deciles were 49:1 (Webb, 1972). The heart of Peru's highland Indian population, known collectively as *Mancha India* (including the departments [states] of Apurímac, Ayacucho, Cuzco, Huancavelica, and Puno), continued to contain more than half of Peru's total lowest quartile and only 6 percent of its highest; Greater Lima, in contrast, had less than 4 percent of the lowest quartile, and 54 percent of its highest.

Within Lima, income disparities, though less extreme, were still marked (22: 1 ratio for highest and lowest deciles); "middle-class status" (i.e., ownership of a car for private use [Webb, 1972], applied to perhaps 6 or 7 percent of all of Lima's households. These income inequalities naturally gave rise to extreme differences in expenditure patterns as well as to amounts of money spent. For instance, an upper-income Lima family in the late 1960s spent

TABLE 1

STRUCTURE OF EXPENDITURES BY SOCIAL STRATUM
FOR METROPOLITAN LIMA, 1968-1969

Type of Expense	Pueblos Jóvenes (23.5%)	Low Stratum (40.8%)	Middle Stratum (33.2%)	Upper Stratum (2.5%)	Total
Food and drink	51.7	48.2	33.1	22.2	43.4
Housing and related expenses	24.8	23.3	38.1	47.1	29.5
Clothing	7.4	8.7	7.9	7.7	7.9
All other	16.1	19.8	20.9	23.0	19.2

Source: Figueroa (1974: 36-37).

only 22 percent of its income on food, whereas poor families spent about half (see table 1). But as Figueroa (1974) notes, "in *absolute* terms, a typical upper-class family spent more for just food and drink than a [squatter] family spent *in total*" (38; emphasis included).

Reform, Participation, and the Velasco Regime

On assuming power in 1968, the military made it quite clear to the country that *change*—reform, experiment, innovation— in Peru's social, economic, and political spheres was to be the hallmark of the new administration. Reform piled upon reform; major policies began to affect the agrarian sector, the educational system, the state itself as a guiding force in the economy, the mass media, basic industry and commerce, and relationships between labor and management.[2]

The military's core objectives included the elimination of the old landed national oligarchy and the creation of new economic structures based on state investment and leadership. To these ends, the military called on the poor to become mobilized and to participate in the Revolution. Participation, therefore, is a key for understanding the Velasco period. But as is discussed later, widespread involvement, originally intended to be a means for bringing about an economic changing of the guard, soon became an end in itself.

Perhaps no military government anywhere in Latin America formulated as many potentially sweeping reforms as did the Revolutionary Government of the Armed Forces.[3] From the moment of seizing power, the military leaders not only maintained a strong, continual rhetorical commitment to restructuring what they saw as the corrupt, clientelistic, and elitist way of handling politics through established civilian parties and electoral mechanisms; they also instituted policies in a variety of social and economic settings to implement their goals. The creation of the Industrial Community, with its goal of worker-ownership and management (Pásara et al., 1974); its analogues in the mining, fishing, and communications sectors; the stimulation of agrarian cooperatives and agricultural sector organizations; and the widely discussed and potentially far-reaching Social Property Law of 1974—all of these touched the lives of millions of Peruvian citizens.

Such penetration by the government was intentional. These policies were all aimed at mobilizing as many individuals as possible into these structures, thereby serving (according to the Revolutionary Government) not only to support the Revolution but also to provide opportunities for citizens to influence decisions that affect day-to-day life both at work and at home in one's community. By mid-1976, about 15 percent of Peru's work force (and, including family members, over 20 percent of the country's total population) had been included in one or more local-level participatory structures (Palmer, 1976).

Nor was the military content to create participatory mechanisms and then assume that citizen involvement would inevitably occur. Almost all sectors and classes of Peru became the object of some mobilization campaign or agency, and the masses—the great bulk of both the urban and rural populations —were especially encouraged to become involved in the Revolution, endlessly advertised as "La Revolución es tuya" (The Revolution is yours).

The Revolutionary Government condemned traditional electoral politics for permitting violence to run rampant, especially in the form of riots, strikes, and rural and urban land seizures. The government announced that such violence had no place in the Revolution, and soon demonstrated two ways by which it would be combatted. First, violence was met with force and simply suppressed. But the more important, long-term strategy lay in demonstrating that new structures of participation would make violence unnecessary. By dismissing established parties and practices and by creating new and presumably more logical and efficient means of interest articulation and aggregation, Peruvian society could enter into a new way of handling its internal disputes and contradictions (Woy-Hazelton, 1979).

A Reformist Military

To explain why the Peruvian military during the Velasco era remained so committed to its role of political organizer requires an understanding of the factors that molded the military's views of its duties.[4] Crucial among these were the several influences that brought the Peruvian military to identify national security with national social and economic development.

In the first place, the Center for Higher Military Studies (CAEM), founded in 1951, early on instituted a specialized year-long course for promising career officers emphasizing matters of national social, economic, and political concern, including seminars concerned with dependency and underdevelopment as threats to national security (García, 1974; Villanueva, 1969, 1972). By the early 1960s, CAEM graduates figured disproportionately in promotions to general. The interregnum military government of 1962-1963 clearly emphasized national development matters.

The Civic Action programs of the 1960s, supported largely by the United States, placed many Peruvian officers into day-to-day contact with basic national realities as they worked on literacy, road building, and school construction programs (Valdez Pallete, 1971). Moreover, the successful conclusion of the brief guerrilla war of 1965 increased the military's self-confidence as an institution and made many officers realize that grinding poverty, resource maldistribution, and other inequities could provoke internal war.

These various elements forged among the officer corps, especially in the army, a unity of purpose for the military as an institution and an identification of national security with autonomous internal development. At first the military permitted civilians to carry out these goals. However, when Belaúnde faltered, and when his legitimacy was further eroded by the International Petroleum Company nationalization agreement that favored United States business interests, the military took over, determined to protect national security by stressing national development (Goodman, 1971; Pinelo, 1973).

Because civilian political institutions had demonstrated (at least to the military) their inability to accomplish these goals due to the partisanship, compromise, and delays inevitable in non-consensual electoral politics, the military refused them any role whatever in the new administration (Delgado, 1973). Such disdain for traditional parties and structures as promoters of development and, therefore, of national security, forced the military to consider alternate structures that would somehow avoid those problems associated with established organizations.

The military's identification of development with national security, along with the failure of civilian government to carry out development goals, led the military leaders to conclude that they had to take and retain control of all major social and political processes. Thus the Velasco regime was unwilling to permit any opposition to its control, or any opposition that appeared to threaten the legitimacy of the military as the governing institution. Any challenge to the military from any quarter became, ipso facto, a challenge to national security.

As a result, a set of policies regarding potential challengers emerged, including the downgrading of political parties, the founding of competing unions, and the placing of restrictions on union membership and participation. In addition, the regime attempted to establish its own popular base through government organizations (such as SINAMOS) or "popular organizations" (such as CNA) that it believed, at least initially, it could control more readily.

Identifying national development with national security gave the military its reformist orientation, but simultaneously set clear boundaries within which the reforms were to be achieved (Wilson, 1975). Although the drive for development originally had top priority, the goal of national security later came to limit development in general and participation in particular.

Corporatist Structures and Populist Appeals

The regime's quest for suitable alternatives to the "old style" civilian party politics led to the important innovation of participation based on place of work or place of residence. Cooperatives, industrial communities, and social property structures were designed to augment the chances for workers, individually and collectively, to become involved in decisions affecting daily life and routine on the job (Knight, 1975). In addition, the urban poor—most particularly the squatters—were treated by the Revolutionary Government as an aggregate sector of society, on the basis of residence in officially recognized neighborhoods

These squatter areas received considerable attention in the form of new governmental agencies, large-scale land title distribution, and some (limited) new technical assistance.

This functionally derived, limited system of interest articulation and aggregation gave the Revolutionary Government a decidedly corporatist bent (Cotler, 1975; Palmer, 1971; Almond and Powell, 1978: 378-380; Stepan, 1978; Malloy, 1974). Schmitter's (1974) definition of corporatism has been widely cited:

> Corporatism can be defined as a system of interest representation in which the constituent units are organized into a limited number of singular, compulsory, non-competitive, hierarchically-ordered and functionally pre-determined categories, certified and licensed (if not created) by the State and granted a deliberate representational monopoly with the respective categories in exchange for observing certain governmentally imposed controls on their selection of leaders and articulation of demands and supports. [94; see Stepan, 1978: 46; O'Donnell, 1977: 49; and Collier and Collier, 1977: 493, for other similar definitions]

Corporatism is thus one type of authoritarianism (Linz, 1970, 1975). And although a typology of authoritarian regimes can be quite complex (Linz, 1975), each type is generally characterized by its efforts to limit political pluralism. Some regimes may simply forbid any but approved political organizations or interest groups; others may permit restricted pluralism. Whatever the case, a major function of limited pluralism may be to reduce or at least to control the levels of popular mobilization and demand-making present in a society (Linz, 1975: 179-180). Such controls can, in general, be implanted in two inter-related ways: one, by creating vertical, multi-tier structures to incorporate citizens along functionally specific lines (as Schmitter notes), and two, by creating large bureaucracies to manage the demands emanating from the new structures. These two remove the regime and its leaders a further step from the citizenry. Both strategies—new participatory structures and new bureaucratic agencies—were tried by the Revolutionary Government; both produced a number of presumably unforeseen problems. By shutting down traditional political organizations and replacing them with alternative mechanisms that had exclusive access to limited, valued resources, the regime hoped to direct demand-making activities. However, the regime also made itself responsible for answering these demands, and simultaneously left itself open to criticism if they were not answered. Those individuals with loyalties to the older institutions played upon the regime's failures, and individuals who placed their faith in the new structures often experienced frustration or resentment when expectations went unmet. In addition, limiting citizen involvement to "approved" organizations could easily overload the system's capacity to respond effectively. Thus, although corporatist strategies had a clear and understandable appeal to the Peruvian military—after all, corporatism does have an apparently logical and efficient sheen—the potential backlashes that failures produced quickly became apparent.

Paralleling these developments, President Velasco and several of his ministers made concerted efforts to become populist figures. Since voting and other electoral means of support had been abandoned, the regime's leaders necessarily turned to rhetoric, personal acts, and policy moves designed to win support from the poor, both rural and urban. General Armando Artola, who as a Minister of Interior (1968-1971) was perhaps the most outspoken and at times unpredictable of these spokesmen, frequently visited Lima's squatter settlements to distribute food, drive a bulldozer, or simply make an appearance. And following the Pamplona land invasion in 1971 (see chapter 7), President Velasco and his wife made numerous unannounced stops in Villa el Salvador, where the government had relocated the invaders. Reciprocally, many squatter settlements sent large, conspicuous delegations to rallies sponsored by the government. But as with corporatist structures, populist appeals can provoke negative as well as positive reactions, especially when promises and rhetoric are not matched by performance.

That the Velasco government paid particular attention to the urban poor, and especially to the squatter areas of Lima, should occasion little surprise. Every regime since World War II (and some earlier; see Stein, 1980) has reacted to the squatter phenomenon in some fashion (Collier, 1975), generally in search of support, electoral or otherwise. Since the Revolutionary Government strongly wished to establish its identity and legitimacy, and since it dismissed existing parties or other mechnaisms in this effort, it had little choice but to appeal to the masses for support.[5]

These appeals were not unique in urban Latin America; Perón's relations with the working classes and poor of Buenos Aires (Kirkpatrick, 1971; Wellhofer, 1974; Smith, 1972), Rojas Pinilla's attraction to the poor of Bogotá (Schoultz, 1972), and Asaad Bucarám's charisma among the poor of Guayaquil (Moore, 1977) come to mind. Yet in Lima, no similar sort of citywide support for a particular politician, president, or military man had ever emerged before. Some observers report that Manuel Odría (president/dictator, 1948-1956) enjoyed considerable popularity among the poor (Bourricaud, 1964). Although this may have been true, Powell's (1969) exhaustive treatment of district-level aggregate voting data argues that Lima's squatters did not vote as a block.

Velasco thus faced no entrenched party opposition in the squatter areas, but he also found no precedent for the poor to act collectively for any national leader. Therefore, although necessity dictated that Velasco look to the squatters, no prior historical experience indicated that he could find easily aroused support in his quest for populist legitimacy.

Centralization and National Control

As noted earlier, the Revolutionary Government's commitment to political organization stemmed in large measure from its identification of national development with national security. This identification implied that all initiatives had to be scrutinized and controlled from the center. Despite its claims of being "a social democracy of full participation," the Revolutionary Government's moves to encourage mobilization and political involvement were all created and directed from above. The government's leaders assumed (consciously or not) that they knew best the country's needs and how to attain them. Such an assumption implied that the poor had to be told what they needed and then also told how they could satisfy these needs. The various sectors of Peru's society and economy learned what was going to be done only as the policies were announced and implemented. Public debate was allowed or encouraged only rarely, and, when it did occur, it was more formalistic than functional (Lowenthal, 1975: 11). Therefore, the regime frequently failed to solicit the needs and desires of the poor, instead assuming that the goals they ascribed to the poor were in fact the most salient needs of the poor. This tendency produced much trouble for both the poor and the government.

The insistence on controlling participatory initiatives and decision-making from the center only exacerbated what for Peru has been a fact of life for centuries: the overwhelming importance of the national political system over regional and local affairs. Although it might be argued that local-level officials and bureaucracies were more attuned to the poor and their needs, all national governments have virtually excluded municipal and district governments from any significant roles.

Such national-level hegemony is nothing new; throughout the colonial and independence periods, and to the present time, power in Peru has always been centralized. Very little authority has been delegated, whether by the Spanish crown, the viceroy, military leaders, or civilian politicians. As a rule, civilian regimes disperse power more than do military, primarily through the legislature. But local government—on state, province, or district level—has traditionally been weak under any regime. Moreover, local officials have been elected on a nationwide basis in Peru only twice (1963 and 1966) since World War I; any concept of home rule has scarcely taken hold.

Lima's overwhelming primacy, discussed in detail in chapter 3, and its multi-faceted presence as national capital, largest city, and political-administrative center mean that its problems have inevitably been seen as, and treated as, national problems. Many administrations have concentrated on Lima, often to the exclusion of the rest of Peru, and have as a byproduct intensified the influence of national over local government.

This centralization of power and resources increased after 1968 in many ways, despite official disclaimers (Wilson, 1975). Local officials throughout the country were appointed, up to and including the mayor of Lima; all law-making and policy-formulating capacities reposed in the executive branch under the president; and all participatory organizational innovations came from this central authority, with little or no public debate or input. State agencies, whether the various ministries, public utilities, or other bureaucracies, exerted a virtual monopoly over resources and juridical powers that were highly valued by the poor. These controls included not only regularization, the distribution of land titles, and the installation of basic community infrastructure but also the means through which these resources could be obtained.

The Regime and the Poor

Now that some of the major characteristics of the urban poor, their places of residence, and the character of the national government have been sketched, it is proper to suggest some of the difficulties the poor and the government found when interacting or confronting one another. By denying the legitimacy of civilian parties and all national-level electoral procedures, the Revolutionary Government faced the dilemma of establishing legitimacy for itself and of first defining and then encouraging support.[6] Its basic strategy of fomenting local-level participation while maintaining central control only exemplified the critical contradictions inherent in this approach. Furthermore, convincing the poor of its good intentions quickly led to expectations by the poor that material assistance and support would be forthcoming. As economic conditions became stagnant and then deteriorated in the mid-1970s, expectations went unmet and frustration and cynicism flourished.

For the poor, authoritarian rule meant that electoral techniques to extract aid became inoperative, and other ways of approaching the system had to be found. The poor, though frequently adept at meeting this challenge, did find it much more difficult—indeed, virtually impossible—to avoid the government's penetration into daily life and community affairs and to maintain any autonomy by which they could pressure the regime (Leeds and Leeds, 1970; Leeds,

1973; Cotler, 1970: 435; Hammergren, 1977: 457). Perhaps the most important problem for the poor emerged from their expectation that political involvement in the new structures promoted by the government would produce material payoffs.

Under the Velasco regime, elites and mass had fundamentally different perceptions as to what political participation was, what its purposes were, and why an individual should have become involved. As Horowitz (1970) succinctly put it, "Masses desire what individuals desire: socio-economic *satisfaction*, not political *mobilization*" (23; emphasis in original). Participation for the poor as an end in itself is useless; it must be a means to a material, beneficial end. If the political system or the intervening bureaucracies cannot produce, the discontent can produce an extremely severe backlash.

Conclusion

The study fills a gap that Schmitter identified in 1971, namely, that many of the studies in Latin America that deal with the military have "focused exclusively on the *causes* of military intervention . . . and have neglected almost entirely its *consequences*" (Schmitter, 1971: 427; also Nordlinger, 1977: chapter 4). For the Velasco period, the most important point is not how the military took over but what they did after they gained power.

To examine the Peruvian military as governors, therefore, the study looks at the relationships between the urban poor and a military regime bent on reform. It identifies the particular characteristics of Lima's poor, the differences between slum dwellers and squatters, inter-community variations and their effect on their inhabitants, and the ways in which the poor become involved. It also looks at the Velasco regime in its formative and its fully developed stages, and analyses what problems and shortcomings made governmental policies err or become counterproductive. In so doing, the study illuminates the day-to-day problems of the poor and the pitfalls inherent in a corporatist political system.

But the study also asks (indirectly as well as directly) some hard questions about the potential for basic change when a country such as Peru is caught in the web of underdevelopment and dependency. The participatory reforms of the Velasco period went well beyond those of any other regime Peru (or most any other country) has ever had. Still, it is proper to ask whether these reforms altered in any significant way the facts of life that produced distorted urban growth in Lima, or whether they gave the urban poor any political independence to govern or to improve their lives. And even if *individual* improvements (material or otherwise) did occur, these cannot be equated with macro-level *structural* improvements such as decreased rural-urban migration, a lessening of political clientelism and internal dependency, or a stronger, more independent national economy. It may be that for the poor and the state alike, solving problems was beyond reach; coping was all that could be expected. Whether that was enough, either economically, politically, or even morally, remains very much open to question.

3. Urbanization, the Urban Poor, and Poor Neighborhoods

Latin America today possesses the fastest population growth rate of any region in the world. In addition, Latin America is even more rapidly becoming an urbanized population. Although the area has long contained a few very large cities, only in the last three decades has urbanization become a truly overwhelming phenomenon.

Peru and Lima are no exception. In 1941, Lima had scarcely half a million people; by 1978 it contained well over 4.5 million. And such growth is not only extraordinarily rapid; it is unprecedented as well throughout its four centuries as a colonial and national capital.

For the first three hundred and fifty years of its life (1535-1885), Lima grew slowly, and for extended periods of time assumed an almost steady state finally reaching 100,000 about 1876 and a quarter of a million during the second administration of August Leguía (1919-1930). Certain national as well as international events gave Lima a strong push. Leguía instituted heavy programs of public works both in Lima and elsewhere; he expanded the provincial road network and linked hitherto unconnected penetration roads with highways bound for Lima; and he broke Lima's old traditional boundaries by building major intra-city axes that opened much previously unurbanized agricultural land for development and speculation. The world-wide economic crisis in 1929 brought hardships to rural Peru, where raw commodities faced an uncertain international market. Many provincial inhabitants and their families chose, or were forced, to move cityward and start again. World War II, with its demands for raw materials and its spread of industrialization and technology, produced changes in public health; Peru's and Lima's infant mortality rate and life expectancy dropped and rose respectively in a short period of time. By 1945, Lima had about 600,-000 people and was about to receive a provincial inundation that has yet to diminish in any serious way (Bromley and Barbegelata, 1945).

Primacy

Perhaps the first impression one receives in observing the relationship between Lima and (as Peruvians, and especially native Limeños, are apt to put it) *lo demás*–"the rest" of the country–is how closely Lima typifies the venerable image of primacy as "the head of Goliath on the body of a dwarf." Virtually all aspects of Lima, and all statistics dealing with its effect on the hinterland, support this notion. Peru's second city, Arequipa, has a 10:1 population ratio behind Lima, and Trujillo, as number three, has a 14:1 ratio. In 1940, Lima was the only city in Peru with more than 100,000 inhabitants, and not until the 1972 census did another Peruvian city surpass 250,000–at which time Lima had reached nearly 3.5 million.

Lima's political, economic, and administrative primacy, however, exceeds its mere demographic importance. Politically, for example, its electoral weight during times of electoral government is clear: it contains between a third and a half of Peru's total eligible voters. Economically, Lima produces three-fifths of Peru's industrial output and four-fifths of its consumer goods, holds over half of the labor force employed in commerce and two-thirds of that in industry, and accounts for over 95 percent of all financial transactions and associated activities–and this with about one-quarter of the country's population (Robin et al., 1972; Delgado, 1971). Administratively, Lima is far more than simply the national capital; it is headquarters for virtually all government activity and decision-making, and is the seat of a highly centralized national governmental apparatus. Various administrations have attempted to decentralize government power and authority, as well as to stimulate industrial investment outside of Greater Lima, but without notable success. President Fernando Belaúnde Terry (1963-1968) initiated local elections throughout Peru for the first time since 1919, but the military takeover in 1968 ended that experiment, and local officials are once again appointed in Lima by the national government.

Primacy, therefore, has at least two aspects. One is demographic, and concerns Lima's size relative to the rest of the country; the other involves delegated and absorbed power in social, political, and economic spheres. These aspects, of course, become mutually reinforcing. Lima would not attract as many migrants as it does if it were not the national capital, the center of all activity, and a magnet for people seeking greater opportunities or an escape from rural drudgery. Although Lima's primacy has historical antecedents, its dramatic population growth since World War II deserves closer examination.

Urban Expansion and Migration Since 1940

From 1940 to 1961, Lima grew from 600,000 to almost 1.8 million (Cole,

1957). And of that increase, well over 50 percent was due to in-migration of people to the city. The 1961-1972 intercensal figures are of the same magnitude, although more pronounced; the 1.8 million became 3.3 million inhabitants in only eleven years. Projections for 1990 indicate 6.7 million inhabitants, indicating that the 1960s annual growth rate of 6 percent and more will decline to about 4 percent. As a recent study concludes,

> . . . the rapidly increasing levels of Peruvian urbanization are strongly supported by migrations from the countryside to the urban centers. The net effect of the interplay between births, deaths, and immigration in the 1940-61 period found 18 persons joining the rural sector for every 19 new persons in the urban group. During the most recent intercensal period (1961-72) the balance has shifted much further; for every 10 new rural inhabitants the urban sector gained 27. . . . Lima alone absorbed 42 percent of the total national population during the 1961-1972 interval. . . . (Lima-Callao) shows a 5.7 percent rate of increase (for the same interval), one which is very high considering the absolute number of urban residents needed to maintain the pace of growth. [Fox, 1972: 17, 27]

Spatially, this growth has occurred in several phases. Until the end of the 1940s, the city developed within a triangular area bounded by Central Lima, Chorrillos, and Callao. But in the 1950-1955 period, these boundaries were broken as large areas along the northern bank of the Rímac River were settled. This expansion, followed by major extensions further north, then east (along the central highway leading inland), and finally south, in effect ruptured the traditional urban shell. Such expansion meant a very rapid growth in the physical space that Lima occupies. In 1952, Lima had an area of 21.3 square miles; this grew by 1959 to 32.7, and by 1967 to 55.7 (Austin and Lewis, 1970: 9-11).

Settlement of the new areas has proceeded in two fundamentally different ways (Deler, 1975; Henry, 1976). The first has been the "classic" growth by private-sector investors who, seldom restrained by the state, open previously barren or cultivated lands for construction of single-family housing or low-rise apartments aimed at middle- and upper-class buyers. For years, speculators have laid out tracts with streets, sidewalks, public lighting, and water/sewerage facilities, waiting for buyers to appear. For the most part, supply has exceeded demand.

The second way in which urban space has been conquered involves spontaneous urbanization and self-help construction. This kink of growth has generally occurred on uncultivated, state-owned lands both within and beyond the old city boundaries. Although squatting has been present in Lima for decades and even centuries (Mangin, 1967a), the great majority of Lima's spontaneous

settlements date from the post-World War II period. The earliest of these neighborhoods grew on hillsides and slopes relatively near the downtown area. By
the mid-1950s, however, significant areas on both sides of the Rímac River had
been absorbed, and by the late 1950s and early 1960s, large-scale land invasions
stretched north and then south some ten to twelve miles from the central city.
By 1979, Lima's squatter areas contained well over one and a half million people, and occupied as much territory as did all of Lima in the mid-1950s.

Despite this remarkable geographic expansion, the downtown districts of Lima have also remained densely populated. Until recently, most migrants from
provincial areas first moved into Lima's low-income, rental slums, referred to
generally as "tugurios." Although many of these migrants later moved on to
other housing in a squatter area or elsewhere, many others remain in downtown slum housing. Such dwellings are the only source of affordable rental
housing for low-income individuals and families. These stagnant or deteriorat-
ing districts of Lima, like the squatter areas, probably contain at least one million inhabitants. Taken together, and roughly speaking, well over half of Lima
resides in either the slums or the pueblos jóvenes.

Slums and Squatter Settlement Differences

But what factors distinguish these two types of dwelling environments? The
most obvious, and also the most crucial for understanding participatory differences, is land tenure. Housing in a tugurio is rented, whereas housing in the squa
squatter settlement is individually owned, a distinction with far-reaching consequences. In the first place, the tugurio normally represents a static or decaying
environment. Few owners of slum housing make efforts to improve their properties, since such improvements may bring on an increase in taxes. Moreover,
the demand for low-income housing in Lima is so extreme that a complaining
tenant can be told to leave if he feels conditions are unacceptable. But the
squatter settlement is basically a low-income residential environment in which
individual heads of families do not rent their land or houses. To say, however, that they *own* their land fully and legally is hardly true; often land titles
are provisional or missing altogether, and promised titles have frequently been
delayed interminably. The major point, nevertheless, is that the squatters live
in permanent settlements, where they avoid rental payments and all of the con-
tractural landlord-tenant burdens.

Nevertheless, the two settlement types are linked with one another. All migration studies indicate that people moving from the provinces to Lima do so
in stages *within* the city (see chapter 5). That is, the first residence in Lima is
almost always in a downtown, central city district, either in a rented room or

apartment or with family members or friends. Few migrants move directly to
a squatter settlement. But the tugurio environment plays a most important role
as a staging area for the migrant, since it permits him to pass a period of time
acculturating himself to Lima and finding reasonably steady employment.[1]
Thus the pueblo joven *pobladores* (inhabitants) have frequently spent considerable time in a tugurio as well (see chapter 5).

Despite this linkage, slum-squatter differences are still fundamental. For one
thing, the squatter settlements constitute an officially recognized universe. Governments since the 1940s have made a variety of efforts to control, coopt, and
otherwise manipulate this potentially valuable urban mass, with the overall result
that the squatters occupy a prominent position for any regime or candidate
(Collier, 1976). Therefore, the pueblos jóvenes have also been investigated, studied, censused, listed, and noticed for some decades now. The slums, on the other
hand, have been accorded little attention, for at least two major reasons: they
are not as compelling and they are not illegal.[2] Many have living conditions
far worse than those of the squatter settlements, but only minimal notice has
been paid by any government. Since tugurios are scattered throughout virtually
all of Lima, most action depends either on the landlord or on the local-level
municipality—an arm of Peruvian government notoriously poor in resources.
Only rarely has the national government become involved.[3]

Because of the recognition accorded the squatters, they have developed ties
with the national government that the central city slums lack. Since before the
1960s, some agency of the national government has been continually responsible for coping with the various service-related needs and problems of the pueblos jóvenes (Collier, 1976). In addition, Law No. 13517, passed in 1961, finally
defined a squatter settlement legally, and also produced a list of officially designated settlements (Manaster, 1968). An unrecognized pueblo joven, or one
founded after the passage of the law, was thus immediately at a disadvantage,
and the primary task of any such settlement was to obtain recognition as soon
as possible. The pueblo joven, therefore, develops a series of linkages with the
national government which the tugurio does not.

Another major difference exists: the squatter settlements generally have
some form of local community-wide organization. Although the details of such
associations vary widely from one community to another, the mere existence
of such an organization separates the pueblo joven from the tugurio, where any
sense of community or belongingness is infrequent at best. Most pueblos jóvenes in Lima have rather remarkable histories of self-help projects based on local
intra-community effort, for the most part revolving around the provision of a
material good or service of some sort.

In sum, the pobladores have gained three key advantages over their slum counterparts: (1) a noticeable position in urban society, due primarily to elite desires to gather support from the poor and to defuse any potentially anti-governmental moves; (2) an organizational strength, born at the time of forma-tion of the community, and generally continuing thereafter; and (3), as a result of the first two, bureaucracies set up to cope with the squatter phenomenon and to provide certain welfare benefits from the government. These three assure the pobladores of greater access to politics, in that they have a consid-erably greater probability that their claims will be incorporated as the basis of policy by government decision-makers. They have thus acquired what Scoble (1968) refers to as the "attentive interest" of relevant authorities.

The tugurio inhabitants, on the other hand, though having an approximate-ly equivalent numerical population, have not become as salient a force. The lack of policies directed toward them—that is, the non-decision by elites to ad-dress the slum problem, the inability and lack of opportunity to organize them-selves, and the resultant absence of government resources—has effectively negated most attempts by the urban poor in the slums to gain access to politi-cal goods and services. One goal of the study will be to investigate how these differences are reflected in individual participatory patterns.

Peru's Economy and the Urban Poor

Most observers (and recent policy-makers in Peru as well) have concluded that the squatter neighborhoods constitute a viable solution to the problem of large-scale, low-income urban housing (Mangin, 1967a, and Turner, 1969, among many others). It is therefore profoundly important and paradoxical that the squatter solution is, at heart, illegal. Just why this illegal solution has become so wide-spread and, indeed, so acceptable to Peru's authorities calls for a look at the na-tion's and Lima's economies, at the nature of employment under late-blooming dependent capitalism, and at the inability of both the public and private sectors to provide housing that is congruent with the economic capacities of Lima's poor.

As was suggested in chapter 1, Peru during the 1960s and 1970s was perhaps a classic case of a dependent nation and economy. A wide range of literature offers much analysis and data to support this contention (see inter alia, Wilson, 1975, especially chapter 4; Ballantyne, 1976; Quijano, 1971; Malpica, 1967; Torres, 1974; Espinoza, 1971; Sulmont, 1975; Gilbert and Ward, 1978). Brief-ly, Peru since World War II has developed high-technology manufacturing en-claves for the production of consumer durables and for agricultural and mining exports. However, such developments were, until 1968, very much under the control of foreign corporations and capital. The emergence of these enclaves affected Peru's labor force in a multitude of ways. In the primary, extractive area of the economy, the modern agriculture and mining sectors employed high technologies, with two major consequences: much of the rural labor force necessarily became landless wage labor, while another part (independent small farmers, or *minifundistas*) was forced to furvive through subsistence agriculture. Many rural artisans, displaced *minifundistas*, and *peones* (landless farm workers), however, could not compete with advanced techniques or with capitalist manufactured goods, and were thus unable to maintain a viable position in the rural economy. This situation, compounded by rising rural population pressures and severely limited arable land (about 5 percent of Peru is presently cultivable), led tens of thousands of rural individuals to migrate to urban areas for alternative employment.

As it grew during the 1960s and 1970s, Lima continued to maintain its economic and political (as well as demographic) hegemony, thanks in no small part to this cityward migration. But even though Lima represented the overwhelmingly most important industrial enclave for Peru, the nature of its development prevented the manufacturing sector from absorbing the migration influx, thereby producing a swollen tertiary sector and a large surplus labor pool available for very low salaries.

Webb (1975) divides urban employment into two unequal sectors; the modern (consisting of establishments with five or more employees) and the traditional (small artisans, domestics, self-employed, etc.).[4] By the late 1960s, when the Velasco regime took power, about two thirds of the urban labor force could be classified as traditional (Webb, 1975: 90). In addition, although this sector was growing twice as fast as the modern sector in size, its share of income grew only half as fast as the non-traditional. Therefore, even though Peru enjoyed reasonably steady economic progress overall during the decade 1960-1970, such macro-level improvements did not affect the poor proportionately (Webb, 1975: 91-92; Roberts, 1978, chapter 5; see also Plotnick, 1975: 109-134).

This pattern of development gives impetus to the creation of a center and periphery. Nationally, Lima (with a very few other urban centers) represents the center; the rest of the country is the periphery. Within Greater Lima, however, the pattern repeats. The upper and middle classes, perhaps along with some highly skilled workers, enjoy the outputs of the technologically advanced modern center, while the majority of the labor force constitutes the periphery, related to the center intimately but disadvantageously.

Due to international and national economic structures and processes, therefore, the urban poor of Lima confront a variety of interrelated obstacles. In the first place, their low, frequently erratic wages (or earnings) prevent them from accumulating savings, either of any significant size or on any regular basis. The poor are thereby excluded from bank loans, mortgages, and other formal credit arrangements.[5]

These conditions and consequences of poverty, however, are juxtaposed with another characteristic of capitalism: the existence, recognition, and protection of private property by the values of the populace at large, by the socio-economic system, and by the nation's leaders and their policies. This acceptance obviously affects the structures and functionings of Lima's economy; perhaps nowhere is its impact clearer than in the housing market. One critically important result, Leeds (1969: 53) argues, is that "solutions to housing problems in capitalist societies by private interest and public authority alike are uniformly in terms of the *private* ownership of habitational units." In searching for a solution for a housing deficit, therefore, almost no effort goes into developing communal housing of some sort. Rather, public and private authorities—and their various clienteles—all direct their energies toward the provision of individually and privately owned dwelling units, often of the single-family type. Such thinking receives constant reinforcement from the government, from private builders, from advertising in the mass media, and from other sources, until the individual family head comes to believe that unless he possesses his own house (and lot), he has not provided sufficiently for himself and his family, and that he has, in some vague way, not done his proper share for himself or for his country (Rodríguez, 1973; Guerrero de los Ríos and Sánchez León, 1977).

This attitude produces strong demands throughout society (from the wealthy to the lowest income levels) for individual, private, single-family housing. However, the private sector produces housing only for those who can participate in the usual mortgage payment system—i.e., the middle and upper classes. For the lower classes who are unable to enter into contractual relationships with banks or other institutions, the alternatives provided by society are limited and, generally speaking, either unattractive or beyond reach, or both. Low-cost rental housing lacks the desired sense of independence; condominium arrangements are largely unavailable or unknown; and most private builders, able to do well financially in the middle and upper classes, decline to provide low-income housing, even if long-term, low-interest mortgaging were available. Some Some members of the working classes, especially union members, affiliate with credit unions, savings and loan associations, and cooperatives of one sort or another; however, many others lack access to such mechanisms.

As for the public sector, all governments since World War II have publicly worried about the housing deficit in Lima, and the military that assumed power in 1968 is no exception. It has paid some attention to the needs for housing; the creation of an autonomous Ministry of Housing indicates a bureaucratic gesture in this direction. However, much of the money actually spent for public housing went into projects that are simply beyond the reach of the urban poor. An early 1970s housing project known as Túpac Amaru advertised *casas de interés social* (literally, "social interest houses"), and although this project may indeed have supplied much needed housing, the financing required that the prospective buyer pay 10 percent down (cash), with monthly payments of roughly US $50 to $75. At the time, the official minimum wage was US $1.50 daily—or about $50.00 a month. Obviously, most of the urban poor could view such requirements only with despair or disbelief.

Both the public and the private sectors have appeared unwilling or unable to supply low-income housing. Therefore, as an analysis of real estate in Lima concluded,

> . . . the [squatter settlements are] the only habitational solutions that urban development in a capitalistic free enterprise system offers to low income groups, and . . . if the characteristics of . . . [Lima's] want ad offers are maintained, an increasingly expanding sector of the society will be affected. [Rodríguez, 1973: 16]

For these reasons and for others to be discussed throughout, Lima has become a city in which the squatter settlement has taken firm root and flourished.

Squatter Settlement Heterogeneity

For anyone interested in the urban poor of Lima, the slums as well as the squatter settlements demand investigation. However, attention quite naturally goes first toward the pueblos jóvenes: they constitute the most visible and intriguing physical manifestation of Lima's growth. At the outset, these settlements appear as largely homogeneous poor neighborhoods. Anyone viewing the pueblos jóvenes for the first time is struck with a welter of mixed impressions: unpaved streets and sidewalks lined with partially completed houses made from brick, wood, straw matting, and other materials; multitudes of small children; if a weekday, a notable absence of men, and, if a weekend, a considerable number of men and women involved in construction work on their houses; a large number of small general stores, cottage industries, and houses offering services of various sorts—sewing, barbering, shoe repair, and the like; an absence of automobile traffic and of noise in general, countered by the presence of a bus line that during the late afternoon rush hour is crowded far beyond capacity; and (for the most part) a lack of one or more basic urban services in most areas—water, electricity, and sewerage.

If the visitor persists in efforts to become acquainted with these areas, and makes trips to a number of settlements, these first impressions will be simultaneously reinforced and modified. The classification *pueblo joven* covers a universe of at least three hundred discrete settlements that differ greatly among themselves. Houses vary from the crudest, flimsiest shelters to substantial, three-story brick and mortar dwellings with considerable financial investment behind them. Some settlements contain only a few score families, while others have upwards of a hundred thousand people; some appear to be little more than a scattering of shacks across desert valley floors and hillsides, whereas others are near the center of Lima and are solid residential districts of the city. The pobladores themselves range across almost every racial and color line: white, black, Indian, and every combination of these three (and others) live in the communities.

In recent years some observers have claimed that any attempt to generalize about the pueblos jóvenes of Lima is a risky as well as a fruitless task, since the differences among settlements are so profound (Leeds, 1969). These differences include size and age; location within the metropolitan area of Greater Lima in relation to the downtown; specific geographic characteristics—hilly, flat, irregular, and so forth; the type of construction, especially in terms of individual dwellings—i.e., the degree to which permanent materials have been used; the manner of formation of the settlement—whether through invasion, accretion, governmental cooperation, or some combination of these; and the particular idiosyncratic events that have had important effects on the development of each of the communities across time.

This partial listing of differences suggests that selecting a few settlements to represent all of Lima's pueblos jóvenes becomes difficult and often frustrating. In the first place, with the normal exigencies that time and money impose, one individual cannot realistically hope to know any more than a handful of communities, except on the most superficial level. To depend on the observations of assistants (except in limited ways) in selecting sites is also unsatisfactory, since initial investigatory trips may be essential in gaining access to a community.

Typologies exist that use a variety of relevant factors; however, these typologies do not include many political aspects of the squatter phenomenon (Delgado, 1971). That is, questions such as how the communities vary as political entities, and how their political interactions and relationships with various governmental authorities and institutions have developed, are not party of any typology. The problem thus becomes one of first identifying those factors of crucial *political* importance.

Land tenure, and the community's legal position, constitute one possibility. For example, what politically relevant differences would emerge through a comparison of two communities that differ in terms of land tenure? Would an individual's psychological commitment to his community heighten or decrease when land tenure became a fact of life? Would demand-making activities by the community increase or decrease?

Another factor concerns the manner in which the settlement was originally created. A settlement founded through massive, well-organized invasion might, all other things being equal, have higher levels of community interaction and trust among its inhabitants than would a settlement founded through accretion or through some form of government collaboration. But the invasion-founded settlement might also undergo a precipitous decline in neighborhood activities once it established itself. Furthermore, the age of a settlement might be important, in that a community twenty-five years old might simply not have the enthusiasm that a recently-founded settlement would possess.

The three fundamental variables utilized for selecting the research communities are: (1) the *age* of the site; (2) the *manner of formation* of the community; and (3) what can best be labelled the *overall developmental level* of the community.[6] This last variable is made up of four sub-variables: (a) the materials used in the construction of the individual dwelling units; (b) the overall population density of the settlement; (c) the type of terrain on which the settlement is located; and (d) the internal cohesion of the community. This last (d) in turn includes such factors as the level or intensity of conflict within the community, the efficacy of the local association, and the success of community-wide activities. The overall developmental level constitutes a "softer" factor than the others and requires much personal observation.

Comparing the Research Communities

Each of the three units that are the keys to understanding political involvement—the individual, his immediate neighborhood, and the national political system—creates different problems for analysis. Since the study treats only one regime in a single country, problems associated with linguistic equivalence and with a whole range of variations and controls found in cross-national studies are irrelevant.

However, choosing individuals and (especially) communities for comparative purposes becomes much more complex. Both minimizing (i.e., controlling) and maximizing differences within these two analytic levels requires the application of distinct techniques on both levels. For the individual, standardized survey data, complemented with heavy participant observational, informant, archival, and other ethnographic information, provide the fullest and most practical ways for gathering reliable data about a large group of people.

The community, on the other hand, presents more serious methodological problems. Obtaining a sufficient number of individuals through administering a survey is relatively simple. But the range of variables that distinguish among poor urban neighborhoods—either slums or squatter settlements—is very large, and the entire universe of squatter settlements in Lima is around three hundred. As a result, "We have more variables than cases. . . . Multivariate statistical analysis is out of the question, since the number of cases is so small. This problem is endemic in comparative analysis" (Smelser, 1973: 77). Moreover, realistically speaking, an N of 300 does not really exist. Each community selected must be studied as an entity in itself in order to identify historical and structural idiosyncracies that influence both its inhabitants and external authorities. Such knowledge requires hundreds of hours in each neighborhood, thereby limiting any single study to a handful of areas.

Walton's (1973) notion of standardized case comparison helps resolve some of these dilemmas. Defined as collecting original data through standardized and reproducible techniques across cases that are meaningfully comparable, standardized case comparison necessitates selecting cases purposively and in accordance with a predetermined set of relevant independent variables. This procedure makes control over both similarities and differences possible, and permits both the maximization and minimization of differences among comparative groups or entities. Standardized case comparison thus not only permits solid, meaningful selection of communities, but likewise allows limiting the number of communities to only a few.

In this sense, the study takes on an explicit comparative cast, despite its being confined to one sector of one society in one city in one country under one regime. Controlling all of these dimensions leaves room for rigorously examining differences that emerge on other levels.

Conclusion

Lima's poor in general have two basic housing alternatives open to them: they can stay in one of the several types of centrally-located slum rental housing (Hirschman's [1970] "loyalty" option), or they can move into one of the three hundred or so squatter settlements (Hirschman's "exit" option). The majority of Lima's migrants are *not* in the pueblos jóvenes (ONPU, 1968); some districts in Lima (especially Rímac, La Victoria, and Central Lima) contain large percentages of slums, inhabited for the most part by migrants who prefer life in the downtown center of the city. All migrants, in other words, do not become squatters, nor are all squatters migrants. Whether a poor individual will move to a pueblo joven depends on the circumstances the poor must face and the choices they must make.

The discussion has sketched in some structural features that distinguish tugurios and pueblos jóvenes from one another, and has also identified three variables—age, manner of formation, and overall development—that influence the political behavior of their inhabitants. The discussion now turns to a more detailed account of six specific communities, to some of the unique events and circumstances that have shaped each of them, and to how each of them fits into the three-variable classification scheme presented in this chapter.

4. Six Low-Income Neighborhoods

Chapter 2 offered some general statements about low-income housing in Lima and suggested that the two principal neighborhoods that the poor occupy—the tugurio (slum) and the pueblo joven (squatter settlement)—are qualitatively different types of environments. By moving on to describe the half-a-dozen areas selected for intensive study, we can begin to appreciate how idiosyncratic events influence the formation and development of each settlement, and how these events in turn shape the relationships among the poor within a community as well as the political linkages between the community and various levels of government. Moreover, since these six neighborhoods will be continually compared with one another throughout the book, they deserve some detailed discussion.[1]

Primero de Enero. This is the newest of the six, and represents perhaps the classic pueblo joven invasion site. The community started to form during the second half of 1967, when a group of three hundred or so families who lived in an older pueblo joven took two steps toward planning an invasion: they hired some outside assistance, and they gained the support of a local district mayor.

The leaders of the group contracted some help to lay out and plan the invasion site prior to the actual move and to help with the move itself when the time arrived. Great care was taken to follow all of the guidelines of the Junta Nacional de la Vivienda (the JNV, or National Housing Board) for planning the settlement—the size of the lots, the width of the streets, the overall density of the population, sufficient green spaces, and the like were all planned in accordance with JNV specifications. The idea was to present the JNV with a completed plan once the invasion was a *fait accompli* and thereby allow community development (e.g., permanent house construction) to proceed immediately.

The second step was to obtain the support of the local mayor, who declared

METROPOLITAN LIMA:
The Location of the Research Communities

that an adjacent piece of land was district property. The mayor also publicly encouraged the families to move into the area, despite the fact that ownership of the land was extremely dubious at best and consequently became a major difficulty.

A day or two after the initial invasion, the police appeared on the scene. The invaders responded by confronting them with the women and children, and the police withdrew shortly thereafter, with little contact and virtually no violence. The present population level of the community—2,080 families—was attained in a few weeks.

After the initial invasion, the pobladores and the government encountered numerous problems. Foremost among them were a very bitter border argument between the invaders and some adjoining housing cooperatives and the refusal of the JNV to accept the plan the squatters had drawn up, since it had not been officially approved. This refusal meant that the JNV, and later its successor, ONDEPJOV, had to produce a survey and a lot plan for the zone; it also meant, as a consequence, that the pobladores were unable to move ahead with permanent house construction, since the possibility existed that the authorities could annul existing lots and force a relocation, thereby causing a loss of time and money. After countless meetings and on-again/off-again agreements, the pobladores and the government finally reached an accord, and the area was officially resurveyed and lots redistributed some four years after the invasion (for a more detailed account, see chapter 7).

The problems Primero de Enero has faced since its inception have created high levels of stress and resentment for its inhabitants. Over and over people complained that they had been saving money and were eager to improve their houses, only to be held back by the lack of approved lots. One of the original invaders, a man who was instrumental in organizing the invasion and seeing it through, said that he had not undertaken such an effort for nothing:

> I didn't come here to live like this; I came here because we were overcrowded, because I needed more room for my wife and the kids. I've got a good job—have had since 1963—and I've been saving to build a decent home. I was one of the first ones here, but I haven't been able to do one thing. The damned government has created more problems than it ever solved.

In 1975, house construction in brick and mortar was well under way for about half of the families; the community had also constructed two elementary schools, which were staffed by the Ministry of Education, and a post office had been built and was operating. No facilities were available; water still came in tank trucks, sewage and waste matter were still discarded in a large open area,

Plate 1. Primero de Enero. Three years after the invasion, temporary housing was still the rule until final lot adjudication.

Plate 2. Pampa de Arena. Brick housing construction was well under way after 6-8 years of occupancy. Tank trucks still circulated, selling water to each household, since running water was unavailable.

and streets were still rudimentary, although the earlier helter-skelter arrangement of houses had given way to regularized blocks.

SINAMOS promoters contacted Primero de Enero in 1973 and, after several fruitless attempts, forced the community to restructure itself in accordance with its scheme (see chapter 8). SINAMOS promised that land titles would be distributed after such reorganization but failed to follow through. Also, SINA-MOS's attempts to exclude previous community leaders from the new organization were both unpopular and unsuccessful. One ex-president of Primero de Enero, a man outspoken in his dislike for SINAMOS, was continually re-named as a delegate from his block; at community meetings, he repeatedly brought up the matter of titles and of other promises not kept, much to the dislike and irritation of SINAMOS personnel.

Pampa de Arena. In late 1963, a fire destroyed a number of precarious dwellings near Lima's downtown wholesale market, in a district known as Tacora. The fire climaxed a long-run argument between municipal authorities, who wanted the land for a new highway, and the inhabitants, who lived and worked in and around the market. Following the fire, which effectively ended the debate, the mayor of Lima, in collaboration with the JNV, arranged to have the affected families transferred to a desert area near two low-income housing projects.

The fire victims were located on the periphery of these projects, and the resettlement area became known as Pampa de Arena. The Tacora group arrived in 1964; some 350 families established themselves in estera mat huts, and the government promised help with housing, water, and so on. Shortly after the fire, other smaller groups of families also found themselves in Pampa de Arena; these were victims of eviction and relocation projects around the city, and by the end of the first year approximately 525 families had arrived.

For the first year, these families were alone. When the first year had passed, the pobladores celebrated in the usual fashion, with fireworks, flagwaving, and similar noisy activities. This noise, however, signaled to some families in a nearby housing project that a land invasion was underway, and by the end of the day some dozens of families had founded a new settlement that began because a land invasion took place by mistake. These invaders—about seven hundred families within the first week or so—continued to increase "owing [in the words of a JNV memorandum] to the impossibility of controlling the arrival of new invaders." By 1967, almost three thousand families had arrived and had founded five totally new zones in Pampa de Arena.

Others grew in similarly accidental fashion: one zone began when a few dozen families invaded the proposed site of a soccer field. JNV archives contain the following note:

On 3 February 1967 (at night) 15 families invaded part of this zone for the stadium; on the 4th of the month this situation was communicated to Headquarters and the necessary support requested to avoid an increase in this initial number.

On the same date communications were sent through Headquarters of the Housing Board to the Guardia Civil and to the Prefecture of Lima, asking their collaboration and guarantees to protect the zone.

As almost an afterthought to outlining the steps taken "to prevent further invasion," the report concludes: "It is estimated that at present approximately 1,000 families now occupy this zone." This document was written on 14 February 1967, some six weeks after the first fifteen families had arrived. The one thousand families now constitute the largest zone in all of Pampa de Arena. Needless to add, the stadium never materialized.

Pampa de Arena continued to grow; more groups arrived through invasion, eminent domain relocations, and other similar transferrals, until by 1970 close to thirty thousand people lived in the area, in some sixteen neighborhood zones. But until the late 1960s, these zones were not organized collectively on any area-wide basis. Several tentative attempts in this direction had been made, but none had been able to arouse much support.

In early 1970, the zones in Pampa de Arena differed substantially, and in a variety of ways. The smallest had fewer than eighty families; the largest, nearly fifteen hundred. Some were highly and successfully organized and had well-built community centers and thriving local associations, whereas others showed almost no improvements. And despite intensive efforts by the government to penetrate the community, these inter-zonal differences persisted into the mid-1970s.

Compared with Primero de Enero, some zones show more advanced levels of consolidation; permanent brick and mortar construction exists in about half the houses, and land titles were distributed in 1971-1972. However, the community as a whole still lacks basic infrastructural services. Water is available only from tank trucks or from scattered public standpipes; electricity exists only from illegally tapped nearby power lines or from individual generators; and such things as sewerage facilities, paved streets, sidewalks, and the like are still a long way off. However, community projects have had some notable successes. For instance, transportation or simply access for any vehicle was a problem for all of Pampa de Arena from its foundation; the sand of the desert valley prevented buses from traveling on all but one access road. In 1967, one zone successfully organized itself to provide *ripio* (crushed rock) for the streets. The project received a good deal of assistance from the then Ministry of

Development, which donated two hundred truckloads of fill. Since that time, other zones have likewise laid down a network of "surfaced" roads, thus allowing buses and private cars (not to mention pedestrians) much easier access throughout the community.

All of Pampa de Arena has developed a vigorous commercial life, and the larger zones have considerably varied, complex marketing and small business systems. Businesses such as *bodegas* (general stores selling groceries, household supplies, kerosene, etcetera), bakeries, and small cottage industries and services—tailors, seamstresses, laundresses, and so on—are very common, as are small restaurants and bars. Each zone also has its own sports clubs, mothers' clubs, school associations, and the like.

Moreover, during the late 1960s most of the zones in Pampa de Arena came into contact with a privately funded community development agency called Acción Comunitaria. Acción's basic goal was to organize the community on a block-by-block basis, thereby not only permitting local elections but also laying the groundwork for the formation of community groups such as savings and loan cooperatives.

Acción's success was mixed; it had almost no luck in some areas, due to apathy and suspicion. However, Acción's efforts did well in other zones; one neighborhood's local association had managed to finish a two-story brick community building that was in almost constant use. The work depended directly on the organization of the zone; each block was assigned a Sunday when it was responsible for having its members donate a day's work in digging trenches, laying bricks, or whatever. In like manner, the development of a savings and loan association rested on the block delegates, who had to see to it that the families in their blocks contributed the specified amount (usually S/40 [about $1.00] weekly). The accumulation of these savings was to go toward a loan from one of the large downtown Lima banks for the installation of water and sewerage systems.

In sum, Pampa de Arena represents the early and middle stages of consolidation. It has, as a community, moved beyond Primero de Enero, and its inhabitants now face the long, steady struggle necessary to upgrade themselves, their homes, and their neighborhood. They can, perhaps, take some comfort in seeing how their positions have improved over ten or more years, but they must also realize that they have an immense amount of work to do if they are to resemble the next community described.

Santiago. This represents the ultimate end-point for a squatter-formed neighborhood: in 1973, it was officially declared *not* to be a pueblo joven, and instead became simply another part of the municipal district of Central Lima. It is this progress that made Santiago an especially attractive research community.

Santiago occupies a long, narrow strip of land on the southern bank of the Rímac River. What is now the community was until the 1920s the old bed of the Rímac; however, work under presidents Leguía and Benavides changed the course of the river and narrowed the channel, exposing a considerable part of the old riverbed.

During the 1930s the land belonged to a Ramírez family, who took advantage of the river's deposits of cobbles to operate a quarry. At the end of the Second World War, some of the workers in the quarry, along with others, began to set up house as squatters in the area that today is the first few blocks of Santiago; the irregular manner in which these "blocks" were formed is still evident. At this time, President Benavides claimed the land had passed to the state, and despite protests by the Ramírez family the land fell under the jurisdiction of the district of Central Lima.

The first of a series of local associations formed shortly after the invasion of the land. Since this invasion coincided with General Odría's accession to power in 1948, it was first called the Asociación de Pobladores Manuel A. Odría, but this name was soon changed to Santiago, and one group, the Asociación de Pobladores de Santiago, soon assumed leadership. From all accounts, the Asociación de Pobladores between 1948 and 1956 was instrumental in maintaining order and regularity in the zone. Those individuals who came after the initial invasion were directed to the Asociación, which controlled the available land and sold the right to occupy a lot (although this was in no way legal, nor did it constitute title to the land). One old-time resident related that he paid S/5,000 to the Asociación in 1947, plus another S/1,000 for membership in the group (over $300). Others, however, were sometimes able to occupy a lot clandestinely and avoid such payments.

The Asociación de Pobladores undertook in the 1950s the installation of water and electricity in the community. These efforts were at least partially successful. But under President Prado's administration, the Asociación became, according to several accounts, less and less responsive to the needs of the community; several tales of funds disappearing and of general mismanagement circulated, and one specific individual was continually reappointed president of the Asociación from 1956 on, thereby increasing discontent among the community.

By 1962, the situation had reached the point where elections had not been held for some years, and a church-affiliated *hermandad* (brotherhood) became the focal point for the emergence of a new organization. The hermandad had broken with the Asociación over a dispute for land for a new church building; since the Asociación had refused to grant permission for a new church to be built, the land was invaded and the church erected under the guidance of the

hermandad and with the assistance of the Misión de Lima. At this time, the
Consejo (spelled with an "s" and not a "c") Local de Santiago, the new organization, took form as a rival to the Asociación, and undertook as its first task
the provision of potable water for the entire community.

The Consejo presented a petition with 3,800 names to the ambassador of
the United States, hoping to obtain funds from the Alliance for Progress. Alliance funds subsequently played a role in the installing of both water and electricity, officially inaugurated on Christmas Day, 1965.

However, the Consejo did not achieve its success without difficulties; the
Asociación opposed the Consejo from the start, labeling it "the enemies of the
people" and referring to it constantly as *el grupito* ("little group"). Any undertaking of the Consejo incurred the animosity of the Asociación; the brouhaha
over paving the streets continued for some years. In one instance, both the Consejo and the Asociación passed flyers throughout Santiago announcing that a
functionary of the Ministry of Housing would be visiting the community to
give out details for the final distribution of land titles. Both organizations
claimed responsibility for sponsoring the ministry representative; on the appointed day, both organizations held simultaneous meetings, with both asserting that
the same person would speak on the same subject, and at the same hour. When
the ministry functionary arrived, he became both highly confused and irritated;
he consequently did not talk about land titles at all, thereby increasing intra-
group hostilities, as well as dissatisfaction with the ministry.

Beginning in 1970, the national government began the distribution of land
titles for Santiago. At the same time, the conflict between the Asociación and
the Consejo became meaningless, since ONDEPJOV implanted a new organizational structure (see the description in chapter 8).

Finally, in 1973, Santiago was officially taken from the list of pueblos jóvenes in Lima. By that time, the community had paved streets and sidewalks
throughout; virtually every house had running water, electricity, and sewerage.
Moreover, Santiago's twelve thousand or so inhabitants enjoy a high level of
community facilities. There are six schools (one secondary), pharmacies, market areas, bakeries, two movie theaters, a Roman Catholic church with a paro-
chial school, an evangelical church, and numerous small shops that sell and repair a variety of goods. A police station now operates, equipped with a patrol
car; mail is delivered house to house. There are open areas for soccer, and a
kindergarten-cum-children's playground.

At the time of field work in 1971, however, the existence of two strong community organizations in open opposition provided a chance to see what effect
such a conflict had on the community as a whole. On the one hand, severe conflict could hinder overall development. On the other, Santiago's successes suggest

that each organization may have felt it necessary to strive for material communal gains for which it could then take credit. The problem of intra-community conflict is treated in a later chapter; meanwhile, Santiago remains the virtual end-point for any pueblo joven—one toward which all may aspire, but which only a minority will probably attain.

28 de Julio. In the early 1940s the then mayor of Lima, Luis Gallo Porras, constructed a new downtown wholesale market that quickly became known in local parlance as La Parada. La Parada always has depended on large numbers of menial laborers, and the unskilled therefore look on the market as a major source of employment. Any large marketing operation also supports and depends on a multitude of secondary industries and businesses: garages, stores, and repair shops provide all variety of merchandise and services. Street vendors and other itinerant entrepreneurs proliferate as well.

La Parada has also created, since its founding, a demand for cheap housing, which in turn has led to squatting and trespassing on nearby land. Since World War II, three hills—San Cosme, Cerro El Pino, and Cerro El Agustino—have been successfully invaded and trespassed on; they were unoccupied and were convenient. 28 de Julio, which has been an official district of the city since 1965, surrounds and covers one of these hills; in 1971, it had fourteen separate communities, located on flat land at the base of the hill and on the hillside itself, and its total population was estimated at a hundred thousand.

The district's major (and only paved) road runs along the northeastern side of the hillside; the flat lands on both sides were haciendas and privately owned until the 1950s. The land was rented to *yanaconas* (tenant farmers), who grew the vegetables and fruit the area produced. The yanaconas paid a rent for a plot of land on which they constructed housing for themselves. But in the early part of the decade, two changes took place: first, the owner lost interest in maintaining the hacienda, and irrigation became more and more irregular; and second, the zone as a whole became increasingly attractive as a housing site for the people who worked in La Parada. Accordingly, the yanaconas paid less attention to cultivation, and began instead to subdivide their plots of land, renting or selling pieces to friends and relatives. A cycle was therefore established: subdivision by the yanaconas, who rented or sold parcels of land to individuals who in turn resubdivided their plots for others. By 1960, the old hacienda lands were entirely converted to housing, and in 1961 Decree Law No. 13517 (the "Law of the Barriadas") declared that 28 de Julio was a *barrio marginal*, thereby absolving the inhabitants of any rent payments.

The physical layout of 28 de Julio, meanwhile, crystallized in a highly irregular and unplanned manner, and the footpaths from the hacienda days now serve as the streets and alleyways for the settlements. A dozen or more

Plate 3. Santiago. Thirty years after its beginning, Santiago lacked only details. Paved streets, sidewalks, electricity, running water, and three-story houses characterize the entire community.

Plate 4. 28 de Julio. Despite thirty years of work, the density of the area's population precluded significant improvement. Its downtown location made people unwilling to move to less crowded but more distant areas.

communities have been created in this fashion along both sides of the main street, including zones A and B of 28 de Julio, which together form the fourth and fifth research communities for the study.

Perhaps the first and most important characteristic of both zones is their population density: approximately 525 people per hectare, or slightly over 200 per acre, inhabit each zone. The average dwelling unit of Zone B is 35 square meters, meaning that each person in the zone has 6 square meters of dwelling space.[2]

The majority of the dwellings have adobe walls; almost none have two stories, making the crowding even more severe. Neither zone ever experienced a large-scale invasion. But the value of the land is evident: one of the leaders of Zone B stated that he had paid US $1,000 for about 200 square meters in 1956 (although legally, of course, the seller had no right to sell and the buyer no title or right to the land he purchased).

Both zones contain a large number of shops, restaurants, bars, and commercial enterprises catering both to the pobladores of the area and to outsiders. Principal among the last are a large number of small garages doing repair work and selling spare parts obtained from dismantling abandoned and stolen automobiles. Many of these establishments were originally located in Tacora; after the fire, they moved into 28 de Julio and now line the first few blocks of the main street. Traffic circulation along this street has improved immensely since a major overhaul in the mid-1960s created a paved highway complete with sidewalks and public illumination. A number of branches of downtown businesses have located here, among them an office of a major Lima bank. However, this street remains the only through main artery of the entire district. Within zones A and B, few of the alleyways permit vehicular traffic other than handcarts, and most of the streets are cul-de-sacs.

The general conditions of crowding and semi-permanent housing provide a rather pessimistic picture; despite intra-community improvements (see below) and a formal classification as a pueblo joven, 28 de Julio in 1971 clearly suffered from built-in blight. Indeed, Delgado (1971) labeled it a *barriada tugurizada*.[3]

Zone A. There were four sections in Zone A in early 1971, with a total of about seven hundred families. These four formed in 1968 in response to overtures by the Ministry of Public Health, which informed the zone that in order to have any chance of receiving governmental assistance, the community would have to establish a viable organization. The four sectors joined together into a Comité 4, which then petitioned the Ministry of Housing and ONDEPJOV for assistance. The government responded with a decree that gave both zones some 55 hectares from an expropriated hacienda nearby.

Comité 4, however, and its backing of government plans—expropriation, re-location, and remodeling—had strong opposition. In the mid-1960s, an organi-zation had appeared with self-appointed leaders. It carried out a census of the zone, charging each family a sum to be included, and then issued identification cards for another sum. It also invited government officials—ministry personnel, senators, deputies, etcetera—to speak to the community, thus giving itself a cer-tain aire of legitimacy. But according to several sources, this group never really undertook any community projects, outside of assigning each house a number.

When Comité 4 appeared, therefore, the older organization formed itself in-to a Comité Pro-Defensa and announced itself as opposed to the remodeling, which it claimed would simply be community-wide demolition. Intra-zonal con-flict, therefore, was intense as the community waited for the government to move on the remodeling and relocation plans.

Zone B. Enrique Pozo, a long-time resident and leader of Zone B, arrived and settled in 28 de Julio in the early 1950s, when the hacienda was still func-tioning. Over the next decade, the zone became more densely inhabited: in En-rique's words,

... conditions in the streets and alleyways became really bad—people threw all sorts of garbage out the doors of their houses, and when the *garúa* [heavy fog common in Lima through much of the year] was bad, the mud came up to your ankles and the odor was terrible. The mud would suck the shoe right off my foot.

The zone once tried to remedy the situation by collecting contributions and then spreading truckloads of crushed rock and sand in the streets. This effort, however, was only a temporary success.

By the early 1960s, sanitary and physical conditions had reached such a point that the community organized itself to attempt some desperately needed improvements. Four groups, each representing the four major streets of the zone, came together to try to install sewerage and potable water. After almost five years of stop-and-start work, and with some technical assistance from the National Housing Board and modest financial aid and donations of piping from the mayor of the district, water and sanitary facilities came into service for over three-fourths of the houses. The savings to the community were substantial, since all the physical labor of digging the trenches and installing the pipes came from the pobladores.

At the same time, the groups undertook to install electric power and light-ing in the zone, and once again the attempt was successful. However, the cost to each family was considerably higher than had been hoped, since the city utility company did not permit the community to contribute labor. Still, about three out of four dwellings obtained electricity, and the main streets of the zone had public lighting.

Installing water and sewerage involved considerably more work than merely digging trenches; in order for the excavations to be done, the streets had to be widened. This opening-up process necessitated dismantling some houses facing the streets and relocating them a meter or so further back. Such relocations changed meandering alleyways into something more closely resembling streets, wide enough for an automobile to enter. This widening also created open spaces for the community, something that had been missing almost altogether in 1965.

The four local sector committees in Zone B were in solid agreement with one another and with the government concerning the relocation project. One leader said:

> . . . there are too many people here now to be able to do anything. We know that if the government's plans go ahead, we're going to have to build everything all over again. But they [the government] say that they'll save the water and sewerage pipelines already installed; we just hope that they do.

Thus in 1971 28 de Julio was a deviant case compared with the other three. Its close-in location, and hence its extraordinary population density, had impeded progress and had made success hard-won indeed.

28 de Julio since 1971. In 1972 and 1973, the national government followed through on its promises to remodel both zones. After repeated censuses and counts of the neighborhoods, the government initiated simultaneous relocation and physical remodeling; somewhat more than half of each zone was assigned (by lottery) land in the expropriated hacienda adjacent to 28 de Julio, and after these families had moved, the zones were literally bulldozed to the ground and then resurveyed, and new, larger lots were assigned to those families that remained. Only a few individual houses were allowed to remain untouched.

By 1975, a comparison of the zones before and after remodeling provided a truly impressive picture. The newly constructed housing on the hacienda land had proceeded well, but the changes in zones A and B were more remarkable still. Streets wide enough for truck traffic now entered both zones, and very substantial house construction had created neighborhoods virtually rebuilt from the ground up. At the same time, the government forced an organizational restructuring of both zones, as they have done in all squatter settlements since 1968 (see chapter 8).

Governmental assistance, therefore, has been absolutely necessary for the two zones to improve themselves. The basic problem—too many people—required more than communal resources; however, it is also true that the remodeling would have occurred even more slowly had the zones themselves not been represented by patient, persistent, shrewd leaders who continually petitioned and badgered the government first for assistance and (once having gained promises) then for carrying through on its commitments.

Sendas Frutales. The last settlement represents the tugurio or slum environment. Due to problems of time and the difficulties associated with gaining access to a slum neighborhood, I collected comparable data from only one large city block of *callejones* in San José, a working-class district of Lima. And although this area may not accurately represent the whole of Lima's slums, Sendas Frutales was an especially fortunate choice for a number of reasons.

San José, the district in which Sendas Frutales is located, came into official being in 1950. But the particular neighborhood in which research was done— three adjoining streets known collectively as Sendas Frutales—dates from at least five years earlier. At the end of World War II, the area lay well outside the limits of Lima and was devoted to truck gardening, orchards, cut flowers, and the like (and hence its familiar, if unofficial, name). The absentee owners of these lands allowed the workers to build small houses and to pay rent on these dwellings. Gradually more houses were built; the land was increasingly subdivided as the original builders-renters clandestinely permitted friends and family relations to occupy small plots and to pay rent to the original renters. As Lima expanded and a major highway cut through, irrigation and agricultural production ceased and the area rapidly became completely residential.

Sendas Frutales thus became, for Lima's poor, a low-income source of housing with considerable appeal. Not only is it right on a major heavily trafficked road with good public transport, it is also in the heart of a working-class, industrial district with nearby markets, schools, and many other attractions. At the same time, however, and because of these reasons, Sendas Frutales has also developed fundamental problems. Many of the landowners have both permitted and encouraged maximum population densities, have held rents at the absolutely highest possible levels, and have made few efforts to install or maintain basic utilities. By 1972, Sendas Frutales had a total population of about ten thousand (official government figures said eighteen hundred families). Housing ranged from modestly acceptable (in terms of both rent and condition) to execrable. One family of five, for instance, had three relatively commodious (600-700 square feet) substantial rooms with plaster, paint, and concrete floors. Another family, however, with seven members and a different landlord, had to construct two precarious rooms (out of second-hand adobe) totaling 120 square feet; no water, sewerage, or electricity were available. The first pays US $6.50

Plate 5. Main street, Sendas Frutales. Around 500 families rented houses of varying quality. Peruvian flags flew to celebrate the district's 25th anniversary.

a month rent, and the second, US $18.00, just for the land alone; the head of the family had to purchase the building materials from the landlord and thus make any improvements or repairs.

Some fifteen individual landlords have land in Sendas Frutales. One owns a single alleyway with about two dozen one- or two-room flats; Ramiro Villarán, the largest landlord (who owns the land of the second family described), collects rents from almost four hundred families.

Although an almost purely residential zone, Sendas Frutales has a reputation as a dangerous, crime-ridden area and is locally referred to as *Chicago chico* (little Chicago). And although a few bars do in fact cater to drunks and prostitutes (much to the dismay of the residents), such crime as exists is almost exclusively external; the area does not harbor criminals and social undesirables. By and large, the families in Sendas Frutales are poor; most heads of families are migrants; some live in the neighborhood by preference, others have found no other alternative. Turnover has historically been high, and Sendas Frutales has for many years been a staging area where families stay for a few years prior to moving on, often to a pueblo joven. This discovery, as seen in chapters 5 and 6, allows a comparison of similar individuals operating under highly dissimilar circumstances.

Until 1970 or so, the residents of Sendas Frutales had few alternatives available to them for improving their surroundings: they could complain to the landlord, they could try to interest some governmental agency (either municipal, city, or national), they could try to do something themselves, or they could leave. All of these options had problems. Confronting the landlord did little, according to the inhabitants; those owners who maintained their properties received few complaints, whereas those who did nothing except collect rents, and who thus received appeals or demands most frequently, had no intention of making improvements, and said so openly. Moreover, if improvements were made, rents automatically rose. Going to the authorities on any level generally produced delays or simply no response; local municipal inspectors ignored conditions or were bought off, and no national agency had the express duty of dealing with central-city rental slum housing. The inhabitants of Sendas Frutales at times made attempts to obtain governmental assistance; during the 1950s, the municipality of San José did not include Sendas Frutales as an "urban zone," since it was at that time still partially agricultural. In 1958, a group of families asked the Ministry of Development to force the municipality to reverse this exclusion and to place the owners and their rental housing under licensing control. This was never done by the ministry.

In late 1972, however, Sr. Villarán attempted to evict a family forcibly; this family and its neighbors just as forcibly resisted. Villarán obtained the aid and protection of the municipal police, and leveled some one hundred or more units, intending to build medium-rise, middle-class apartments. The people, meanwhile, went to Msgr. Luis Bambarén, Lima's official Bishop of the Pueblos Jóvenes; he in turn contacted a lawyer and the colonel in charge of the zonal office of SINAMOS. After threats, counter-threats, armed (literally) confrontations between Villarán and his tenants, meetings, and many lengthy open letters in Lima newspapers addressed to President Velasco, the SINAMOS colonel (with questionable authority) declared Sendas Frutales to be a pueblo joven. All parties acknowledged that this resolution was temporary; a presidential decree would be necessary to make it take effect.

The repercussions were varied and immediate as President Velasco, the Ministry of Housing, SINAMOS, the landowners, and the pobladores all found themselves in a classic showdown. First the landowners and then the renters (calling themselves "los pobladores del pueblo joven Sendas Frutales") published detailed accusatory letters in a Lima paper; President Velasco issued a formal order revoking the SINAMOS resolution, and turned the whole matter over to the Ministry of Housing; the head of the SINAMOS office delayed in carrying out this order and was promptly transferred; the pobladores twice marched on the SINAMOS office; and the landlords issued notices of eviction that were countered by SINAMOS personnel. Finally, a year or more later, the original SINAMOS resolution was permanently revoked, and Sendas Frutales was declared to be an "urbanización popular," an ambiguous classification. Such a move was unacceptable to the pobladores, and was rejected in a mass meeting. A period of wheel-spinning ensued, ending when President Velasco was replaced in August of 1975 by General Francisco Morales Bermúdez. Shortly thereafter, the pobladores of Sendas Frutales again paid for a letter in a newspaper, continuing to plead for a final decision classifying the neighborhood as a pueblo joven. But by late 1976 the whole matter was still undecided.

The Six Neighborhoods Compared

The six communities selected can now be compared with one another by use of the three variables identified in chapter 2—namely, age, manner of formation, and overall development. Sendas Frutales, the slum community, is a rather distinctive settlement, and is not perhaps directly comparable with the other five.

The following chart shows that the five squatter areas range across these three variables in such a way as to represent the basic stages of squatter growth.

Plate 6. Alleyway housing, Sendas Frutales. The poorest quality, newest housing generally had the highest rents. Twenty square meters here cost US$20 monthly; official minimum wage was US$50.

Primero de Enero, with its estera-mat shacks and recent official lots, occupies one end; Santiago, which has ceased to be a pueblo joven, occupies the other. Pampa de Arena lies between the two, as do zones A and B of 28 de Julio. However, whereas Pampa de Arena has a good deal of potential it can still develop through its own efforts, the two neighboring zones of 28 de Julio were stalemated until the government provided the one good the community itself could not: more physical space so that infrastructural investments and improvements could occur.

The sample of five pueblos jóvenes thus includes neighborhoods of varying ages, formed through a variety of ways, and with considerable differences of physical development and internal cohesion. Choosing two contiguous zones in 28 de Julio allows for a close examination of the role of a strong community organization. Since both areas are virtually the same in density, age, and manner of formation, any variations may be logically traced to organizational efforts and successes. The five squatter areas are thus standardized cases, and are well suited for comparison. They were thus selected purposively and not randomly.

Whereas these five communities cluster together nicely, Sendas Frutales clearly remains the odd case. Two goals warrant its inclusion. First, since many of its past and present inhabitants in fact live in squatter areas, it offers a glimpse of the circumstances that force a great many people to establish spontaneous communities. Second, and more important, it is a qualitatively different kind of environment, one that imposes certain built-in constraints and limitations on those who live in it. Since the inhabitants of Sendas Frutales and a couple of the squatter areas resemble one another quite closely (see chapters 5 and 6), the impact of the slum as compared to the squatter neighborhood on the individual can be delineated quite nicely. Poverty, in other words, remains a constant; what varies is the immediate locale, its legal status, and (hence) the behavior of its residents.

FIVE LIMA SQUATTER AREAS

		Primero de Enero	Pampa de Arena	Santiago	28 de Julio (2 zones)	
I.	Age	New (3 1/2 years)	Medium (6-12 years)	Old (25 years)	Old (25 years)	
II.	Manner of formation	Massive group invasion (1,000 initial families)	Smaller group invasions (50-100 families); government relocation	Small group invasions with subsequent consolidation	Gradual subdivision and accretion on an individual basis	
III.	Overall development	Actual: low / Potential: medium to good	Actual: low to medium / Potential: medium to very good	Actual: medium to high / Potential: medium	Actual: low / Potential: low to high	
A.	Materials of construction	Entirely provisional	Mixed, moving toward permanent	Entirely permanent	Semi-permanent (adobe, some brick)	
B.	Density	Low (120/acre)	Low	Medium (200/acre)	High (250/acre)	
C.	Terrain	Flat to inclined	Flat to inclined	Flat	Flat	
D.	Location within Lima	Distant (14 kms. from downtown)	Distant (12 kms.)	Medium (4 kms. from downtown)	Close (6 blocks from central market)	
E.	Internal Cohesion				Zone A	Zone B
	1. Perceived conflict	Very low	Low-medium	High	High	Low
	2. Efficacy of local association	Good	Strong	Poor	Poor	Strong
	3. Successful community undertakings	Many	Some	Some (past)	Few	Many

Part II. The Urban Poor and Their Spokesmen

5. Poverty, the Pobladores, and and Their Neighborhoods

In their attempts to improve their communities, Lima's poor confront long-term problems as well as short-term, specific influences. The particular regime in power provides an instance of the latter; an administration can influence community life by its promulgation of specific politics, by its distribution of resources, or by its general attentiveness to the poor. These regime-specific matters are treated in chapters 6 and 8.

But a more pervasive influence on both the urban poor and the regime comes from the existence of widespread poverty and the inability of a regime to modify that presence in any substantial manner. This incapacity results in large part from the interrelatedness of poverty's different causes in a dependent nation-state. In the macro sense, poverty exists on a national basis because a particular country simply lacks any useful resources, or trained personnel to exploit available riches, or both. Or a country's distribution system can be deficient, either by accident or intent, rendering sometimes large portions of its population poor. On an individual basis, a person can be absolutely destitute or can be below some established standard of material comfort for his society. But a person may also perceive himself as relatively deprived of material benefits or as having inadequate access to such benefits. And finally, a welfare agency or outside observer may label someone as poor who may never have seen himself as such (see Eames and Goode, 1973; Bloomberg and Schmandt, 1970; Tussing, 1975; Caiden and Wildavsky, 1974, chapter 2; Harrington, 1977; Lipton, 1977, especially chapters 2, 3, and 4).

As was noted in chapter 2, Peru and Lima both suffer from extreme inequalities of income and wealth. Although neither the nation nor its capital would have wealthy populaces were their incomes equitably distributed, the maldistribution of income obviously intensifies and maintains the poverty so common in Peru and Lima. Lima's poor do not simply lack money; the whole physical and social environment—the need for public services, public education, health standards, welfare services—promotes a structural, dynamic, and self-maintaining process (Caiden and Wildavsky, 1974: 46-47).

This chapter examines the basic essences of poverty as they influence Lima's poor in a variety of ways. As a start, in what objective ways can Lima's poverty be measured? To what extent do Lima's poor see themselves as poor? How have these perceptions been affected by previous experiences? Next, how do the poor see their immediate surroundings and their needs? To what degree do poor neighborhoods vary in their degrees of coherence in addressing these needs? And finally, how do the poor conceive of solutions for their most pressing problems? How do these solutions vary among the neighborhoods?

The following examination of these questions will sketch in some of the inherent differences among the poor, both as individuals and as inhabitants of distinct dwelling environments. But more important, it will provide the background against which both the poor and the national government must function. In other words, this chapter is concerned with how life goes on for the poor, regardless of particular regime or type of regime. Migration patterns to and within Lima, for example, or the types of employment the poor hold, are not apt to be affected dramatically from one regime to another, since many of the basic sources of poverty reside in the dependent nature of Peru's economy (see chapters 1 and 3). So although the poor and their immediate surroundings are treated more or less *in vacuo* here, this treatment is intentional. It may also be peculiarly appropriate, since the poor are frequently left to their own devices for solving their problems. Divorcing the poor and their neighborhoods from regime-specific considerations provides an understanding of how the poor have been able to fend for themselves, and also a context for judging how sensitive government policies were to the structures and mechanisms the poor had created.

Migration to and within Lima

The poor who make up the sample living in the research communities do not differ markedly from other samples drawn in Lima's squatter settlements.[1] The sample shows that those individuals who migrate to Lima (about 80 percent of the total sample is migrant in origin) are apt to have the following characteristics:

1. They are young, generally under twenty-five, and have been educated outside of Lima.
2. They are the inhabitants of small villages and towns of under ten thousand in the central and south-central regions of Peru.

3. They are boys and men who have worked, and whose fathers have worked, in small subsistence agriculture and who have not visited Lima previously.
4. They have spent their childhoods in the large middle range of Peruvian provincial environments.
5. They depend on, and receive, considerable assistance from family members, both in making the move and in settling into the city on arrival (Dietz, 1976: 10-25).

On arriving in Lima, over two-thirds of the sample initially moved into some type of slum rental housing in the central districts of Lima. Less than a fifth moved into a pueblo joven, and only a tenth went directly to the address where they were interviewed.

Table 2 presents information dealing with each point of the migration sequence within the city: length of time at each step, the type of dwelling environment, with whom the individual lived, the gross job classification he had while there, and his reason for leaving. Although these data are in many ways self-explanatory, several points deserve elaboration. More than half of the sample, for instance, made more than one move before arriving at their present site (i.e., the site where the respondent lived at the time of the interview). Approximately one-third of the remaining half moved on to a third site, until the N falls to 14 for those who lived in four places prior to settling at the present site. These moves are not of short duration; the mean length of residency exceeds three years at all sites.

Comparing job classifications at the first site with the present occupation reveals that the migrants experience considerable, though limited, mobility across time. 66.3 percent and 18.2 percent of the migrants worked first in lower manual and upper manual jobs on or immediately after arrival in the city. By the time they had reached the squatter communities, these figures had shifted to 41.4 percent and 48.3 percent respectively. But these gross job classifications hide some significance, since an individual may remain within the same classification and still better his employment in terms of job stability, income, and possible advancement. For instance, a man may begin as a street vendor but later become an unskilled factory worker. He has remained in the same gross ranking but has in many ways bettered his situation.

Detailed job classification comparisons make the migrants' mobility more dramatic. For first employment in Lima, workers in the four lowest and most menial occupations—street vendors, agricultural laborers, unskilled service workers, and other unskilled workers—made up almost 40 percent of the migrant sample; those in moderately skilled upper manual jobs—small merchants, taxi and bus drivers, skilled factory and construction workers, and other skilled workers—totaled less than 20 percent. By the time of the interview, the

TABLE 2
THE MIGRATION SEQUENCE WITHIN LIMA

	First site (N:413)	Second site (N:221)	Third site (N:71)	Fourth site (N:16)	Present site (N:527)
Time in years					
Under 1 year	9.8%	4.0%	8.5%	6.3%	1.9%
1-2 years	26.8	28.5	32.4	25.0	7.8
3-5 years	27.3	35.1	21.1	37.5	34.4
6-9 years	13.2	16.4	18.3	18.7	22.3
10 and over	22.9	16.0	19.7	12.5	33.6
Type of housing					
Private house	29.6	33.8	25.0	66.7	72.5
Apartment	7.5	6.7	8.3	6.7	–
Callejón, quinta	48.8	39.6	30.6	6.7	27.0
Tugurio	4.6	6.2	8.3	–	.6
Rented room	2.4	7.6	12.5	–	.2
Other	7.0	6.2	15.3	20.0	.2
Job classification*					
Low manual	66.3	62.5	58.3	53.3	41.4
Upper manual	18.2	29.9	31.9	33.3	48.3
Lower non-manual	2.2	4.0	6.9	–	6.1
Upper non-manual	–	–	–	–	1.0
Inactive	13.4	3.6	2.8	13.3	3.0
With whom respondent lived					
Lived by himself	15.3	18.7	20.6	–	1.7
With relatives	56.5	29.3	20.6	25.0	4.6
With friends	9.1	7.1	2.7	–	–
With his own family	15.6	40.4	49.3	62.5	93.4
Other	3.6	4.4	6.8	12.5	.4
Reason for leaving site					
Work situation	15.5	12.3	11.1	26.7	x
Economic necessity	5.8	5.0	6.9	6.7	x
Bad housing conditions	17.7	12.3	9.7	–	x

	First site	Second site	Third site	Fourth site	Present site
To acquire own house, land	21.3	37.3	31.9	33.3	x
Change in family status	21.5	18.2	12.5	20.0	x
Displacement	5.5	3.6	6.9	6.7	x
Problems with landlord	1.8	.9	1.4	–	x
Found better housing	5.8	3.6	9.7	–	x
Other	5.3	6.8	9.7	6.7	x

*Lower manual:	unskilled workers, street vendors, agricultural laborers, tenant farmers, sharecroppers, subsistence farmers, soldiers, policemen, etc.
Upper manual:	skilled workers and craftsmen, vehicle operators, small retail merchants, salesmen in grocery stores, small commercial farm owners, etc.
Lower non-manual:	office workers, sales agents, sales clerks, supervisors and foremen, farmowners and managers of medium and large-size farms, etc.
Upper non-manual:	professionals, technicians and semi-professionals, managers, executives, employers in non-farm business and industry, etc.
Inactive:	retired, too old to work; too young to work; student

percentages had reversed almost exactly.

This shift in occupational rankings from lower manual to upper manual during the intra-city sequence is considerably more important than any mobility that occurs during the rural-to-Lima movement (see Cornelius, 1975, chapter 2). A comparison of the last job held before arrival in the city with the first job taken following arrival reveals that 77.8 percent of the migrants stayed within the same occupational ranking—generally lower manual. The migration sequence *within* the city is, therefore, the period during which upward mobility occurs, if it is to occur at all. The final move—out to a squatter settlement—represents a step taken only when the basic requirements for existence in Lima have been met (a steady job, a fairly well assured income, and an acquired familiarity with the city). An examination of the reasons for moving from one site to another within the city (see table 2) shows that economic reasons (a change of work site, or a change of actual job) decline while family reasons (marriage, or an increase in the size of family), along with the desire to become a homeowner, assume increasing salience.

Adjustment and Satisfaction

In the most general sense, the sample shows an overwhelmingly positive response to Lima. In answer to the question, "Are you glad that you came to Lima, or would you prefer to have stayed in your home town? " 95 percent said that they were satisfied with having migrated. Preferences were based on the presence of more readily obtainable employment in Lima and an overall better environment—answers such as more entertainment, more attractive suburbs, wider streets, and a better place to raise children were commonly voiced. The disadvantages of Lima most frequently mentioned included problems with employment[2] and environmental factors (climate, traffic congestion, a hectic pace of life, and so forth), followed by the presence of crime and delinquency; high cost of living and housing problems were also both mentioned. Nevertheless, the move to Lima is, for the most part, permanent and satisfactory.

The shift to the squatter settlement itself is likewise permanent for the migrant, who views this move as the end point of migration and as a place of consolidation: 88.2 percent of the pueblo joven sample stated that they planned to remain where they were, as far as they knew at the time of the interview. However, fully two-thirds of the Sendas Frutales sample planned to move. Furthermore, when confronted with a hypothetical question that asked them what they would do if an attempt were made to relocate them elsewhere, almost half of the squatters rejected the notion outright. Thirty percent said that they would go if they could perceive clear benefits, such as full title to the land, and 5 percent responded that they would go only under pressure. The migrants appear to be individuals who have gone through a good deal of movement within the city, who have obtained relatively stable and assured incomes, and who have moved to the squatter settlements in order to consolidate their achievements by establishing a permanent residence.

One other item bears directly on the phenomenon of migration to the city: the ease of adjustment that the migrant has in Lima. When asked if getting used to Lima had been more or less difficult than he had expected (or about equal), half replied that there had been no difference between expectations and the actual situation. A quarter said that it was easier to get along than they had expected, and another 25 percent thought that it had been harder. Four-fifths of the migrants said that they had not had a job waiting for them when they arrived in Lima, yet only a quarter felt that they had encountered a great deal of trouble in finding their first jobs. Almost two-thirds found work within a month after their arrival, and only 8 percent needed more than six months. Migrants are by no means the only persons to encounter employment problems in Lima; indeed, such difficulties make migrant-native differences fade. A native Limeño summed up the occupational situation when he said, "It's the same for everyone, because I'm a Limeño and I can't get a steady job."

These findings, along with those of similar studies both in Peru and elsewhere, go far toward refuting a commonly held assumption about the urban poor (especially squatters): that since they have been socialized in a rural setting, they will undergo severe stress as they adapt to the city, if in fact they are able to do so at all. Much of the earlier literature dealing with rural-urban migration presumed that an individual moving from the countryside to a city would necessarily find the move difficult. The lack of urban employment skills, along with the size, heterogeneity, and impersonality of the city, supposedly makes adjustment difficult, forcing the individual to change his way of life drastically.[3]

Such assumptions are no longer tenable, given the weight of empirical evidence that finds just the opposite. As the Lima sample clearly indicates, the move to the city does not occur in a vacuum in which the individual is subjected helplessly to the city. Kin and *paisanos* provide considerable assistance (see Lobo, 1976; Lomnitz, 1977); jobs do become available, generally in a short time, and a fair amount of socio-occupational mobility does take place. Although a fair number of migrants to Lima doubtless fail to become acculturated, it is probably safe to guess that they constitute a marked minority.[4] For the majority, neither the initial entry into Lima nor long-term consolidation seems to offer insuperable obstacles.

Poverty and the Pobladores: The Sample

The people in the pueblos jóvenes and the tugurios have thus far been referred to as "the urban poor," but just what that term means remains vague (Musgrove and Ferber, 1979). Does poor imply destitute, or unemployed, or unemployable, or low-income, or some combination of these? And are the people in the sample poor in some absolute sense, or only relatively?

To begin, table 3 reveals that slightly less than half of the pobladores in the sample brought home US $50/month or less, which in 1970-1971 was the official minimum income in Lima; two-thirds reported incomes of less than US $100/month.[5] Squatter and slum inhabitants overall show only slight differences, although inter-squatter settlement differences are at times substantial (e.g., Santiago is clearly the wealthiest). But table 3 also shows that the large

TABLE 3

ECONOMIC AND EMPLOYMENT CHARACTERISTICS OF SAMPLE, BY COMMUNITY OF RESIDENCE

	Primero de Enero (N=93)	Pampa de Arena (N=111)	Santiago (N=104)	28 de Julio A (N=59)	28 de Julio B (N=55)	Sendas Frutales (N=105)	Total Sample (N=527)
1. Head of household monthly income:							
US$ 50/month or less	53.3%	54.8%	30.9%	56.1%	49.0%	45.1%	47.7%
US$ 51-100/month	16.5	15.8	16.5	15.8	11.8	24.5	18.9
US$100/month or more	30.2	29.4	52.6	28.1	39.2	30.4	33.4
2. Is currently saving money on a regular basis	38.5	35.6	29.8	42.6	46.0	45.4	38.6
3. Present occupation of head of household:*							
Lower manual	47.3	44.5	24.3	33.9	40.0	50.5	40.6
Upper manual	48.4	49.1	54.4	52.5	49.1	39.0	48.4
Lower non-manual	3.2	2.7	11.7	5.1	7.3	6.7	6.1
Upper non-manual	–	–	1.9	3.4	–	1.0	1.0
Retired, unemployed	1.1	3.6	7.8	5.1	3.6	2.9	4.0
4. Head of household employed in factory	15.2	14.0	28.9	12.5	18.5	20.6	18.7
5. Length of time employed at present occupation:							
3 years or less	17.6	9.6	11.8	7.1	7.7	16.5	12.3
3-10 years	62.6	57.1	35.5	39.3	36.5	45.4	47.6
Over 10 years	19.8	33.3	52.7	53.6	55.8	38.1	40.1
6. "Very" or "reasonably" satisfied with present occupation	56.5	72.1	68.4	80.3	84.9	75.8	71.6

*For definitions of these classifications, see table 2.
All differences are significant at .01 level or beyond, x^2 test.

majority have steady employment (generally in skilled and unskilled manual jobs) and have held these jobs for over ten years. Three out of four find their jobs satisfactory, although fewer than two out of five can save regularly on their income. Less than a fifth work in a factory; however, many pobladores describe such work as highly desirable, and include it along with owning their own business as an ideal work situation.

By external or absolute standards, the pobladores in the sample are clearly poor; Webb's (1972) criterion of middle-class standing (owning an automobile for private use) includes only 7 percent, and almost all of these use their car (or truck) for their work. But the tenure of employment, along with the unemployment rate (as measured by the number of male heads of household actively searching for work, but unable to obtain it), goes strongly against facile denunciations of the squatters as unemployed and unemployable. In addition, the people in the sample are also not "marginally" employed, nor are they overwhelmingly found in service-related jobs in the tertiary sector.[6] Only 11 percent work in the most unskilled or menial of jobs (street vending, heavy or repetitive unskilled manual labor), and employment overall shows considerable variety: skilled and semi-skilled construction workers (17.0 percent), skilled service workers (10.8 percent), bus, truck, and taxi drivers (10.2 percent), semi-skilled factory workers (8.8 percent), and small merchants (7.9 percent). Thus, perhaps the safest overall descriptive label is the *urban working poor*— always with the understanding that within this broad classification lies considerable diversity.[7]

Insofar as other socio-economic characteristics go, the pobladores represented in the sample are relatively young heads of established families with modest amounts of education (see table 4). They are clearly not newcomers to Lima; despite the fact that four out of five are migrants, three-quarters of the total have spent over ten years in the city (or are native); half of those with less than five years' residence live in Sendas Frutales, not the squatter areas.

These data show that the pobladores make up the blue-collar, semi-skilled working class of Lima. They are the people who drive Lima's buses and trucks and taxis; they sometimes work in its factories; they build its buildings, or wait on its restaurant tables, or sweep its streets, or operate its markets. In addition, they buy building materials, consume food and beverages, go to soccer games and movies, and send their children to school. If they depend on the city for a livelihood, the city also depends on them. Lima's middle and upper classes may take the pobladores for granted, or may (when they think of them) be fearful of them, or may ignore them altogether; nevertheless, the wealthy districts of the city would not exist, and could not function, without them.

In addition, the pobladores do not see themselves as downtrodden or as the

TABLE 4

SOCIO-DEMOGRAPHIC CHARACTERISTICS OF LIMA'S POOR, BY COMMUNITY OF RESIDENCE

	Primero de Enero (N=93)	Pampa de Arena (N=111)	Santiago (N=104)	28 de Julio A (N=59)	28 de Julio B (N=55)	Sendas Frutales (N=105)	Total (N=527)
1. Marital status							
Married	52.7%	37.6%	82.9%	59.6%	63.7%	59.5%	63.4%
Free union	41.9	29.7	15.4	23.7	14.5	16.2	24.1
Single, other	5.4	2.7	5.7	6.7	21.8	14.3	8.5
2. Number of children							
None-2	46.6	21.6	27.2	28.6	28.8	48.5	33.9
3-6	49.8	60.3	59.2	48.2	51.9	43.5	51.6
Over 6	3.6	18.1	13.6	23.2	19.3	8.0	16.5
3. Total number of people living in house							
1-4	33.4	13.5	17.3	9.2	24.4	48.5	25.5
5-8	63.4	62.5	52.9	62.7	47.3	42.9	55.2
Over 8	3.2	24.0	30.8	28.1	28.3	8.6	19.3
4. Length of time in Lima							
Under 5 years	10.9	2.7	–	3.4	–	17.1	6.3
5-9 years	32.6	22.5	4.8	3.4	10.9	18.1	16.5
Over 10 years	43.5	63.1	63.5	66.1	66.8	41.9	55.7
Native	13.0	11.7	31.7	27.1	22.3	22.9	21.5

5. Age

Under 30	54.8	19.8	15.7	10.2	16.4	35.3	26.9
30-39	34.4	53.1	27.5	30.5	32.7	35.2	36.6
40-49	8.6	21.6	32.4	25.4	18.2	21.9	21.5
Over 50	2.2	5.4	24.4	33.9	32.7	7.6	15.0

6. Observed socio-economic status

Low	40.9	70.3	17.3	48.2	54.5	60.0	48.5
Lower-middle	59.1	27.9	41.3	30.4	34.5	28.6	37.2
Middle	–	1.8	35.6	19.6	10.9	11.4	13.0
Upper-middle	–	–	5.8	1.8	–	–	1.3

7. Educational attainment

None	1.1	–	–	–	–	–	–
1-3 years primary	11.8	39.8	15.5	31.6	38.9	16.7	24.4
4-complete primary	60.2	37.0	37.9	43.9	27.8	46.1	42.9
Some or all secondary	27.9	22.3	40.8	19.3	31.5	34.3	29.8
Beyond secondary	–	.9	5.8	5.3	1.9	3.0	2.7

8. Languages spoken

Spanish only	62.4	55.5	70.9	55.9	50.9	56.2	59.4
Spanish and Quechua	34.4	40.0	21.4	39.0	43.6	32.4	34.1
Spanish and Aymara, other	3.2	4.5	7.7	5.1	5.5	11.4	6.5

Note: All differences are significant at .01 level or beyond, x^2 test.

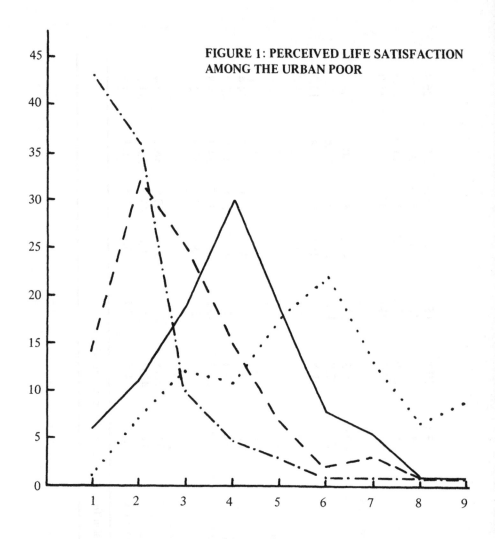

FIGURE 1: PERCEIVED LIFE SATISFACTION
AMONG THE URBAN POOR

Question: "Here's a picture of a ladder. . . . the top of the ladder represents the
best possible life for you, and the bottom represents the worst possible."

———————— Where . . . do you feel you stand at the present time?

— — — Where do you think you were five years ago?

• • • • • • Where do you think you will be five years from now?

—·—·— (Migrants only) Where were you when you first arrived in Lima?
N varies from 403 to 515.

dregs of the city. The pobladores have, by their own perceptions, moved up in the world by coming to Lima; figure 1 shows steady progression across time and on into the future, as well as significant perceived progress derived from migration itself (compare with Cornelius, 1975: 25-26). Yet, though mobility has been achieved in the past and is expected in the future, the poor are not naively sanguine about their prospects. For example, a third of the sample has shifted from one gross job classification to another (e.g., from lower manual to upper manual; see table 2) since coming to Lima, and 40 percent have improved similarly when their work is compared to that of their fathers. But such occupational progress, the pobladores realize, cannot continue; less than 5 percent felt that they would show any further job mobility in the next five years. The positive expectations for the future shown in figure 1, therefore, are not related to any substantial occupational advancement, but instead to an overall optimism that life in general can (or perhaps must) improve.

Views of Lima and Peru

One last area concerns the poor and their impressions of Lima and Peru (table 5). In general, and not surprisingly, the sample as a whole has a good deal to say about Lima, favorably and otherwise. A majority is pleased with Lima simply as a place to live and raise a family; Primero de Enero's high response to such factors is clearly atypical, and probably reflects the inhabitants' satisfaction in having invaded land successfully. The slum subsample from Sendas Frutales is enthusiastic about Lima in all respects. As for Lima's disadvantages, environmental difficulties predominate everywhere except in Primero de Enero; crime, especially delinquency (petty theft, breaking and entering), is also a serious problem. But almost a fifth of the sample has nothing bad to say about the city.

The sample's view of Peru's problems generally reflects neighborhood concerns and the precarious nature of living under conditions of poverty. Employment problems, lack of money and of education, and low levels of industrial development are all frequent responses; fewer than one in twenty mention international affairs. Despite the overwhelming preponderance of rural-origin migrants in the sample, agrarian or rural problems also rank low.

Politically, the most revealing datum lies in the minimal criticism directed toward the government. This finding corresponds to many other studies (see especially Mangin, 1967a; Nelson, 1969, 1979; Portes, 1971) that point out the lack of structural blame among Latin America's urban poor. Additional evidence comes from an item that asked the sample to identify the principal causes of poverty. Over half mentioned lack of work, and more than a fifth

TABLE 5

PERCEPTIONS OF LIMA AND OF PERU, BY COMMUNITY OF RESIDENCE

	Primero de Enero (N=93)	Pampa de Arena (N=111)	Santiago (N=104)	28 de Julio A (N=59)	28 de Julio B (N=55)	Sendas Frutales (N=105)	Total (N=527)
1. Perceptions of Lima							
a. Aspects most liked							
—Economic conditions (jobs, wages, stability of work)	5.7%	15.9%	27.0%	21.6%	22.7%	14.5%	17.7%
—Environment (family life, recreation, cultural life, public services)	91.4	50.0	59.6	43.1	54.5	30.1	54.7
—Living and housing opportunities, landownership	1.4	3.7	3.4	9.8	–	–	2.9
—Opportunities to progress	–	6.1	–	–	2.3	6.0	2.6
—Educational opportunities	–	3.7	2.2	2.0	–	7.2	2.9
—Everything	–	18.3	5.6	23.5	20.4	42.2	18.1
—Negative response	1.4	2.4	2.2	–	–	–	1.2
b. Aspects most disliked							
—Inadequate public services	6.7	2.9	3.2	1.9	–	3.2	3.3
—High cost of living	5.6	5.9	2.1	1.9	–	3.3	3.9
—Employment difficulties	5.6	12.7	8.5	3.7	8.0	1.1	6.8
—Environmental difficulties (overcrowding, noise, pollution, etc.)	26.7	26.5	37.2	37.0	38.0	36.2	32.9
—Poor social relations (lack of friends, neighbors, feelings of isolation, etc.)	1.1	7.8	2.1	5.6	2.0	7.4	4.5

—Crime, delinquency	48.9	19.6	29.8	18.5	10.0	14.9	25.0
—Housing problems	5.6	3.9	4.3	3.7	4.0	7.4	5.0
—Nothing disliked	—	20.6	12.8	27.8	38.0	24.5	18.6
2. Peru's most important problem							
—Lack of employment	45.0	37.4	32.5	22.9	17.8	21.1	30.4
—Low wages, high cost of living, lack of low-cost housing, poverty	7.9	13.6	7.3	10.4	21.1	16.2	13.1
—Social problems (delinquency, etc.), health problems	11.2	14.2	6.5	13.5	11.1	17.8	12.9
—Education	23.2	14.2	22.0	16.7	24.4	18.4	19.5
—Urban problems in general, rural problems in general	—	5.8	5.7	8.3	7.8	7.6	5.6
—Lack of industrialization	11.3	7.1	17.1	12.5	8.9	12.4	11.5
—Bad government	1.3	3.9	1.6	3.1	2.2	2.2	4.4
—Other (foreign affairs, overpopulation, centralization, etc.)	—	3.9	7.3	1.0	6.6	8.6	4.6
3. Element most necessary for Peru's progress							
—Hard work by citizens	33.7	47.3	23.0	35.6	33.3	9.8	30.0
—Government planning	65.2	49.1	66.0	61.0	64.7	86.3	65.6
—God's help. Luck	1.1	3.6	11.0	3.4	2.0	3.9	4.4

Note: All differences are significant at .01 level or beyond, x^2 test.

said lack of education. But these answers are intended as *individual* deficien-cies—i.e., with proper education or work, individual poverty would disappear—and are not translated into systemic shortcomings. Portes's (1971) discussion of the "migrant ethic" in Latin American cities summarizes the point well: the poor "lack a pervading sense of 'grievance' against the social order since eco-nomic opportunities offered by the new . . . city are perceived as potential to be actualized by personal action rather than as legitimate rights to be automat-ically granted by reason of sheer physical presence" (716).

It may well be a cliché that people prefer to feel that they improve over time, despite what an outside observer or "objective" evidence may suggest to the contrary. For Lima's poor, W. I. Thomas's famous apothegm, "If men de-fine situations as real, then they are real in their consequences," clearly holds true: if the poor think that their progress has been significant, *then in fact it has*—and it is this definition of the situation by the actor that becomes essen-tial for understanding attitudinal and behavioral patterns (Elder, 1973). The poor thus view Peru's problems in concrete terms; abstract doubts about poli-tics or the nature of the economic system are virtually absent. The poor also indicate that they feel that such problems are solvable; hard work along with government planning can do what needs to be done.[8]

Whether the migrants are marginal members of Lima's society depends on the definition or conceptualization of the term (Perlman, 1975; Lloyd, 1979: 57-68, especially 60-62). Park's (1928) discussion of marginal man as caught between two cultures (e.g., rural and urban) provided the foundation for mar-ginality as a sociological concept in the United States, although, as Peattie (1974) notes, *marginalidad* (marginality) as a Latin American concept devel-oped to a large degree independently. Marginality was first applied in Latin America in an ecological sense: settlements or neighborhoods, generally poor, illegal, or improvised ones, were marginal to the city. As Germani (1972) notes, it was but a short step to label the way of life and the occupations of the people in these areas as marginal. Politically, marginality then came to be conceptualized (Vekemans, 1969) as lacking involvement in decision-making on all levels of society and as being unintegrated into "mainstream" urban so-cial and economic systems.[9]

Portes (1977) and Perlman (1975) offer perhaps the strongest case against the concept. Portes notes two basic faults. First, the supposed "marginals" consistently take advantage of every opportunity available to them; "their prob-lem [does] not lie in a cultural inability to take advantages of opportunities, but in the nonexistence of opportunities" (Portes, 1977: 98). The data offered here certainly agree; if nothing else, the existence of squatter settlements in the first place argues that the poor have forced the social system to permit an illegality to become tolerated, accepted, and even grudgingly made part of public policy and of elite political calculations (Collier, 1976). Second, the urban poor are integral, necessary, and central components in the urban system; "it is precisely their form of integration, the way in which they are forced to participate, not their lack of participation, that is reflected in their situation" (Portes, 1977: 98). The people in the sample are clearly involved; they work and consume, perform vital tasks for Lima, and provide a large, cheap, and reasonably skilled labor pool.

The final choice as to whether the urban poor—whether slum dwellers or squatters—are marginal thus depends almost entirely on usage and definition. But in agreement with Perlman (1975) and her conclusions about Rio and its *favelados*, Lima's poor are not *marginados*. They may well be dependent on the city, and unable to counter the macro-level structures that control them, but they are not divorced or apart from the city. But their form of integration (or malintegration) probably constitutes their major problem, and is clearly one of the major structural conditions that in effect define rational political behavior for them (see chapter 1, note 9).

In sum, the pobladores express a modest, consistent pride in themselves, their futures, Lima, and their nation. Cynicism and discontent exist side by side with optimism and satisfaction (Mangin, 1967a; Nelson, 1969; Portes, 1971). All things considered, Santos's (1975) comment merits repeating: "The general attitude of the [poor] is that it is better to be poor in Lima than anywhere else" (344).

Pobladores and Their Neighborhoods

Although concentrating on the poor as individuals or in the aggregate, the analysis thus far has taken note of a number of significant inter-community differences. Some neighborhoods are clearly wealthier, more highly developed; some are inhabited by people with higher educations or better jobs. Although such diversity has a certain intrinsic interest, it is much more germane to see how these variations translate into politically relevant activities. The preceding SES data can thus be viewed as underlying factors that both support and guide involvement directed at resolving community problems. Inter-neighborhood differences become essential here, since they are critical for understanding how the poor both shape and respond to their immediate surroundings. But such perceptions will not make much sense until we know more about how the pobladores feel toward their neighborhoods. What sorts of investments— psychological as well as material—have the pobladores made? How satisfied are they with their communities? What problems are the most pressing? How

TABLE 6

PERCEPTIONS OF LOCAL NEIGHBORHOOD: PERMANENCE OF RESIDENCE, BY COMMUNITY

	Primero de Enero (N=93)	Pampa de Arena (N=111)	Santiago (N=104)	28 de Julio A (N=59)	28 de Julio B (N=55)	Sendas Frutales (N=105)	Total (N=527)
1. Time in residence in local neighborhood							
2 years or less	1.1%	13.5%	2.2%	5.9%	2.3%	26.6%	9.7%
2-5 years	98.9	36.0	9.8	3.9	9.1	21.3	34.4
6-9 years		50.5	19.6	9.8	18.2	22.3	22.3
10 years or more			68.5	80.4	70.5	19.8	33.6
2. Feels land tenure is secure							
Yes	55.8	69.7	82.2	24.1	22.6	—	56.6
No	44.2	30.3	17.8	75.9	77.4	—	43.4
3. Reaction to hypothetical eviction							
Accept	25.2	47.9	35.2	74.1	60.8	77.7	49.4
Resist	74.8	52.1	64.8	25.9	39.2	22.3	50.6
4. Improvements planned for house	69.3	91.9	73.9	76.3	74.5	8.3	64.8
5. House constructed by respondent							
All	44.1	24.3	30.6	37.9	64.8	5.1	31.2
Some	54.8	60.4	63.5	29.3	24.1	3.0	41.0
None	1.1	15.3	5.9	32.8	11.1	91.9	27.8

6. Total time devoted to house construction (if any)							
Under 1 year	63.2	75.0	7.5	54.5	60.4	57.1	38.5
1-4 years	36.8	14.8	16.3	29.5	33.3	28.6	34.5
5 years or more	—	10.2	76.2	16.0	6.3	14.3	27.0
7. Total money spent on house construction (if any)							
Under US $125	59.8	51.4	2.6	33.3	30.5	50.0	38.5
US $125-250	35.9	36.5	23.1	38.1	41.3	50.0	34.5
Over US $250	4.3	12.1	74.3	28.6	28.2	—	27.0
8. Present residence seen as permanent	93.9	93.6	74.0	87.5	97.9	33.3	78.2

Note: All differences are significant at .001 level or beyond, x^2 test.

well do the people get along with their neighbors? What, in essence, is the community-generated context in which political problem-solving develops, and how does this environment differ from community to community?

The term *community* refers on one level to a geographically defined and bounded—at least in the minds of its inhabitants—residential clustering of families. But community also concerns things held in common; ideas or beliefs or values can provide such a binding agent, and so can jointly held needs (Keller, 1968; Mollenkopf, 1973; Gans, 1962; Lomnitz, 1977; Clinard, 1966). These mutual elements generate and maintain certain types of organizational activities that allow the locality's inhabitants to engage in concerted actions and to achieve collectively ends that cannot be achieved alone (Coleman, 1971: 658; Huntington and Nelson, 1976: 15; Cornelius, 1975).

Success at solving communal problems does not, of course, depend solely on the presence of an organization (although some organization is doubtless a necessary ingredient); a whole range of other factors may be crucial, including past efforts and their perceived efficacy, vigorous leadership (Lloyd, 1979: 193-196), formal and informal contacts with resources and persons external to the neighborhood, and so on. In addition, the spirit talked of above—the feelings of communality based on shared elements—may be fundamental to any or all other factors, for without a base of support, a leader or an organization can do little.

There are numerous ways of analyzing the presence and the intensity of a locality's sense of community; I shall use three principal areas critical to a neighborhood's ability to pull itself together in the face of collective problems. These three are *community affect*, or one's dedication to the community as a permanent place of residence; *satisfaction* with the neighborhood as a place to live at present and in the future; and the quality of *inter-personal relations* present in the neighborhood. Each of these, both separately and jointly, plays a major part in determining how well a locality can handle its problems (see Cornelius, 1975, chapters 4, 5, and 6, for a parallel study in Mexico City).

Community Affect.[10] The extent to which an individual may be willing to take part in local problem-solving activities depends in considerable part on his commitment to that neighborhood. Table 6 suggests a number of patterns and tendencies. In the first place, all of the squatters see their present residences as permanent, and plan to invest further in their homes on top of sometimes considerable investments already made, in terms of both money and time. Specific differences mirror specific conditions; for example, the two zones of 28 de Julio manifest considerable willingness to be moved elsewhere through eviction. But these data are a clear indication of the tenuousness of 28 de Julio's situation and the pending (at the time of field work) expropriation of land to relieve overcrowded conditions. Another instance: Primero de Enero's perception of land tenure is the lowest, after 28 de Julio; however, its resistance to a hypothetical eviction is the highest. Such a pattern doubtless emerges from the newness (three years) of the community and its successful invasion: the pobladores are determined to remain and make good.

Sendas Frutales shows variant patterns throughout. Its population is almost evenly composed of short-term and long-term residents; three-quarters are willing to go somewhere else, only a third intend to stay permanently, and housing investments are minimal. The slum environment clearly does not have the capacity to provoke permanence, due to the lack of land ownership and the structural differences between slum and squatter settlement discussed earlier in chapter 3.

Satisfaction with Neighborhood. Lima's poor have good and bad things to say about their neighborhoods, and both the compliments and the complaints vary considerably across locales (see table 7). Not unexpectedly, home ownership among the squatters ranks high, especially in the newer areas, followed by two environmental aspects: peacefulness, and a feeling of having good neighbors or friends or relatives nearby. Location plays a mixed role, rating high in some (especially 28 de Julio, with its closeness to central Lima) and much less in the truly peripheral areas. Primero de Enero's pobladores again show their enthusiasm for gaining a place to live, but this is a feeling that trails off markedly in older communities.

Insofar as complaints are concerned, those squatter neighborhoods without water, sewerage, or electricity clearly feel the lack: when basic services are missing, their absence transcends everything else. If such facilities exist, then complaints move in a number of directions. Some feel that their neighbors are unfriendly or that the area is unsafe; others fault the lack of a variety of services such as paved streets and sidewalks, schools, or police protection. One in ten finds nothing to fault. Sendas Frutales does not show as considerable variation here; location and neighborliness count high, and delinquency and an overall lack of services account for most complaints.

In more general terms, the pobladores in all six locales are not overly harsh; satisfaction is strong more often than not in all of the pueblos jóvenes (less so in Sendas Frutales) and most feel that their neighborhoods are making (and will continue to make) modest progress. Again—and with reason—those in rental slum housing are substantially less sanguine.

Inter-Personal Relations. [11] Investment in, and affect toward, a community can occur simply because a person finds the location useful or because he has no alternative and must accept his situation. Likewise, satisfaction with a neighborhood can exist for many idiosyncratic reasons. In other words, neither affect

TABLE 7
PERCEPTIONS OF LOCAL NEIGHBORHOOD: SATISFACTION, BY COMMUNITY

	Primero de Enero (N=93)	Pampa de Arena (N=111)	Santiago (N=104)	28 de Julio A (N=59)	28 de Julio B (N=55)	Sendas Frutales (N=105)	Total (N=527)
1. Perceptions of community							
a. Aspect most liked							
Peacefulness, tranquility	3.2%	23.6%	48.5%	6.9%	9.1%	19.4%	20.4%
Home ownership, no rent	85.0	41.0	5.8	18.9	18.1	9.7	30.8
Facilities available (schools, transportation, streets, etc.)	1.1	3.6	5.4	1.7	5.4	11.7	5.8
Location (central, near work, etc.)	1.1	1.8	16.5	43.1	45.5	30.1	19.3
Other (good neighbors, relatives nearby, clean air)	9.6	30.0	20.4	29.3	21.8	29.1	23.4
b. Aspect most disliked							
Lack of basic services	83.6	67.4	9.5	21.5	10.5	19.4	38.3
Lack of communal facilities (streets, schools, land titles, etc.)	4.8	8.7	34.9	12.6	25.1	21.4	17.9
Location, environment	—	6.7	12.6	7.2	10.4	5.1	6.7
Character of neighborhood (poor neighbors, delinquency, etc.)	11.8	10.5	24.3	39.3	33.3	37.1	29.2
Nothing; everything is good	—	5.8	18.9	19.6	20.8	13.3	11.9

2. Overall satisfaction with neighborhood							
Good	52.2	52.2	62.5	56.0	65.5	41.2	53.9
Fair	40.2	40.5	33.7	30.5	32.7	40.2	37.1
Poor	7.6	7.3	3.8	13.5	1.8	18.6	9.0
3. Perceived progress of neighborhood							
Rapid	—	8.3	13.5	25.4	63.0	2.9	14.5
Slow	63.7	78.7	85.6	62.7	37.0	63.7	69.6
None	36.3	13.0	1.0	11.9	—	33.3	16.0
4. Believes neighborhood will improve during next five years	96.6	98.2	94.2	98.3	98.1	83.7	94.4

Note: All differences are significant at .005 or beyond, x^2 test.

TABLE 8

PERCEPTIONS OF LOCAL NEIGHBORHOOD: INTER-PERSONAL RELATIONS, BY COMMUNITY

	Primero de Enero (N=93)	Pampa de Arena (N=111)	Santiago (N=104)	28 de Julio A (N=59)	B (N=55)	Sendas Frutales (N=105)	Total (N=527)
1. Neighbors seen as friendly							
All	19.6%	29.7%	26.0%	49.2%	50.0%	40.0%	33.5%
Some	77.2	61.3	61.5	47.5	40.7	49.5	58.1
None	3.3	9.0	12.5	3.4	9.3	10.5	8.4
2. Residence of closest friends is in same community	28.3	52.4	31.9	76.8	72.0	38.8	46.0
3. Perceived unity in neighborhood							
Strong	–	22.2	7.1	16.9	37.0	13.9	14.6
Fair	91.4	54.6	37.8	42.4	42.6	32.7	51.1
Minimal	8.6	23.2	55.1	40.0	20.4	53.5	34.3
4. Neighborhood seen as having conflicting groups present	–	39.1	54.9	82.0	50.0	19.7	37.6
5. Neighbors seen as willing to help one another	47.0	51.0	28.0	30.5	43.1	32.0	38.6

Note: All differences are significant at .005 or beyond, x^2 test.

nor satisfaction may produce the spirit of community mentioned earlier unless a third ingredient is added—namely, the ability of a neighborhood's inhabitants to get along with one another.

Table 8 offers evidence that most pobladores view their neighbors with a reasonable degree of friendliness and trust and that many have their closest friends in their same neighborhoods. Perceived unity varies greatly across localities. Primero de Enero and Pampa de Arena manifest low levels, along with Zone B of 28 de Julio; Zone A and Santiago, however, contain people well aware of the divisive organizational problems (at the time of interviewing)—indeed, over four out of five in Zone A see conflict present, as do over half in Santiago. The great majority of these respondents can also identify by group as well as by individual leaders just what the sources of conflict are, and judge such conflictual activities detrimental to their neighborhoods. Half or less of each area feels that neighbors are willing to help one another, but a number of respondents remember some incidents vividly. For instance, various pobladores recall neighbors joining to help out in cases of illness or death, others mention having helped one another in house construction, and many remember community successes achieved through neighbors working together.

The data concerning these three areas—neighborhood affect, satisfaction with the area, and inter-personal relations—suggest that despite sometimes considerable inter-locality differences, most pobladores are quite favorably disposed toward their place of residence and their neighbors. That conflict exists is inevitably the case, and a minority of the sample shows signs of alienation and dislike for both neighborhood and neighbors. Some Lima natives complain of being surrounded by *provincianos;* others see their neighborhoods as simply a place to live and nothing more, and still others, especially in the newer areas, despair of obtaining even basic services. Nevertheless, most are clearly determined to stay where they are and are as clearly convinced that progress will occur. Overall, three-quarters answer affirmatively to the question, "Do you think that (name of community) has changed since you have been here?" It is worth noting that half of those answering affirmatively (90 percent of both Primero de Enero and Sendas Frutales answered negatively) credit their community's residents for whatever changes have taken place.

The data in general also support a pattern that Goldrich (1970), Mangin (1967a, 1967b), and others have noted: as a squatter locality progresses and gradually solves its problems, the spirit of community—the amalgam of "shared activities, experiences, and values, common loyalties and perspectives, and human networks" (Keller, 1968: 90-91)—atrophies. Simple age does not correlate with this decline; both zones of 28 de Julio have residents with strong attachments to their neighborhoods. But Santiago, easily the most developed and successful, also has the lowest levels of community unity, neighborliness, and general satisfaction. Before analyzing why this should be the case, it is necessary to see if and how these general community-related perceptions and feelings influence specifically political activities.

Communal Problems and Political Participation

Chapter 1 defined political participation as individual or collective efforts to provide neighborhoods with communal goods, sometimes but not always through attempts to obtain a favorable distribution of governmental resources. By sketching in the pobladores' views of themselves and perceptions of their neighborhoods, two major parts of the study start to come together: how communal problem-solving is undertaken, and the ways in which the pobladores act to confront their most pressing needs.

The inhabitants of the six neighborhoods have definite ideas about their communities, and table 9 reflects a considerable degree of variation across localities. When a basic utility—especially water—is missing, such an absence produces a clear, strong felt need around which a community might well mobilize. In areas that enjoy at least a modicum of services, the pobladores perceive a wider range of other needs—paved streets and sidewalks, schools, police protection, and so forth. In a couple of neighborhoods, land titles are especially salient. But in general terms, the greater the degree of development, the wider the variance in perceived objective needs.

Table 9 also shows that poor neighborhoods do not agree on the proper resources for combatting their problems nor on what factors are most important. A solid third of the respondents feel that they can handle their own problems internally and that external aid is not only unnecessary but in some cases might be an actual hindrance. A long-term migrant market-stall owner in Pampa de Arena, and a block delegate to the local organization, described such an instance:

> The Fathers of Families of Pampa de Arena [the local association] had trouble with some bad leaders who took over the association; we voted them out and made them leave, but we didn't have any trouble. Some neighbors wanted to complain [to the national government], but I argued that would cause more problems than we already had. Who needs someone to tell us how to run our own association?

In addition, a majority of pobladores overall judge "hard work by the community's residents" to be the most important of four fixed alternatives for local improvements;[12] only in Santiago and Sendas Frutales is this not the case, and for understandable reasons. Santiago has reached the point where almost everything that can be done locally has already been done, whereas Sendas Frutales can do virtually nothing for itself until and unless its juridical status changes fundamentally. In the other four neighborhoods, the pobladores (sometimes by a two-to-one ratio) evince a thoroughgoing faith in their abilities to confront the problems that face them. While acknowledging the need for government aid in certain instances, many pobladores have strong feelings as to how, when, and where this aid should be present—feelings that have at times run counter to government policies.

The pobladores appear to have distinct ideas as to who can contribute to community welfare. The salience of the presidency probably means, to a large extent, just what it says: the president himself is seen as a potentially crucial source of aid and not simply as a symbol of the government. The frequency with which neighborhoods will send and publish letters to the president not only indicates the high profile of the office, it also reveals that the pobladores recognize that when outside aid or resources are necessary or useful, these resources exist on the national level of government, not the local.

Given the faith in and preference for intra-community problem-solving, but also given the recognition the poor accord to outside governmental aid (but see Cornelius, 1975: 174-177), we can now turn to an analysis of how the pobladores do in fact become involved in using both internal and external resources.

Participation in Communal Problem-Solving

Table 10 suggests that the pobladores in the six neighborhoods undertake the resolution of communal needs in a number of ways and that involvement varies considerably across communities. Within the squatter neighborhoods (i.e., excluding Sendas Frutales), two-thirds of the sample have lent a hand at least twice in some sort of community effort. For this segment, the most common projects include providing a school or market (33.5 percent), improving streets or sidewalks (26.8 percent), or struggling with the lack of potable water (26.5 percent). At times, these projects are almost literally community-wide; three-quarters of Zone B in 28 de Julio worked on the water project, and two-thirds of Primero de Enero contributed in some way to building the neighborhood's ten-room elementary school. Most help out with manual labor (ditch-digging, brick-laying, and the like), by helping to organize the project during its initial stages, by contributing money for supplies, or by drumming up support from neighbors (or some combination of these). Fully four out of five participants classify their efforts as successful; another 10 percent say that the project is still incomplete; only a tenth feel that they had failed. Failure rate

TABLE 9

COMMUNAL PROBLEMS AND SOURCES OF AID, BY COMMUNITY

	Primero de Enero (N=93)	Pampa de Arena (N=111)	Santiago (N=104)	28 de Julio A (N=59)	28 de Julio B (N=55)	Sendas Frutales (N=105)	Total (N=527)
1. Most important neighborhood problem							
No water	61.3%	89.2%	18.3%	72.9%	16.4%	22.9%	47.6%
No electricity	–	9.9	–	3.4	–	30.5	8.5
No paved streets	–	–	22.1	1.7	27.3	23.8	12.1
Lack of other facilities (markets, schools, etc.)	–	–	51.0	6.8	19.9	8.6	14.3
No land titles	37.6	–	1.0	8.5	21.8	–	10.1
Other	–	.9	7.6	6.8	14.6	14.4	7.5
2. Location of resources needed for resolving neighborhood problems							
Within community	45.1	36.4	23.0	29.8	18.9	28.7	31.3
External to community	54.9	60.9	77.0	68.4	56.6	68.1	64.8
Both, other	–	2.7	–	1.8	24.5	3.2	4.0
3. Most important factor for community improvement							
Hard work by residents	58.7	70.9	39.8	55.2	60.4	38.1	53.2
Governmental aid	39.1	29.1	46.6	43.1	35.8	54.3	41.7
Luck, God's help	2.2	–	13.6	1.7	3.8	7.6	5.2

4. Ranking (by mean of 1-9 scale) of persons or groups who might aid in solving communal problems

President Velasco	6.9
School teachers	5.2
Municipal authorities	4.8
Police	4.7
Priests	4.5
Newspapermen	4.3
Mayor of Lima	4.3
Local leaders	4.3
Private groups	3.5

was highest in Zone A of 28 de Julio (37.5 percent), where community action had been both low and ineffective, doubtless due to the high level of intra-neighborhood organizational conflict. No other neighborhood had an unsuccessful rate of over 20 percent.

The squatters also become involved in petitioning local leaders and national agencies for help, although these are less common activities. Those who report going to see their local associations' leaders have done so largely to inquire into (or complain about) land tenure and the lack of definitive titles or to ask for the organizations' aid in some project. The poor see these visits as a good deal less efficacious; only a third feel that they have been useful, and almost a half report outright failure. Such perceptions, nevertheless, do not necessarily reflect badly on community leadership. On the contrary, the problems that provoke the petition (especially land adjudication) are for the most part outside the ability of local leaders to solve; all they can do in turn is petition national authorities for aid or resolution of the problem.

For those pobladores who have taken the time and devoted the energies and resources necessary for visiting a government agency—most commonly, the Dirección (Bureau) of Pueblos Jóvenes—land problems again dominate the motives cited. And, once again, success is much less evident; only a third feel that they accomplished what they set out to do. Only 30 percent call their efforts useless, nevertheless, since an equal percentage consider their business with the bureau *en trámite* (still pending). Finally, the pobladores also rate their interactions with local leaders and national authorities as courteous, and feel that they received a good deal of attention.

Thus the squatters in the five pueblos jóvenes have not only had some considerable experience in problem-solving using both intra- and supra-local resources; they also feel that their efforts have by and large paid off (or at least may have a chance to do so) and that they have been listened to. In sum, what they have tried has worked. Some disappointments have occurred, of course, and delays often cause the respondents to complain about endless visits to offices, work parties called off, money invested fruitlessly, and the like. But by and large, the squatters' modest and frequent successes probably tend to reinforce these peaceful, non-disruptive activities and to make them both acceptable and worth repeating.

Sendas Frutales: A Deviant Case. Being a slum area, Sendas Frutales has had far less luck in dealing with its relevant authorities. Collaborative undertakings constitute rare and exceptional behavior, since the payment of rent effectively discourages any sort of dwelling improvement. In addition, the inhabitants of Sendas Frutales normally have only two options open to them: they can appeal to their landlords, or they can go to the Municipality of San José, the district

TABLE 10

COMMUNITY-RELEVANT PARTICIPATORY BEHAVIOR, BY COMMUNITY

	Primero de Enero (N=93)	Pampa de Arena (N=111)	Santiago (N=104)	28 de Julio A (N=59)	B (N=55)	Sendas Frutales (N=105)	Total (N=527)
A. Problem-Solving Behavior							
1. Frequent involvement in communal activities (more than one instance)	79.5%	71.9%	52.4%	54.2%	84.3%	8.7%	43.9%
2. Recent involvement in communal activities (within past year)	51.1	63.9	14.7	22.4	27.1	2.0	41.3
3. Has petitioned local leaders about communal problem [1]	54.8	32.7	11.5	34.5	34.5	35.3	33.5
4. Has been to ONDEPJOV for any reason [2]	50.2	28.4	32.7	44.8	49.1	61.5	42.0
5. Has petitioned ONDEPJOV about communal problem [2]	46.2	23.6	12.3	40.8	40.9	4.8	24.2
B. Politically-Relevant Behavior							
1. Member of some local association	54.3	27.3	12.7	30.5	29.6	2.9	25.0
2. Attended local meeting within past three months	76.3	52.9	18.3	62.1	58.2	8.0	43.0*
3. Member of local school association	17.4	27.3	26.5	27.1	24.1	23.1	24.2
4. Member of three or more voluntary organizations	10.9	21.9	18.8	20.4	32.7	16.3	19.2*

Notes: [1] In Sendas Frutales, substitute "landlord" for local leader.
[2] In Sendas Frutales, substitute "Municipality of San José" for ONDEPJOV.
Inter-community differences not significant at .001 level by x^2 test.

of Lima in which they reside. About a third of the sample has tried the first alternative; visits stem from concern over dilapidated conditions, non-functioning toilet and bath facilities, the need for improved water and electric service, or trouble with the rent. However, only 20 percent count their efforts as even partially successful; the rest describe landlords who refuse to listen and/or comply, who are indifferent, or who tell the poblador to resolve his problems himself. And for the handful of people who have gone to the Municipality of San José, most feel that they have wasted their time and that district authorities inevitably side with tax-paying landowners and not their tenants (if the authorities become involved at all).

The slum-dwellers simply do not have the same possibilities open to them for communal problem-solving as do the squatters. This lack of opportunity is due to the existence of rent payments and the ownership of land by private individuals; it is also due to the unwillingness of a series of national administrations (including the post-1968 Revolutionary Government) to provide the policy and bureaucratic framework through which a tenant can ask for assistance. Under such circumstances, any widespread involvement or mobilization is most unlikely, and only the blatant eviction actions of Villarán (chapter 4) coalesced the previously atomized neighborhood into taking the unprecedented step of appealing to the salient politico-religious figure of Bishop Bambarén. Msgr. Bambarén changed the whole tenor of previous landlord-tenant patterns by being an effective spokesman who had contacts and visibility the poor did not.

The Successful Resolution of Communal Problems

All of the findings presented thus far support the major conclusions of Cornelius (1969), Nelson (1969, 1979), Portes (1972), and many others, namely, that the urban poor in Latin America tend strongly to be politically non-disruptive, that they view their experiences as positive, and that they are unwilling to risk what they have gained by participating in violent or anti-establishment behavior. For the large majority of the sample, the city and the pueblos jóvenes and the government function satisfactorily. Migrants of rural origin do not expect the world to be given to them; they are willing to save and invest and defer gratification of immediate needs for long-term gains, and they feel that these investments do (and will continue to) pay dividends. The pobladores obviously are not naive or even easily satisfied. But Lima has permitted them to move beyond what could have awaited them in their home towns, and, relatively speaking, improvement has occurred, despite the problems and needs that all pobladores recognize.

These general conclusions, however, still do not explain why communities differ so markedly in their levels of involvement. Why is it, for instance, that Zone A of 28 de Julio can obtain such wide cooperation on some project, while Zone B cannot? Why does involvement apparently taper off as a community progresses? And, more generally, what sorts of communal needs provoke wide-spread involvement? In response, certain factors appear to explain why mobi-lization does or does not occur in a neighborhood. These are the character of the need or the issue involved, the felt stakes or investments of the pobladores, and the leadership's ability to organize internally and to petition externally.

The needs over which widespread community involvement has arisen have generally been truly *collective*. In other words, to mobilize a community, a need not only must be present, it must also be a salient, pressing disadvantage to everyone in the neighborhood, must be unavoidable and constant (i.e., not be an intermittent issue), and must be too costly for one person to supply indi-vidually (Mollenkopf, 1973). The presence of such a need is probably a neces-sary but not a sufficient factor for successful mobilization. Second, the pobla-dores must feel a major personal, emotional stake in their community and in the need to resolve some issue such as the one described. Common suffering or felt deprivation such as illegal land tenure can produce such a stake, at least for a while; so can a communal experience such as mass participation in a land inva-sion.

The emergence of effective leadership is a crucial final success factor. Leader-ship exerts an influence in a variety of ways; these include the formation and maintenance of (by the perceptions of the majority of the pobladores) a strong, effective community organization, the exclusion or suppression of intra-community conflict, and the capacity to resolve perceived problems (e.g., through delivering needed resources) by obtaining supra-community resources when ap-propriate (Cornelius, 1975, chapter 6; Giusti, 1971; Hodara, 1965-1966; Paredes, 1973: 207-232).

The circumstances that provoked wide neighborhood response had these three elements in common. The lack of a water system in Zone B of 28 de Ju-lio, for instance, was such a need. It created a sense of common suffering and hence a widespread stake in its resolution; and the community responded to aggressive leadership that was able to organize internally and to tap external re-sources. In contrast, the need was equally great in Zone A, and presumably the stakes were comparably intense. But Zone A could not avoid severe, divisive internal conflict that thwarted organizational attempts and crippled petitions for outside assistance.

Another reason for the aggregate differences in communal involvement lies in the straightforward fact that older communities are apt to have done almost everything that they can by and for themselves, and have also resolved their

most pressing needs. As a result, little consensus exists as to what is most important (as in Santiago; see table 10), and little remains that can be achieved
solely by internal self-help. With a disagreement about needs that are not truly
pressing and that cannot be resolved internally, community mobilization becomes close to impossible even with the best leadership, and problem-solving
declines to petitioning external sources for aid, carried out by a small coterie
of pobladores who may not have wide support.

Conclusion

These findings contribute to a continuing discussion in the social sciences
concerning the effect of the urban environment on migrants from provincial
areas. One school of thought, beginning with Deutsch (1963) and Lerner
(1958), argues that residence in a city presents an individual with increased
exposure to political information, groups, parties, and pressures, thereby increasing political participation. This "social mobilization" view contrasts
sharply with the "anomie" school, which emphasizes the alienation supposedly
inherent in the city. Migrants, dependent on the traditional bonds of family,
kin, and a close-knit rural community, find themselves uprooted, without norms,
and marginalized when they move into a city. Thus the social mobilization approach predicts increased participation, often of a radical tendency; the anomie
approach looks for apathy and withdrawal (Fisher, 1975).
  The findings here do not present a clear case for either theory; participation
is much lower in the slum than in the squatter setting, but other individual-
level differences between slum dweller and squatter are insignificant. In attempting to square theory with data, two major points need to be made. In the first
place, any theoretical generalization that attempts to predict the behavior of
all migrants in *all* urban areas runs the great risk of simply being too sweeping
to be useful. As Cornelius (1969) notes,

> . . . the most serious deficiency of the conventional wisdom in this area lies
> in its broad conceptualization of the population flow into urban areas as an
> undifferentiated mass responding in uniform fashion to a given set of condi-
> tions or stimuli, to which all migrants are presumably exposed. [110]

Although some generalizations can of course be made about migrants and their
backgrounds, Lima's migrant (or native) poor are not individuals who will react
to the city in identical fashion. Social mobilization or anomie theories are, fundamentally, aggregate theories based on suppositions about macro-level social
and demographic movements—yet they claim to predict micro-level individual

attitudes and behavior patterns. Therefore, given the macro nature of the theories, but also given the large variety and differentiation among migrants, migration patterns, and urban dwelling environments, it is not at all surprising to find theory and data uncomfortably juxtaposed.

Second, the theoretical perspectives of both schools do not permit any detailed inclusion or discussion of the effect of *differing neighborhood types* on the migrant (Cornelius, 1975: 132-134; Eisinger, 1976: 14-17; Greenberg, 1974, chapters 3 and 4). The data and descriptions have clearly shown the different effect that a neighborhood can have on its inhabitants, but neither theory is capable of the sort of community-level differentiation necessary.

In general terms, therefore, neither theory is especially accurate; perhaps neither can take account of community-level structural differences. Local-level conditions influence political behavior very strongly, and any theoretical statement that does not take such differentiation into account, or that does not have sufficient flexibility to account for such local-level variation, will thereby be deficient (Clark, 1978).

Huntington and Nelson (1976) argue that "individual mobility leads to higher socio-economic status and thus to higher levels of political involvement" (95). But individual mobility, when coupled with successful organizational neighborhood activity, may (as shown here) paradoxically produce a decline in continued local-level involvement. Lima's squatters initially undertake individual mobility and collective political action simultaneously, counter to what Huntington and Nelson seem to claim (1976: 95). If both individual *and* community progress occur, then collective activities diminish, as in Santiago. But individual progress with only partial communal change (e.g., in 28 de Julio, Zone B), or early community progress with little individual SES progress (Primero de Enero), may permit or encourage both mobility and organization to occur.

Thus both individual and neighborhood participation are subject to numerous influences. The next task is to probe into the structure of participation, to identify those pobladores who become active in their communities, and to describe how these activists differ from their less involved neighbors. The activists are the people who most frequently interact with external political authorities; knowing something about them will let us understand the nature of elite-mass involvement more fully.

6. Modes of Participation and the Community Activist: An Empirical Analysis

Until recently, many studies of participation have posited that involvement occurs along some sort of continuum, ranging from total non-involvement to very active full-time dedication to political activities (see, e.g., Milbrath, 1965: 18; Goldrich, 1970, discusses politicization among the urban poor in Peru and Chile in the same way). However, Sidney Verba and Norman Nie (and associates) during the early 1970s offered an alternative concept of participation. They proceeded as follows:

> Most studies of participation have . . . paid little attention to the question of the alternative ways in which citizens participate . . . Most studies have been of participation within the context of electoral politics. . . .
>
> Our view differs. We wish to look beyond the vote as a means of activity and beyond the electoral system . . . There are many types of activists engaging in different acts, with different motives, and different consequences. [Verba and Nie, 1972: 44-45]

And again:

> Fundamental to our approach is the notion that [participation] is a multi-dimensional phenomenon . . . Most studies . . . have focused upon two modes of activity within the electoral process—voting and campaign activity. We add to these dimensions of activity two non-electoral ones . . . citizen-initiated contacts . . . [and] cooperative activity with other citizens . . . to influence governmental officials. [Verba, Nie, and Kim, 1971: 10-11]

Using this assumption as a basis for an extensive cross-national study, Verba and his colleagues investigated similarities and differences in participation among seven countries—Austria, India, Japan, Nigeria, the United States, the Netherlands, and Yugoslavia (Verba and Nie, 1972; Verba, Nie, and Kim, 1971; Verba, Nie, et al., 1973; Kim, Nie, and Verba, 1974; Verba, Nie, and Kim, 1978). These nations all differ from one another along an enormous variety of dimensions: party systems, electoral laws and practices, literacy and overall rates of development and mobilization, income, and ethnic complexities and cleavages. However, the first six are (or were, at the time of the study) fundamentally democratic, electoral nation-states with open competition between or among two or more parties for public office. Yugoslavia, alone among the seven, has a setting in which political participation might predictably take on qualitatively distinct modes, due in large part to the much different role elections play in political life, to the fundamentally distinct party system, and to the broad variety of self-government or self-regulated institutions present in that society. Despite all differences, however, Verba, Nie, et al. identified four closely parallel modes of participation in each nation. In the first five countries, these modes are labeled campaign activity, voting, communal activity, and personalized contacts. In Yugoslavia, however, campaign activity is replaced by another mode described as self-management, leading the authors to conclude that "the Yugoslavian case represents . . . a most interesting example of the way in which the political structures in a nation can affect the general ways in which citizens take part in political life" [Verba and Nie, 1972: 248]. Moreover, the authors make a highly important comment when they note that the Dutch survey data produced a fifth mode of political activity "that had no direct parallel elsewhere" (249), thereby suggesting that the four original modes, though distinctive, are by no means exhaustive of all possible modes of political involvement.

These findings—first, that participation in a variety of nations exhibits features of multi-dimensionality; and second, that political participation patterns can apparently be modified by significant structural differences within a political system—represent major steps in comparative research across nations. But despite the inclusion of Yugoslavia, it can be argued that Verba's work is limited in that *the seven nations differ from one another in degree but not in kind.* All seven are electoral regimes of some variety; none is (or was, at the time of data collection) a truly authoritarian or dictatorial no-party system. The comparisons, therefore, though cross-national and indeed cross-cultural, are not *cross-systemic*, since no country operates under a non-electoral regime. Applying the multi-dimensional model of participation to the specific case of the urban poor will not only test the generalizability of the approach; it will also allow a deeper look into the way communal involvement is structured (cf. Cornelius, 1975: 90-93; Verba, Nie, and Kim [1978: 331-339, 384-386] list other studies using the Verba-Nie approach).

Two Modes of Participation

As a beginning, table 11 sets down five specific political acts that occur, and are available, to a poblador (see also table 10).[1] The first activity, by far the most frequent, involves an individual's voluntary participation in local-level community activities; the second inquires into how recently such activity took place. These are both *communal involvement*, since they concern participation in collaborative, cooperative projects within a community undertaken to solve a communal need, utilizing intra-community resources. The last three, however, differ in that they involve both individual and collective acts aimed at extracting some benefit from political authorities (whether local or national) by influencing the decisions of these authorities; these three activities can be labeled *demand-making* (Cornelius, 1975: 167).

Both communal involvement and demand-making are participatory kinds of political behavior in which the pobladores become involved. Whether these five activities are in fact part of an overall participatory dimension, or whether they separate into two distinct modes, however, are empirical questions.

One rough way of estimating how well these two different types of activities are *intra-* as well as *inter*-related is presented in table 12A, using product-moment correlation coefficients. Two findings emerge: first, all five variables are modestly well related with one another (all coefficients significant at .001 or less); and second, the coefficients *within* the two sets of related activities are considerably stronger than *across* the two sets. However, such findings, though useful, are inadequate for testing the hypothesis that distinct modes of participation may exist. In order to accomplish this task, table 12B presents the results of two states of a factor analysis, first with a principal components (unrotated) solution, and then with a rotated oblique solution.

Table 12B's principal components solution indicates that all variables do indeed belong to some common dimension of activism and that this dimension explains approximately 35 percent (and in one case almost 50 percent) of the variance in each activity and accounts for almost half (46 percent) of the total variance among the five variables.

A clearer picture of communal involvement and demand-making as distinct modes of political participation emerges from an examination of the oblique rotated factor solution in table 12B (see Verba and Nie, 1972: 64). This solution offers confirmation for the predicted distinction between collaborative, intra-community attempts to satisfy a communal need and attempts to petition local and national leaders for additional assistance or aid. Moreover, these

TABLE 11

FIVE POLITICALLY RELEVANT ACTIVITIES

1. Have you collaborated with other inhabitants of (community's name) in any sort of community work?
(Scored for frequency of collaboration) 73.3%

COMMUNAL INVOLVEMENT

2. Have you ever worked or cooperated with other residents of (community's name) to try to meet some need or solve some problem of (community's name)? When did you do this?
(Scored for participation within the past year) 38.5%

3. Have you ever personally, alone or with other residents of (community's name), gone to talk with some official of the local association about some problem or need?
(Scored for affirmative answer) 33.1%

DEMAND-MAKING

4. And have you ever personally, alone or with other residents of (community's name), gone to talk with an official of the National Office of Pueblos Jóvenes about some problem or need?
(Scored for affirmative answer) 32.6%

5. Are you acquainted with the National Office of Pueblos Jóvenes near Unidad Vecinal No. 3? Have you ever gone there?
(Scored for affirmative answer) 37.1%

(N varies from 415 to 422)

TABLE 12A

CORRELATION COEFFICIENTS AMONG FIVE
PARTICIPATORY VARIABLES

Participatory Variables	Correlation Coefficients				
	1	2	3	4	5
1. Frequent involvement	—	.52	.30	.21	.22
2. Recent involvement		—	.35	.26	.17
3. Local demands			—	.44	.28
4. National demands				—	.52
5. Office visit					—

TABLE 12B

FIVE-VARIABLE ACTIVISM INDEX: PRINCIPAL AND
OBLIQUE ROTATED SOLUTIONS

Participatory Variables	Principal Component (Unrotated)	Oblique Rotation	
		Communal Involvement	Demand-Making
1. Frequent involvement	.65	.85	−.03
2. Recent involvement	.68	.87	−.01
3. Local demands	.71	.38	.49
4. National demands	.73	.00	.87
5. Office visit	.64	−.10	.86

modes revolve around the pobladores' place of residence, and deal largely with efforts to resolve either directly (collaborative effort) or indirectly (making a demand to a political leader) some pressing need. Both modes are also clearly non-disruptive in nature. Yet neither can be interpreted as involuntary, coerced, or ceremonial; both involve attempts to ameliorate a perceived need, although only one specifically centers on attempts to influence a government official and the distribution of goods and services.

However, the oblique rotated solution also implies that still another mode (or modes) of participation may be present. Although the equivocal performance of locally-directed demand-making loads more heavily on the generalized demand-making mode than on the communal involvement mode, the loadings do not differ greatly (.49 and .38). This lack of a clearly defined, unambiguous loading suggests that local-level demand-making may constitute yet a third mode of participation.

The Modes of Participation: Some Further Analysis

Examining this ambiguity and the reasons behind it involves taking a somewhat circuitous path. There are several models that examine the causal relationships between the location of individuals in their class structure, their involvement in organizational life, their levels of political participation, and the attitudinal and cognitive variables that link them. In order to investigate these relationships at the individual level, Nie, Powell, and Prewitt (1969) posited a model that links social structure and organizational involvement to political participation by way of attitudinal and cognitive pathways. They conclude that social structure and organizational involvement represent two distinct paths to participation. Involvement is more directly linked to participation; socioeconomic status is mediated by intervening attitudinal variables. We can apply similar causal interpretations to the data for the pobladores; the formal technique employed here in fitting the empirical results to the causal model is path analysis.[2] The major utility of path analysis lies in its clarification of relationships suggested by previous empirical results and theory.

Variable in the Model. The model here has seven variables. First are two *input* or exogenous variables, which are the individual's objective socioeconomic position and the political effects of his membership in the local community association. Second are four *intervening* variables that tap both attitudinal and cognitive aspects of an individual's political life; third is the *dependent variable,* which is participation. The four intervening variables attempt to represent the linkages between social structural and organizational characteristics and their relations to political participation. Nie, Powell, and Prewitt summarize the causal argument for the sequence as follows:

> Economic development alters the social structure particularly in terms of the class structure, secondary group structure, and residence patterns in society. The increase in socio-economic status and organizational complexity (which are concomitants of urbanization) changes the patterns of political socialization. Greater numbers have those politically relevant life experiences which lead to increased political information, political awareness, sense of efficacy, and sense of citizen duty. These attitudes and cognitions, in turn, lead to increased levels of political participation. [1969: 808]

The intervening variables in the model are: 1) *commitment to community*, similar to Almond and Verba's (1961) "citizen duty" scale, which is measured by an index of the sum of four dichotomized variables; 2) *political information*, which is composed of seven dichotomized variables, and whose intent is to get at the individual's access to sources of political information; 3) *political efficacy*, which is composed of two dichotomized variables dealing with perceived treatment in a hypothetical encounter with government; and 4) *political attentiveness*, which is operationalized in an index of seven variables that aims at an individual's ability to recognize significant political characters and events. The exogenous variables are: 1) *socio-economic status*, which is a standard scale composed of measures of education, occupational status, and income, and 2) *organizational involvement*, which is a single variable measuring membership in the local community association.

The Path Analytic Model. The model presented in Figure 2 is strong and relatively parsimonious, explaining 43 percent of the variance in the dependent variable. The model emphasizes the limited relationship between socio-economic status and political activism; any correlation between the two variables is mediated through the positive effect socio-economic status has on an individual's access to political information. Because the population residing in squatter settlements has such a limited SES range, however, we must look elsewhere for an explanation of participation among squatters. As is shown later on, the activist poblador varies only slightly from his inactive neighbor on almost every SES indicator.

The factor with the greatest explanatory power in the model is membership in the local association.[3] Nie, Powell, and Prewitt suggest that organizational involvement, though propelling individuals into political life, does not do so through increasing their propensity to acquire political information, their sense of political efficacy, or their political attentiveness (Nie, Powell, and Prewitt,

1969: 813); this analysis supports their findings in part. Nie, Powell, and Prewitt found that 21 percent of the correlation between organizational involvement and participation is accounted for by the paths through the attitude variables, and that a full 58 percent of this correlation is accounted for by the direct
path between them. The Peruvian data show a similar proportion: 22 percent
of the correlation is accounted for by indirect effects, and the direct effects
account for 75 percent. Again, the relationship between involvement and activism when mediated by socio-economic status is almost non-existent in the present study.

Participation and Organizational Involvement: A Re-analysis

Although the close-knit relationship between organizational involvement and
activism parallels many other findings, the fact that local-level involvement explains such a large percentage of activism provokes the following question: Is
organizational involvement here in fact a distinct, separate explanatory variable? Or is *organizational involvement by and of itself an additional mode of
participation?* To examine this possibility, we can expand the five behavioral
activities in table 11 by adding two variables that deal with organizational involvement (see table 13).

The first hint that organizational involvement may be merely another mode
appears in table 14A. Not only do correlation coefficients continue to be modestly strong (and universally positive), but also the coefficients within three new
arrangements of the seven variables are noticeably higher than across the three.
The average coefficient within each group is nearly .50; the average outside is
about .30. Although this finding suggests that a poblador may tend to work
within a single area of activity—i.e., that an individual is more apt to become involved in communal projects *or* in local affairs *or* with the national political system, rather than *across* modes—we still do not know if all seven activities still constitute variations of an underlying participation dimension, or if three discrete
modes do in fact exist. To proceed, therefore, we shall repeat the factor analysis steps outlined in table 12B.

Three Modes of Participation

Table 14B presents a principal-components, unrotated solution that utilizes
the seven variables from table 13. The first component demonstrates very
clearly that all seven activities do jointly constitute a participation dimension;
all seven have positive and approximately similar associations with this component. The first component, moreover, contributes almost 45 percent toward

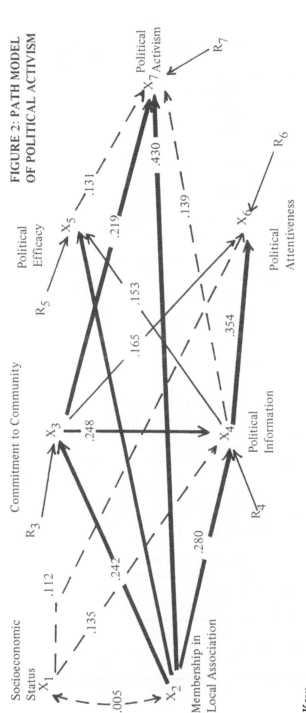

FIGURE 2: PATH MODEL
OF POLITICAL ACTIVISM

Key:

1) All paths shown have path coefficients of at least twice standard error.
2) Heavy black arrows indicate path coefficients of at least .200 (four times standard error).
   Light unbroken arrows indicate coefficients of at least .150 (three times standard error).
   Broken lines indicate coefficients of at least .100 (twice standard error).
3) Residual paths (R_X) and variance explained (in parentheses) for dependent variables:

R_3= .970 (06%) R_4= .900 (20%) R_5= .940 (12%)

R_6= .884 (22%) R_7= .756 (43%)

TABLE 13
SEVEN POLITICALLY RELEVANT ACTIVITIES

COMMUNAL INVOLVEMENT	1. Have you ever collaborated with other inhabitants of (community's name) in any sort of community work? (If yes) How many times? (Scored for at least two such instances)	73.3%
	2. Have you ever worked or cooperated with other residents of (community's name) to try to solve some problem or meet some need of (community's name)? (If yes) When did you do this? (Scored for participation within past year) . . .	38.5%
LOCAL ORGANIZATIONAL INVOLVEMENT	3. Are you presently a member of the local association? (Scored for affirmative answer)	30.5%
	4. In the past three months have you attended a meeting or assembly here in (community's name)? (Scored for affirmative answer)	51.4%
	5. Have you ever personally, either alone or with other residents of (community's name), gone to talk with some official of the local association about some problem or need here in (community's name)? (Scored for affirmative answer)	33.1%
NATIONAL-LEVEL INTERACTION AND DEMAND-MAKING	6. Are you acquainted with the National Office of Pueblos Jóvenes near Unidad Vecinal No. 3? Have you ever gone there? (Scored for affirmative answer)	37.1%
	7. Have you ever personally, either alone or with other residents of (community's name), gone to speak with some official of the National Office of Pueblos Jóvenes about some problem or need here in (community's name)? (Scored for affirmative answer)	32.6%

(N varies from 414 to 422)

TABLE 14A
CORRELATION COEFFICIENTS AMONG SEVEN PARTICIPATORY VARIABLES

Participatory Variables	Correlation Coefficients						
	1	2	3	4	5	6	7
1. Frequent involvement	—	.52	.32	.35	.30	.22	.21
2. Recent involvement		—	.35	.43	.35	.17	.26
3. Local member			—	.43	.53	.30	.43
4. Attendance at meeting				—	.40	.22	.31
5. Local demands					—	.28	.44
6. Office visit						—	.53
7. Office demands							—

TABLE 14B
SEVEN-VARIABLE ACTIVISM INDEX: PRINCIPAL AND OBLIQUE ROTATED SOLUTIONS

Participatory Variables	Principal Component (Unrotated)	Oblique Rotation		
		Communal Involvement	Local Community Involvement	National-Level Interaction
1. Frequent involvement	.61	.89	-.09	.11
2. Recent involvement	.66	.77	.17	-.04
3. Local member	.74	-.01	.80	.08
4. Attendance at meeting	.68	.32	.59	-.09
5. Local demands	.78	-.04	.83	.06
6. Office visit	.56	.10	-.10	.93
7. Office demands	.68	-.06	.33	.70
% total variance	44.6			

the amount of variance explained.

But the final results generated through factor analysis (the rotated oblique solution in table 14B) offer significant evidence that the three modes now hypothesized—communal involvement, local community organizational involvement, and national-level interaction—do in fact exist. Three modes are readily identifiable; one occurs in each factor and the great majority of other variable loadings are consistently low.

The differences between the original bi-modal and the new tri-modal participation indices deserve some discussion. In the first place, factor analysis has revealed that *organizational involvement*—so often classified as a strong explanatory variable affecting political participation—*is in this case one mode of participation.* Such a finding suggests that the close relationship between associational involvement and political activity noted in many studies may be in fact somewhat misleading.

Of the first two modes, the original demand-making mode has disappeared; its local-level item has become part of the new local involvement mode, while its national-level item has moved into the new national interaction mode. The manner in which this split in the original demand-making mode occurs suggests that the *referent* toward which the activity is directed is stronger than the *form* of the activity. Although the pobladores may make demands on both the local and the national level, they are more likely to do one or the other, not both. In other words, although some pobladores are locally oriented, and others nationally, the probability of an individual's presenting demands on both levels may be lessened by the fact that to do so requires transcending the two different arenas of activity, the local and the national.

This tri-modal structure of participation lends considerable empirical credence to the original definition of participation as "individual or collective efforts to provide neighborhood with communal goods, sometimes but by no means always through attempts to obtain a favorable distribution of governmental resources." It was argued in chapter 1 that activities not directed at external governmental actors or resources could justifiably be included as political participation. The factor analysis performed here indicates that, for the pobladores, externally directed political activities make up a subset of a broader type of participatory behavior that does not necessarily involve supra-community linkages, actors, or resources.

Case Studies of Political Involvement

The identification of these three modes offers a quantitative, statistical analysis of how the pobladores try to resolve some communal problems. However, it may be useful to complement these findings with some descriptions of how these modes actually function in practice. It would be possible to relate dozens of specific episodes, incidents, and attempts (both successful and unsuccessful) from each of the communities; those included here are intended to be representative.

Communal involvement. Of the four zones in Pampa de Arena, San Jerónimo Lídice had the most widespread success in community action programs. A number of important communal activities were being carried out simultaneously in 1971. Sunday afternoons were set aside for work on neighborhood projects. By early 1971, San Jerónimo had a community center under way. To pay for the cost of materials (brick, cement, reinforcing steel, window frames, and so forth), each family in the community was assessed a weekly fee of S/40 (then equivalent to US $1.00). Moreover, each family in one or two specific blocks (chosen on a rotating basis) was responsible for providing manpower for the manual labor involved (or else paying an additional quota). On one particular Sunday, approximately two dozen men and women were working at digging trenches for piping and tubing, mixing mortar, and laying brick; some of the men worked on construction crews during the week, and therefore acted as foremen. At the same time, the community had solicited assistance from the Ministry of Health, and a pre-school vaccination clinic had been set up. To raise additional funds, a *gran kermesse* (roughly translated, a neighborhood bazaar) was held, with games of chance as one of the highlights. Finally, the neighborhood was in the process of electing new block delegates to the local association; one family in each block was responsible for the ballot box as well as the duty of going from house to house to remind residents to vote.

Although the variety of activities that were occurring on this particular Sunday was somewhat unusual, the idea of block responsibility on a regular basis is typical of any number of squatter settlements. San Jerónimo's system was perhaps more strongly institutionalized than many; indeed, a neighboring zone had failed completely in its attempt to emulate such a scheme. Perhaps San Jerónimo's success can be ascribed to the presence of several leaders, both formal and informal, who had dedicated themselves to nurturing local improvements.

Local organizational involvement and national-level interaction. We shall describe here a series of meetings that exemplify not only the two modes identified earlier, but also how the two modes relate to communal problem-solving. Local associational meetings frequently (but not always) either are the result of, or they result in, interactions with national-level authorities. However, each of these activities may occur without the other. The case described here shows how local meetings and national-level activities reciprocally influence one another.

Plate 7. Parents wait in line at the temporary community center for immunizations provided for their pre-school children under a Ministry of Health program.

Plate 8. Men and women lend a hand to continue work on the new center. Each family contributed an afternoon of labor every few weeks.

Plate 9. The community also held neighborhood elections; the outgoing block delegate manned the ballot box.

Plate 10. A bingo game as a fund-raiser might collect US$20 or so during the afternoon. Beer and soft drinks were the prizes.

As was suggested in chapter 4, the first few years of Primero de Enero's existence were made difficult because of a bitter dispute between the invaders and several cooperatives over land and the right to build on it. The disagreement became extremely intense, both because the association had paid out S/150,000 (US $3,750) for a share of the land and because the land in question was level and close to the highway leading into Lima. This made the land particularly attractive for establishing residence.

The National Office for the Development of Pueblos Jóvenes (ONDEPJOV) reopened its field office in Primero de Enero because of a national campaign to award land titles to the residents of the pueblos jóvenes. However, the association-cooperatives dispute necessarily had to be resolved before definitive land titles could be awarded. Social workers from ONDEPJOV and architects assigned to the titling program contacted the association (as well as the cooperatives) and announced that the problem had to be resolved or else the association would face the possibility of missing out on the granting of titles.

However, the threat by ONDEPJOV was somewhat idle. The agency was under pressure from its superiors at the office of the prime minister to proceed promptly with the titling program. It was extremely unlikely, therefore, that the agency could bypass Primero de Enero, and, most important, the *leaders of the association knew it.* Thus, when ONDEPJOV notified the association that *titulación* would have to begin, the association told ONDEPJOV that it would have to have a community assembly and a vote. On a damp, cold Sunday evening, about 150 pobladores met in the local straw-mat community center to discuss whether to go ahead with ONDEPJOV's plan before the matter of the disputed land was settled. The vote was unanimous against any cooperation.

Two days later, the association leadership met again with ONDEPJOV. At that time, personnel of ONDEPJOV suddenly revealed that the cooperatives were willing to divide the disputed land, that the S/150,000 would be returned until the issue of the value of the land was settled, and that all remaining surveying and road leveling would start the following week. When this agreement was typed and drawn up, the association and ONDEPJOV both signed, the association went back and informed the residents of the community, and work actually did begin within ten days.

This case suggests a number of salient features about interactions among the poor at an organizational level and between the poor and the national government. Most significantly, the poor, through their leaders and by means of local meetings, can and do have an impact on what the government does. The original intention of ONDEPJOV was to proceed with some remodeling and to distribute land titles while ignoring the dispute between the association and the cooperatives. However, the unwillingness of the residents of Primero de Enero to simply "go along" gave the personnel at ONDEPJOV no choice but to confront another, separate issue and to resolve it as well. The ability of the community to recognize that ONDEPJOV could be forced to accomodate the community and to change its original plans (rather than the reverse) suggests the active role that residents can and do play.

In sum, the three modes of political participation empirically identified and described here are meaningful and useful ways in which the pobladores can help to provide communal goods. They are not the only means available to the poor, as we shall suggest below. Nevertheless, they are probably the most common methods employed, *precisely because they do work.* The poor will reject other potential means of participation if they are not instrumentally successful. Huntington and Nelson (1976) suggest that the tendency for individuals and groups to try to influence the government will be influenced by their access to alternative means of pursuing their goals. If non-political means are at least as promising as political channels, people will invest their time and energy accordingly.

The Distribution of Participation among the Pobladores

Identifying three modes of political involvement now allows an examination of the distribution of the pobladores in each mode, as well as in overall activism. Table 15 reveals first that for each individual mode, national-level involvement appears to be the least likely way of participating; only 25 percent of the pobladores score one or two on this mode, whereas three out of five have participated

TABLE 15
DISTRIBUTION OF POBLADORES IN PARTICIPATORY ACTS: OVERALL AND BY MODES

Communal Involvement		Local Organizational Involvement		National-Level Interaction	
Raw score		Raw score		Raw score	
2	56.2% High	3	19.4% High	2	24.2% High
		2	14.5		
1	22.4 Low	1	26.3 Low	1	20.4 Low
0	21.4	0	39.8	0	55.2

in community development projects of some sort. But how, and in what ways, do the pobladores become active? Clearly, some may participate very little, and others may become involved in one specific way or another. Within the modes identified, some five types of activists emerge immediately:

1. *Total activists*–engaged in all three modes.
2. *National contactors*–confined largely to contacting and petitioning national-level government personnel.
3. *Local members*–involved almost entirely with the local community organization.
4. *Problem-solvers*–engaged in community development projects and in little else.
5. *Inactives*–involved in little political activity of any sort.

By dichotomizing each mode (zero or one is low, two or three is high), it becomes possible to see how many pobladores fall into each type. Table 16 reveals the number in all five classifications. Three-quarters of the pueblo joven sample (313 of 422) fit into one of these types, indicating that a majority of the pobladores do not engage in political activity that crosses modes or that necessitates operating simultaneously on two different levels of government.

However, some pobladores do in fact cross modes, involving themselves in ways other than the five originally hypothesized. What are these types, and how important are they? Table 16 distinguishes them in the following way:

6. *Problem solvers/national contactors*–engaged in community projects and national-level petitioning.
7. *Contactors/demanders*–involved nationally in demand-making and locally in the community organization, but not in community collaborative efforts.
8. *Local community activist*–participatory in both local modes, but not with national-level petitioning.

The first two (6 and 7) together account for only an additional 8 percent; neither appears to be a common combination. But the last classification–the local-level activist–represents a sizeable percentage of our total, containing some 16.3 percent of the sample, and fully 25 percent of the pobladores when the inactives are excluded. This finding, however, should be no surprise; that individuals who participate in community projects are also involved in their community's association is only logical.

These three combinatorial participant types, moreover, reinforce the conclusion that the *arena* provoking activity is stronger than the *mode* of activity. Types 6 and 7 (above) are cross-level as well as cross-modal in nature; both are infrequent. But type 8, which is cross-modal but concerned only with local affairs, actually represents the third most numerous of all eight types. The

TABLE 16

DISTRIBUTION OF TYPES OF PARTICIPANTS

	National	Local	Problem-Solvers	%
1. Total activists	High	High	High	12.7
2. National contactors	High	Low	Low	3.7
3. Local members	Low	High	Low	2.7
4. Problem-solvers	Low	Low	High	21.4
5. Inactives	Low	Low	Low	35.0
				75.5% (N=313)
6. Problem-solvers/national contactors	High	Low	High	5.8
7. Contactors-demanders	High	High	Low	2.4
8. Local activists	Low	High	High	16.3
				24.5% (N=98)

Total N=411; 2.7%, or 11 pobladores, were excluded because of missing data.

pobladores, therefore, display a tendency to confine their political activities either to their local communities or to the national system, although they combine modes within the local setting quite frequently.

The Activist Poblador: A Profile

We now know a good deal more about how the pobladores can become involved; however, nothing has yet been said about what sort of individual becomes involved in politics. In other words, do those pobladores who are highly participatory have perceptions or attitudes or values that are different from those of their inactive counterparts?

To begin to answer this question, those pobladores who have participated in six or seven of the activities in table 15 can be labeled activists. Likewise, any poblador who has involved himself in none or only one of these same activities can be called inactive.[4] Thus categorized, 23.5 percent (N-99) of the pobladores are activists, 23.7 percent (N-100) are inactives. In essence, we are talking about the most and least active quartiles.

Table 17 reveals that the activist and the inactive differ along many important dimensions. It is true that no differences exist along any socio-economic lines; income, education, and occupation are virtually identical. The activist is, however, more likely to be a migrant. But along all variables that involve the local neighborhood and its inhabitants, the activist consistently displays a more positive, optimistic perspective, and emerges (not surprisingly, considering his own involvement) as having considerable faith in his and his community's ability to improve conditions. Nowhere does this belief emerge more strongly than in the activist's perception of the efficacy of hard work as opposed to government assistance for local betterment: three-quarters of the activists rank their own efforts as most important, whereas 60 percent of the inactives opt for governmental aid (see chapter 5, note 12).

In addition, the activist is involved in a broad range of politically relevant activities and belongs to a greater number of voluntary associations than the inactive. And, finally, the participant poblador is open to political stimuli more frequently, and more commonly sees himself as well informed and interested in politics.

If any relationship in sociology and political science has been shown to be persistent, it is the direct correlation between overall SES and participation (see summary and sources in Milbrath, 1965). The analysis thus far has suggested that such indicators are not particularly useful when SES does not vary widely; the participants among Lima's poor are still poor. But several dimensions exist where strong differences occur. The activist poblador shows a marked

TABLE 17
ACTIVIST/INACTIVE COMPARISONS

	Activist (N=99)	Inactive (N=100)
A. Socio-economic status		
1. Migrant	87.9%	75.0%
2. Manual employment	88.8	89.0
3. High job satisfaction	29.2	33.3
4. Income less than $100/month	76.3	74.8
5. Six years or less of school	67.3	62.9
B. Community-related perceptions		
1. Residence seen as permanent	93.3	81.6*
2. Neighbors seen as friends	96.0	82.8*
3. Community unity seen as high	82.3	56.7*
4. Neighbors seen as mutually helpful	48.9	28.4*
5. Local problems not needing outside aid	38.5	22.1*
6. Most important factor for community		
a. Hard work by inhabitants	76.3	30.3
b. Government help	22.7	60.6
c. Other (fatalism)	1.0	9.1*
C. Politically-relevant behavior		
1. Block delegate to local association	20.6	2.0*
2. Acquired land through invasion	70.4	53.7*
3. Member, local school association	33.0	10.0*
4. Member, local neighborhood association	78.7	1.0*
5. Member, three or more organizations	52.1	23.0*
D. Political Stimuli		
1. Listens or watches news daily	85.7	67.0*
2. Reads newspaper daily	91.9	65.3*
3. Discusses politics frequently	51.0	21.0*
4. Attempts to be informed	62.4	35.1*
5. (Migrants only) More interested in politics since migration	47.6	25.3*

*Significant by x^2 test at .05 or beyond. These differences hold true within all five squatter settlements.

preference for group activities, whether by favoring the use of local resources in his community or by belonging to at least a couple of voluntary associations. This preference, in turn, is supported by the very noticeable degree of personal efficacy the activist attributes to himself and his neighbors in solving problems; the activist has a strong faith in his abilities to provide for communal needs.

The likelihood that his optimism and his efforts will, in fact, be successful may be aided by the activist's involvement with his local community as well as with the national political system; his greater knowledge doubtless springs in large part from his broader and more intense exposure to the media and his more frequent participation in political discussion. His commitment to his community is not only manifest in his perception of it as a place of permanent residence; it also appears in the substantial investments of time, money, and energy implied by the fact that he is indeed an activist. In a word, the activist poblador is above all else *involved*—psychologically, cognitively, affectively, and behaviorally.

Activism and the Five Communities

As a final point, we can ask how the various types of participants are distributed across the five communities. Table 18 presents suggestive data for each community and for the types of change that might be expected across time. First, we can look at each community individually.

1. *Primero de Enero.* This community is unique in a number of ways. Perhaps the most important is that the number of inactives is less than the number of either total activists or local activists. This recent invasion settlement, therefore, contains a very large percentage of pobladores involved primarily in local-level activities and in all three modes (in fact, 46.2 percent of *all* total activists in the entire sample are in Primero de Enero). Considering the pressing nature of their communal needs, the pobladores' concentration on these cross-model and cross-level participatory activities is understandable and (from their perspective) pragmatic. The almost total absence of individuals who concentrate solely on demand-making nationally mirrors at least two conditions unique to Primero de Enero: the existence of many projects that can be done with local resources, and the frustration with and lack of confidence in the national government.

2. *Pampa de Arena.* Although inactives make up the largest single category in Pampa de Arena, problem-solvers and local activists are not far behind; these two together make up about 70 percent of the community's population excluding inactives. But the percentage of total activists is the next to lowest of all five settlements, and contacting-demanding as a discrete activity has not emerged to

TABLE 18
TYPES OF PARTICIPANTS BY COMMUNITY

Participant type	Primero de Enero (N=92)	Pampa de Arena (N=107)	Santiago (N=101)	28 de Julio A (N=58)	28 de Julio B (N=54)
1. Total activist	26.1%	8.4%	3.0%	15.5%	13.0%
2. National contactors	–	.9	5.0	6.9	9.3
3. Local members	1.1	2.8	2.0	3.4	5.6
4. Problem-solvers	9.8	27.1	25.7	12.1	31.5
5. Inactives	22.8	30.8	55.4	43.1	16.7
6. Problem-solvers/national contactors	6.5	3.7	4.0	6.9	11.1
7. Contactors-demanders	–	2.8	1.0	8.6	1.9
8. Local activists	33.7	23.4	4.0	3.4	11.1

any meaningful degree. Basically, Pampa de Arena appears to be a settlement in which local-level involvement has diminished somewhat and in which activity in general tapered off after the first few years following the land invasions.

3. *Santiago.* More than half of Santiago is inactive, and another quarter is strictly problem-solvers; total actives and local actives together make up only 7 percent. The high level of development reached in Santiago has paradoxically brought about a marked decline in participation, for a number of reasons. First, all major communal undertakings have been accomplished, and the various needs of the settlement do not provoke the same unanimity or urgency more basic needs might spark in a less-developed area. In addition, Santiago consolidated itself and "filled in" over twenty years or more, and comparative newcomers may have settled when many communal needs had been satisfied and were thus taken for granted. The remaining needs of the community are those that require much time, energy, and perseverance and outside assistance; most pobladores are apparently unwilling to make such efforts.

4. *28 de Julio.* As noted earlier, data come from two contiguous but substantially different zones of 28 de Julio. Since size, age, location, general SES, and a number of other important variables can, in effect, be held constant, we can see if the successes of Zone B are reflected in the types and levels of participatory activity.

Zone A has at least one anomaly: it has the second-highest percentage of both total activists and inactives. It also has the lowest number of local-level activists of any community (3.4 percent), and ranks only 12 percent in problem-solving. But more than 15 percent can be classified as contactors-demanders on either the local or the local and national levels. Zone A, in effect, appears to have little confidence in itself; its energies go into contacting and demanding but not into the more mundane sphere of problem-solving.

Zone B, on the other hand, has the lowest level of inactives anywhere (16.7 percent), the highest number of problem-solvers (31.5 percent), and three times as many local activists and almost as many total activists. Too, a tenth of Zone B operates as national petitioners. Overall, this zone has the broadest spread across all participant types; its attempts to improve its circumstances have created individuals who cover all fronts in trying to bring about change.

Once again, the data indicate that the local community organization declines over time and that the strongly cohesive sense of "community" so evident in new settlements fades over time as improvements take place. The older the settlement, the fewer the number of activists of all descriptions (this tendency is especially evident when 28 de Julio is excluded). But when (as in the case of 28 de Julio) improvements are slow in coming, or when (as in Santiago) a community has succeeded in those major improvements that they bring about by themselves, demand-making as a way of political involvement becomes relatively more common, carried on by a small core of participants who spend increasing amounts of time petitioning external authorities for aid.

Involvement in a Slum Environment

Sendas Frutales offers an instructive comparison to the five squatter neighborhoods. That its deficiencies are as pressing as those of any pueblo joven offers no argument; that it has been unable to confront its problems either through self-help or (until very recently) through petitioning governmental agencies is equally obvious. When field work was being carried out, no neighborhood organization as such existed, despite the efforts of the local parish priest to establish such a group.

Chapter 5 indicated that slum involvement across a variety of participatory activities is quite low. Table 10 showed only minimal involvement in communal problem-solving, in petitioning landlords for improvements, or in going to the Municipality of San José for help. Examining these acts in the same way as was done for the squatters (see table 19), nevertheless, shows that participation still has identifiable modes; for those who are involved, one nexus of activity revolves around local community improvements through collaborative projects or organizational involvement, and the other deals with directing petitions at various outside authority figures.

However, involvement remains extremely low. Fewer than a twentieth of Sendas Frutales's inhabitants have taken part in all five activities, and 70 percent have not participated in any of them. These figures, of course, were gathered prior to the 1972-1973 showdown involving the inhabitants, the landlords, SINAMOS, President Velasco, and Msgr. Bambarén (see chapter 4), and this confrontation has undoubtedly had a major politicizing effect on the populace. The fact that the inhabitants of Sendas Frutales refused to accept President Velasco's decision denying the neighborhood its status as a pueblo joven argues a sense of community and cohesion not present in the 1971 data. Moreover, the pobladores mobilized US $40,000 within less than a year, indicating that savings and a willingness to invest in neighborhood improvements needed the opportunity to germinate. What changed Sendas Frutales was the blatant and illegal move to evict a family, leading to the equally unprecedented countermove by the people of enlisting aid from an outside source of power—namely, Bishop Bambarén. The eviction threat escalated the whole landlord-tenant confrontation from a highly unequal but institutionalized arrangement to a much more fluid pushing match in which the previously superior landlord was suddenly confronted not only by external authorities but also by organized (instead

TABLE 19

SLUM NEIGHBORHOOD FIVE-VARIABLE ACTIVISM INDEX: PRINCIPAL AND OBLIQUE ROTATED SOLUTIONS

Participatory variables	Principal component (unrotated)	Oblique Rotation	
		Communal activity	Petition/ grievance
1. Community involvement	.48	.77	−.21
2. Attendance at meeting	.65	.72	.09
3. Visit to municipality	.71	.52	.40
4. Petition to landlord	.41	.20	.82
5. Municipality demand-making	.65	.19	.70

of atomistic) opposition.

A Slum-Squatter Comparison

To illustrate the effects of such a change, we can compare the two communities that, on the surface, appear to be the most different in terms of participatory involvement—namely, Primero de Enero and Sendas Frutales, the recent invasion site and the slum area respectively. Primero de Enero, as was pointed out, has the highest level of poblador involvement; more of its inhabitants are activists than inactives, and only 14 percent reported that they had participated in no community activities. Sendas Frutales, on the other hand, has extremely low involvement levels.

Yet these two areas resemble one another reasonably well along demographic and SES-related dimensions. Income levels, occupation, migrant-native ratios, and other similar indicators show no significant differences. In addition, turnover among tenants in Sendas Frutales is high because it acts as a staging area for people who eventually move on to residence in a squatter neighborhood. Therefore, the residents of these two communities differ in their involvement levels *not* because attitudinal or SES variables predispose one group toward activity and the other not but because the legal and structural definitions of each community differ so drastically.

That individuals can move from one setting that inhibits and discourages participation to another that demands intense involvement suggests that attitudinal and behavioral changes supposedly required of migrants moving to and within a city may not be anywhere near as severe as many accounts have claimed. Not only do the Peruvian data suggest that adaptation to a new situation goes relatively smoothly for most migrants; a recent study of problem-solving in the United States concludes that "past residential history has little impact on (an individual's) mode of response to problems where he lives at present. . . . *The choice of a strategy for responding to neighborhood problems depends . . . on the type of neighborhood a person lives in*" (Orbell and Uno, 1972: 476). People do, in a word, adjust to the particular demands, limitations, and exigencies of a specific neighborhood. Moreover, they can and do adapt rather quickly to a new set of circumstances when they move.

Indeed, even without moving, significant changes in behavior occur if conditions warrant, as evidenced by the attempt to declare Sendas Frutales a pueblo joven. The mere hint that the community might exist under a new legal status sufficed to provoke some basic changes and responses among its inhabitants.

Such findings reinforce the conclusions in chapter 5 that neighborhood-specific conditions play a significant role in influencing political behavior (see Cornelius, 1975: 133-134). Of course, not every individual will react to a specific setting, or to change, in like fashion; after all, Sendas Frutales does have *some* activists, and almost a quarter of Primero de Enero is inactive. Social, economic, and psychological characteristics will always play roles in determining participation, but knowledge of them is not sufficient to explain or predict behavior.

Additional Modes of Participation

The application of the Verba-Nie "modes of participation" analysis to the area of communal involvement by Lima's urban poor has some specific advantages. It allows a closer dissection of how communal improvements are undertaken, how (and to what degree) the poor pool their efforts, and how such activities vary not only across settlement types but within squatter neighborhoods as well. The analysis also offers one way of identifying those individuals who are the most active.

But though these all constitute advances in understanding, the approach has some built-in limitations. Foremost among these is that this sort of dimensional analysis depends entirely on the numbers and kinds of questions asked (Rusk, 1976: 584-585). That is, additional modes of a substantively different nature cannot be identified because the respondents were not asked about them.[5]

Although collaborative undertakings, local organizational involvement, and nationally-directed demand-making (and their counterparts in the slum setting) may well cover a range of important behaviors, no claim can be made that they provide an exhaustive identification of the ways in which the poor act to improve their communities. Indeed, the descriptions of the six neighborhoods in chapter 4 contain numerous examples of activities that cannot reasonably be subsumed under any of the modes identified. In Primero de Enero, the pobladores petitioned the Minister of Housing directly, purposely circumventing established bureaucratic channels. In Zone B of 28 de Julio, a group of neighbors made large picket signs and displayed them prominently during a parade in which President Velasco took part. Most prominently, perhaps, a small group in Sendas Frutales enlisted the aid of Msgr. Bambarén. And at least half of the six neighborhoods have purchased space in Lima newspapers to publish a letter addressed to President Velasco, calling on him to resolve some crisis.[6]

Lima's poor commonly use this last technique as a means of attracting attention (see Cornelius, 1975: 148-150, for a similar example from the Mexican case; see also Portes and Walton, 1976: 75-80). The following letter deals with the efforts of Sendas Frutales to have President Francisco Morales Bermúdez (Velasco's successor) clarify and make final the classification of the area as a pueblo joven:

Open Letter to the President of the Revolutionary Government of Peru

The undersigned, representatives of Pueblo Joven "Sendas Frutales of San José," . . . in a desperate attempt to look for a definite solution to our housing problem, and in hopes of avoiding the abuses of which we are victims, fall back upon you so that you may, within the highest concepts of justice, resolve the irregular situation that has confronted us for some years.

In this Pueblo Joven, declared to be such by Resolution 493-73-PL-ZR-MQ granted by SINAMOS on 18 September 1973, live some 1,800 families that are formally and systematically being harrassed by those who attribute to themselves the quality of landowners, with the goal of throwing us out so that the zone will revert to those who consider themselves owners.

[After a brief history of the problem, the letter cites numerous decrees and laws that, according to the authors, should forbid the supposed owners from evicting families or from collecting various charges in lieu of rent.]

Not only do we see ourselves harrassed through legal injustices, but also we are victims of physical threats, above all on the part of Ramiro Villarán, who has threatened one of our association's directors with a revolver; the authorities have knowledge of this fact, and guarantees have been solicited.

[The letter then responds item by item to a previous letter published by the landowners and to the move by then President Velasco to change Resolution 493, making Sendas Frutales an *urbanización popular* and not a pueblo joven.]

In such fashion, Mr. President, we declare that in the meetings with the Director General of Pueblos Jóvenes we have at no time accepted the revocation of Resolution 493; moreover, the General Assembly of Pobladores rejected absolutely the reversion of the lands to the pseudo-landowners, a move that would mean a regression that has no proper place in the present-day process in which our Country lives—that is to say, the rolling-back of the free exploitation of the poor. At the same time, the same Assembly re-affirmed its decision to continue fighting the expropriation and the rectification of Resolution 493.

Mr. President, the irregularities and abuses are evident, not only through this letter but also because they can be proven at any time. Because of this we come to you not only to denounce the situation but to have the situation defined by confirming and expropriating the zone declared as a Pueblo Joven.

We have confidence in the humanitarianism and socialism of our revolution; and in the solution of the problem described we equally reaffirm our militant support of the Revolutionary Process of the Armed Forces.

                                        Lima, November 23, 1975.

The act of signing and then paying to publish this letter did not bear any immediate fruit, nor is it likely that the Sendas Frutales spokesmen believed that it would. Rather, the letter represents one of a series of petition-demands aimed at a variety of sources that the pobladores hoped would resolve the issue in their favor. Political participation, it should be emphasized, does not necessarily or even usually occur as separate acts. Rather, a community's inhabitants will, separately and collectively, become involved in a variety of activities simultaneously if they feel that such involvement bears a reasonable chance of success.

Whether or not the writing or signing of such a petition actually constitutes a discrete mode of political activity cannot be ascertained, and it may be unimportant one way or the other. What *is* relevant is that involvement in petitioning (e.g., letter-writing) or demonstrative behavior (e.g., displaying placards or posters, or marching en masse on a government office) are relatively infrequent activities, at least compared with the modes identified earlier in this chapter, and are put into practice only when other, more conventional techniques prove ineffective. Also, only a small number of individuals actually sign a public letter (although many may contribute to its costs), and probably only a minority ever participate in a protest demonstration of any sort.[7]

Activists, Participation, and Authoritarian Rule

The urban poor in Lima clearly become involved in a variety of behaviors aimed at communal improvements. These range from straightforward community involvement—the simplest of all—to interaction with national government personnel, an act that may involve considerable time and sophisticated knowledge of governmental bureaucracy (see chapter 7). The step-by-step discussion here demonstrates that participation is not a uni-modal, either/or situation in which pobladores are either active or inactive; rather, involvement occurs in a variety of ways, and community-specific conditions strongly influence both the mode and the degree of participation.

In addition, the finding that local-level organizational involvement is not a strong explanatory variable vis-à-vis participation, but is in fact *one mode of participation,* may be a discovery of potentially broad significance. Although studies have repeatedly pointed out that organizational membership explains a good deal about political participation, the Peruvian data indicate that such explanatory power may be spurious and that associational involvement appears to be so closely correlated *because it is in fact* participation. Reanalysis of existing data will, of course, be necessary to see if this finding holds for other situations as well, but the treatment of organizational membership and participation as discrete behavior may have to be reformulated.

The major point throughout, however, has been to indicate that pobladores do become involved in a variety of ways, and although the analysis cannot claim to be an exhaustive treatment of participation, the modes discussed make up some of the most common, and simultaneously the most crucial, ways the pobladores act to maintain a sense of community and to derive assistance from supra-local sources. The empirically identified modes admittedly concentrate on behavior that is unexceptional, conventional, and non-disruptive—qualities that probably characterize poblador political behavior in general. The combination of poverty, perceived upward mobility, fear of sanctions or reprisals, a strong deference toward authority, and a desire to protect past gains produces a situation in which unnecessary risk-taking is avoided except in extreme cases of want or dissatisfaction.

Whatever the type of activism, therefore, poblador participation is aimed at achieving incremental changes designed to *cope* with a situation and improve on it rather than to *eliminate* the conditions that provoke squatter settlements in the first place. National-level interactions aim at influencing outputs and their distribution, not at participating in the actual decision-making processes that allocate resources. Local-level communal involvement and organizational activity attempt to better a situation but do not challenge larger systemic characteristics that created the circumstances. As was noted in chapter 5, this absence of structural blame is widespread among the Latin American urban poor, due to the prevalence of an individualistic ethic of promotion through personal effort, and to the migrant's view of the city as an opportunity and his belief that success depends on *himself* and that failure is due to an individual's lack of hard work, patience, or will power.

What do these conclusions mean for the pobladores and their government? Considering that the activists are the most apt to be positive about their situation and are simultaneously the most likely to interact with the authorities, the probability of disruptive tactics due to acute discontent or dissatisfaction is slight. Instead, *the person who is an activist is precisely the sort of person the government would prefer to have represent the poor.* [8] The activist has a recognized stake in the status quo and is generally unwilling to risk violence or confrontation. Therefore, the activist may not only operate in ways acceptable to the government but may also try to keep conflict within his community at a minimum. Both tendencies are without doubt of considerable value to any government, and the military is no exception.

Participation and Military Rule

This last point leads at least indirectly to a basic question: To what extent are the modes of involvement examined here unique to authoritarian rule? Is there anything about these participatory activities, in other words, that would suggest that their existence is due to the presence of a non-electoral political system? Since one major goal of the entire investigation lies in describing participation under military rule, it is important to discuss if and how these types of participation function any differently under authoritarian as compared to electoral rule. [9]

In the first place, all of the modes identified have undoubtedly operated for many years in Lima's squatter areas under a variety of civilian and military governments. Self-help improvement has been a highly distinctive characteristic of the pobladores ever since squatter neighborhoods emerged in Lima decades ago and is probably unaffected by national regime type. Likewise, vigorous local organizations have involved people in their communities, again regardless of national politics. And finally, as Leeds and Leeds (1976) suggest,

The relationship between the Peruvian . . . pueblos jóvenes and the political order external to them has tended more and more to focus on an increasingly diversified bureaucratic structure rather than to deal with competing parties because the latter compete so undependably. Because a complex administrative apparatus has been set up to deal with settlements, . . . the means for getting rewards tend to be seen as associated more with the bureaucratic establishment. [219]

This points at the heart of the matter in two ways. First, for the pobladores, whose community problems are long-term and only incrementally solvable, continuity among external resource allocation authorities is imperative. Contacts with specific bureaucrats and agencies therefore become especially valuable (see chapter 7). And second, as a corollary, bureaucratically-directed demand-making assumes crucial importance under non-electoral rule because most other channels of petitioning (e.g., political parties) disappear.

With parties and campaigning in abeyance, it might be thought that loss of the possibilities for pressuring candidates, for using the vote, or for engaging in any other such activity would be a serious blow to poblador leverage. Likewise, the one-way chain of command and the issuing of orders from the top would seemingly allow little chance for initiating pressures from the bottom. And finally, the fact that the government first discouraged and then forbade independent, autonomous organizational initiatives would not appear to permit the pobladores to attempt any sort of united, large-scale demand-making.

However, each of these restrictions deserves consideration from the pobladores' perspective. In the first place, the suspension of the electoral process permitted the energies of the squatters to be concentrated on bureaucratic targets rather than dispersed in searching for candidates and parties that were most willing to listen to problems or to promise solutions. With time, money, and resources always in short supply, being able to focus political energies on a specific government agency possibly worked to the pobladores' advantage. Indeed, when demands did occasionally overload the political system, it may well have been the bureaucrat who suffered the personal wrath of the president and who took the blame for ineptitude (see chapter 7).

Such a state of affairs rested largely on the fact that the military very much wanted, and actively courted, public support. Speeches by President Velasco and others repeated that the government and its reforms favored the lower classes and that for reforms to be successful these same lower classes had to participate actively in attaining the goals of the Revolution. In effect, the government placed itself in the position of being the friend or sponsor of the lower classes (rural as well as urban). More important, these groups started to act as if they took the government at its word. The pobladores thus occupied a salient

position in the military's efforts to build support. Although the military doubtless tried to manipulate the pobladores, as we shall see in chapter 8, this control
became a two-sided proposition.

Perhaps most important, the Revolutionary Government's desire for lower-
class support produced two beneficial (for the poor) results: programs aimed
specifically at the lower classes and a self-induced willingness by the Revolutionary Government to respond to demands and needs. In a sense, the absence
of the vote conceivably may even have been a gain. That is, since Peru maintains a literacy requirement as well as other administrative impediments that
often minimize the lower-class vote (even though voting is by law obligatory),
politicians and parties normally focus their campaigns and promises on the middle and upper sectors of Peruvian society. By negating the electoral process, the
military in effect removed obstacles that previously suppressed lower-class demand articulation. Indeed, some of the restrictions associated with authoritarian
rule thought to smother successful demand-making may have been peculiarly
beneficial to the lower urban classes; political energies became concentrated and
hence more effective, and bureaucrats were forced to respond more efficiently.

Conclusion

To an outside observer with preconceptions based on democratic theories,
ideals, or practices, participation implies popular control, the vote, access to
decision-making, and the like. But such preconceptions, valid within their own
context, cannot act as standards by which to judge other societies. The activities
here called participation constitute for Lima's poor vital means for improving
their surroundings and for gaining access to public resources. The pobladores
define rational behavior (see chapter 1, note 9) at least partly in terms of the
nature of the regime. Individual-level decision-making necessarily takes context
into account to deal not only with long-term constraints such as poverty but
also with short-term considerations such as regime types. The values, preferences, and goals of the poor may remain constant, despite shifts in regimes, but
the means for attaining these ends—i.e., rational behavior—will change in accordance with the changes promulgated by the elites.

Certain modes of behavior become dominant under authoritarian rules as
political parties and other related electoral mechanisms simultaneously become
unavailable or irrelevant. That is, it is not a matter of an electoral regime's permitting one set of behavior patterns, whereas another, distinct set emerges under
military rule. Indeed, and as was pointed out, long-term needs and bureaucratic
continuity insure that certain patterns and relationships will persist despite
shifts in regime incumbents and even in regime types. But the *number* of chan-

nels available for involvement, and the *salience* of specific modes of participation, will both change as the nature of the national political system itself changes over time. And to bring matters full circle, the poor may in turn alter the national system as they respond in predicted as well as unforeseen ways to policies and rules from above.

Lima's urban poor have a variety of means available to them for coping with their community's needs. Communal-level participation has a rather complex structure that is influenced fully as much by the type of community (slum or squatter) and its own unique circumstances as by psychological predispositions or values. Those individual pobladores who are most active are also firmly dedicated to their neighborhoods and are probably unlikely to try disruptive, antigovernmental tactics in their quest for external resources.

Finally, the importance of the modes identified lies in the nature of the national political system and its authoritarian character. Since alternative modes dependent on electoral politics are at present irrelevant, local-level autonomous efforts and bureaucratic petitioning assume particular salience. The next chapters indicate how communal needs are translated into politicized demands and how neighborhood representatives actually present these demands to appropriate bureaucracies and authorities.

Part III. The Urban Poor and the Revolutionary Government

7. National-Level Political Demand-Making

Of the several ways Lima's poor have for improving their neighborhoods, demand-making directed at the national level can now occupy center stage. Intra-community cooperative efforts and local organizational activities are of course vital to any settlement; if for no other reason, these sorts of behavior take up most of the time that the pobladores have to invest.

But the major goal of this study has been to focus on how Lima's poor can operate under a regime that has attempted to control the political activities of all groups in Peruvian society. Thus the issue here becomes the examination of how the urban poor have been able to function, given the ability of the political system to manipulate access to resources and control political behavior. Chapter 6 concluded that although poblador demand-making interactions with the national bureaucracy exist under any regime, such behavior necessarily assumes extraordinary salience under military rule because other, electoral-related participatory modes disappear or become irrelevant. A national demand-making mode clearly exists; it is the intention of chapter 7 to describe in detail how this mode operates and to investigate whether the poor perceive it as useful or successful. Proceeding in this fashion will overcome the objection of Leeds and Leeds (1976), who rightfully complain that

> The existing literature tends to treat the population of . . . low-income groups generally in isolation, rather than in the contexts of the wider political structures in which they in fact do operate.
>
> . . . Any analysis of political behavior or organization among . . . an urban proletariat must include an extensive discussion of the channels available for such a population to operate through, the pressures and constraints upon the population which limit its operation and give form to its attitudes and behavior, and further, [the] policy with regard to such a population on

the part of the external governing bodies which ultimately close or open or shift the channels. [202]

In effect, political participation has hitherto been treated as a dependent variable: the study has examined what participation is, how it is structured, and who becomes participatory. Now, however, political participation shifts and becomes the independent variable, thereby permitting an analysis of the influences that participatory activities have on the delivery of services, the quality of life, and treatment by authorities. Rather than asking how the poor become involved, we can now examine the consequences participation has on governmental performance and outcomes, and ask whether or not the poor view their participatory activities as efficacious.

National-level demand-making exists on a formal basis because the national political system has created a large bureaucratic apparatus to cope with the needs of Lima's poor. Although the Revolutionary Government closed off many ways of demand-making or of creating pressure through political means, its strong rhetorical commitment to the masses of Peruvian society forced the regime to allocate resources to these sectors. This has meant in turn maintaining (despite bureaucratic shufflings) many of the *modi operandi* present before the 1968 coup. One constant across regimes has thus been the bureaucracy, which continued to be staffed basically by the same employees as previously, except on the highest levels.

Discussing how a demand is placed, however, and what sorts of strategies are available to the poor depends on knowing how a communal need becomes a politicized demand. Every poor neighborhood in Lima has an array of problems that it cannot solve; every community probably also has at least some activists who are willing to take the time to look for assistance. But what translates needs into those demands that are eventually articulated to external authorities? Only after understanding why a need becomes addressed to the political system—i.e., becomes politicized—can we properly treat the question of how the poor and the government interact.

The Emergence of Politicized Needs

In spite of their clear preference for the city over the rural areas and their satisfaction with their neighborhoods, Lima's poor are under no illusion that they live in the best of all possible worlds. Their communities need many things, and although an area such as Primero de Enero obviously suffers far more material deprivation than Santiago, few pobladores anywhere feel that they lack nothing.

In chapter 5, the pobladores showed (in table 9) that each community develops its own constellation of particular needs and that agreement and intensity over these needs varies inversely with the neighborhood's overall development. In answer to the question, "In your opinion, what are the most urgent or serious problems or necessities here in (name of neighborhood)? Which of these problems or necessities is most important for you?" what the pobladores do *not* mention is as important as what they do. For instance, housing receives no priority—not because housing is not needed, but rather because most pobladores prefer that the government and its agencies stay out of the actual construction process and that they be free to build when and as they are able.[1] Housing thus is not a politicized need, since it is a problem the pobladores prefer to solve by themselves. Some needs are exclusively politicized (e.g., the provision of land titles), some are mixed (e.g., a joint effort at installing a water system, with labor supplied by the community), and others are seen as uniquely individual responsibilities, as purely local matters, or as both.[2] Those that are either mixed or totally politicized are of primary concern here.

An Analytic Model of Demand-Making

Figure 3 presents a model of the process by which some objective condition is translated into a politicized need. The first stage concerns the identification of an objectively bad condition and its transformation into a subjectively relevant problem. It is during this first stage that inter-community differences over communal problems emerge. Two neighborhoods (for example, Primero de Enero and Santiago) both lack paved streets and sidewalks—an objectively bad condition. However, Santiago's residents manifest great concern over this condition, thus making it a subjective problem, but no one in Primero de Enero mentions it, because it ranks well down on a list of priorities. As Nelson (1976: 7) notes, the same objective conditions thus give rise to varying problems, depending on an individual's sets of values and a community's context.[3]

When a communal, subjectively important need emerges, the poblador next judges whether that need is reasonably amenable to solution in the immediate future or whether it may have to be taken up at a later date. Many squatter areas, for instance, might very much wish to have a community-wide potable water system. But until both the people and the government have funds for such an undertaking, and until the government is ready to schedule a project of such size, it will simply have to wait (although occasional prompting by the pobladores is clearly possible).

The pobladores must then decide whether intra-community resources are sufficient or whether outside assistance is required. This decision may be

FIGURE 3: PATHS AND DETERMINANTS OF PROBLEM-SOLVING AND DEMAND-MAKING ON LOCAL AND NATIONAL LEVELS

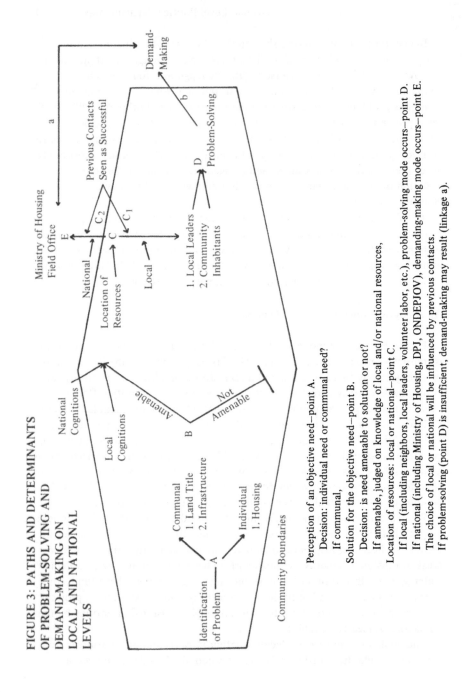

Perception of an objective need—point A.
   Decision: individual need or communal need?
   If communal,
Solution for the objective need—point B.
   Decision: is need amenable to solution or not?
   If amenable, judged on knowledge of local and/or national resources,
Location of resources: local or national—point C.
   If local (including neighbors, local leaders, volunteer labor, etc.), problem-solving mode occurs—point D.
   If national (including Ministry of Housing, DPJ, ONDEPJOV), demanding-making mode occurs—point E.
   The choice of local or national will be influenced by previous contacts.
   If problem-solving (point D) is insufficient, demand-making may result (linkage a).

obvious; it may, on the other hand, involve considerable calculation as to internal resources, which include not only money and time but the potential costs involved by local leaders in attempting to mobilize people for some cooperative project. This aspect of the process may obviously involve neighborhood meetings and discussions; it also depends on the individual and collective poblador knowledge of local circumstances and of the national government's intentions.

If internal resources are at first deemed sufficient, and a community attempts to remedy its problems internally, it is always possible that the effort will fail, thereby provoking local leaders or representatives to seek outside aid. In the early 1970s, there were a variety of potentially useful external agents for Lima's poor, including governmental bureaucracies, Church-related organizations (Caritas, local parishes, Msgr. Bambarén and his activities), charity groups (Oxfam, Junta de Asistencia Nacional or National Welfare Board), private community development agencies (Acción Comunitaria del Perú, international volunteer groups from Germany and Britain, U.S. Peace Corps), and others (Rodríguez et al., 1973, list 26 such groups). Many communities had access to and utilized several such resources, but the Oficina Nacional de Desarrollo de los Pueblos Jóvenes (ONDEPJOV, or the National Office for the Development of the Pueblos Jóvenes) and the Ministry of Housing bureaus directly responsible to the squatter settlements constituted the crucial access point to the national government. Knowledge of these offices, their personnel, and their policies and plans was essential for all pobladores.

As multi-staged as demand-making appears to be, it becomes compounded by the fact that many factors can short-circuit the process (Dahl, 1971, chapter 6). An individual poblador may not know enough of the political system to be able to present a problem in the appropriate place. Or even if he has proper knowledge, previous experience with a bureaucracy or an official may make him reluctant to proceed if he has been turned down in the past or if a petition was ignored. And finally, everything else may be present, but if a community leader knows that his constituency cannot be mobilized, or that there is a strong difference of opinion (or too much apathy) within his area, then the demand may not appear.[4]

The Revolutionary Government and the Urban Poor

Since World War II, national administrations in Peru have had three attitudes toward the squatter phenomenon: to ignore them, thus leaving the pobladores to their own best devices; to attempt to coopt them and make them serve as a political base; or to promote attitudes and behavior patterns that foster the self-help tendencies already present in squatter communities (Collier, 1976).

The passage of Law No. 13517 in 1961 (Manaster, 1968) during the last year of President Prado's administration did a number of things: it officially recognized the squatter phenomenon; it outlined the types of aid that the government would make available to the squatters; and it indicated that such aid would flow toward those settlements that had demonstrated an ability to undertake self-help, bootstrap projects. Law No. 13517 was still operative in 1968 when the Revolutionary Government took over and began to develop a policy toward the urban poor. From the beginning the pobladores in Peru's squatter settlements were a major target for the Revolutionary Government. In the earliest months, ministers and other high officials of the government made frequent Sunday visits and speeches in Lima's pueblos jóvenes, asking for support and defending their takeover in the name of helping the poor.

The first moves in implementing these promises came through the construction of multi-laned divided highways that fed the major squatter settlement areas north and south of central Lima. These highways replaced unpaved and battered roads that had never been designed for heavy bus and vehicular traffic; they have made movement into and out of downtown Lima much more manageable for the thousands of pobladores who must commute daily.

The Creation of ONDEPJOV. While other infrastructural improvements began, the Revolutionary Government also moved to form new bureaucratic agencies to service the squatter population. Only two months after the coup, the government announced the creation of the Oficina Nacional de Desarrollo de Pueblos Jóvenes, inevitably referred to by its acronym ONDEPJOV. ONDEP-JOV emerged while the Revolutionary Government was replacing the old Junta Nacional de la Vivienda (National Housing Board) with a Ministry of Housing, and shortly after the Catholic Church had on its own initiative named Msgr. Luis Bambarén as the Bishop of the Pueblos Jóvenes (see Michl, 1973: 162-166). ONDEPJOV announced soon after its formation that Msgr. Bambarén would be a member of its Executive Committee.

ONDEPJOV was to coordinate all governmental activities aimed at or associated with the squatter settlements and to act as the government's cutting edge for penetrating, organizing, and mobilizing the inhabitants of the pueblos jóvenes. Actual projects such as leveling streets, regularizing lots, and installing services fell to a variety of ministries and quasi-private entities; ONDEPJOV's tasks were to coordinate and plan such projects for all implementing agencies. Although not a ministry, ONDEPJOV was directly responsible to the prime minister, an indication of the priority the Revolutionary Government assigned to its tasks.

ONDEPJOV operated under a set of definitions and guidelines laid out in the decree that had established it; among these was the following statement:

The pueblos jóvenes [are composed of] groups of people who have developed their own neighborhood organization and who have tried to solve their problems and, by means of their participation based on common interests, to integrate themselves into urban life.

These groups of people are located on the outskirts of, and in some cases within, major cities of the country that are undergoing rapid urban expansion, due in large part to the phenomenon of nation-wide migration; these communities by their own initiative occupy the lands on which they hope to build homes. Although these areas require running water, sewerage, electricity, and public transportation, they already contain incipient communal services such as schools, churches, markets, medical posts, police stations, and recreational facilities. [ONDEPJOV, 1969: 3]

This statement, which preceded the enunciation of the decree-law establishing ONDEPJOV as an official agency, is remarkable for its positive tone: nowhere is eradication mentioned, and nowhere are the settlements interpreted as something to be denigrated. Rather, much is made of the squatters' initiative in solving their own problems. The proper role of the government is one of collaborating, assisting, and coordinating these efforts, working within the structures the pobladores themselves have created.

ONDEPJOV acted for about eighteen months as the sole director and coordinator for governmental policies in the squatter settlements of Lima and twenty-one other cities. As it began to assume shape, the Revolutionary Government also became more sure of itself and its goals. As a result, the directions in which ONDEPJOV moved served as an indicator of governmental thinking; two of these directions are especially important.

In the first place, ONDEPJOV started a widespread program of making definitive land titles available (at a nominal cost) to the pobladores through a new, streamlined program. Title distributions, moreover, were soon joined to renovation programs, with the result that ONDEPJOV distributed titles only after a community had been "regularized"—i.e., after its streets had been leveled and straightened, and after lots had been officially surveyed and boundaries adjudicated. Employing the old Junta Nacional de la Vivienda's six-part scheme,[5] ONDEPJOV concentrated on neighborhoods that were the easiest in which to work. At the same time, however, those that offered the greatest difficulties and that presumably had the most severe dwelling and infrastructural deficiencies were left untended or placed toward the bottom of the list. Some significant renovation projects were announced, but they encountered innumerable delays, mainly because of insufficient funding.

One result of ONDEPJOV's encouragement of neighborhood improvement projects was that such projects had to have the approval of ONDEPJOV and its social workers, engineers, and architects. In addition, ONDEPJOV soon developed (by choice as well as necessity) a timetable by which communities were assigned a place in the work flow of the agency, thereby further limiting the participatory initiative of the pobladores, and creating for them the need to master the art of working in and through a centralized bureaucracy (see below).

The second major thrust of ONDEPJOV concerned the agency's rapid emergence as community organizer. The urgent need that the Revolutionary Government felt to legitimize itself with and thus gain support from "marginal" groups led to ONDEPJOV's adoption of a neighborhood organization plan based in considerable part on Msgr. Bambarén's Church-related groups. Moreover, ONDEPJOV declared that for regularization and land title distributions to proceed, a pueblo joven would have to organize itself according to the approved format.

Several descriptions of the plan are available (Michl, 1973; Stepan, 1978: 170-174). Briefly, ONDEPJOV's directives described and encouraged community reorganization on the grounds that a settlement must be well organized in order for community projects to succeed and that all communities should have similar structures so that all could be treated equally and could respond equally to government decrees and policies. With this assumption, ONDEPJOV's goal became one of implanting a grass-roots organization based on three representatives elected from each block or unit of the settlement in question. These three individuals—labeled secretaries of coordination, organization, and economy— constituted Neighborhood Committees; all the secretaries of coordination in turn elected from their members a General Committee of Promotion and Development. This General Committee then elected from its members a Central Governing Board (Junta Directiva Central) comprising six members: a secretary general, a sub-secretary general, and secretaries of organization, economy, culture, and publicity. These six thus constituted the elected leaders of the community and acted as the linkage between the settlement and the government for all negotiations, as well as being the group responsible for passing government directives on to the community at large.

The Revolutionary Government gave two reasons for such a policy. First, it was argued, only a united, organized community could develop and maintain the spirit of collaboration necessary for self-help improvements and for using external assistance efficiently. Second, the new structure would eliminate the frequent tendency of one group or individual to act as a permanent leader, often to their or his personal gain (see Cornelius, 1975, chapter 6, for an analysis of such circumstances in Mexico). But such a policy also gave the Revolutionary Government both the rationale and the means for penetrating into the grass-roots associational life of all pueblos jóvenes and for dictating not only how a neighborhood would be organized, but who could serve as elected block and committee members. Such control emerged from apparently innocuous requirements for election that could in practice be quite exclusionary. These pre-requisites were that all candidates 1) reside in the community they represent, 2) be over eighteen years old, 3) be steadily employed, and 4) have no police record. Stepan (1978: 173) argues, however, and correctly so, that each or all of these were subject to interpretation so as to prevent "undesirable" (from ONDEPJOV's viewpoint) individuals from being elected or to ensure that outside political leaders and/or anti-Revolutionary elements did not gain a foothold.

ONDEPJOV thus created for itself the ability to control (at least partially) as well as encourage mobilization in the squatter settlements. It also developed leverage for seeing that its schemes were implemented and that the neighborhood leaders selected were acceptable according to its own standards. These steps by a government agency were significant departures as compared with the policies of any previous administration (see Collier, 1976), and thus changed poblador-state relationships to a noticeable degree.

The DPJ and the Pobladores: A Study of Bureaucratic Demand-Making

At the time of field work in 1970-1971, ONDEPJOV was the ultimate authority for the pueblos jóvenes throughout Peru, and various agencies within the Ministry of Housing had the responsibility for implementing policies and for dealing with the pobladores on a day-to-day basis. The bureaus most concerned with such ongoing work were the Dirección de Pueblos Jóvenes (the DPJ, or Office of Pueblos Jóvenes) and its sub-directorates, the General Office of Community Promotion and the Office of Urban Community Development. These offices almost always worked together, since any project in a squatter area necessarily involved architects, engineers, social workers, and other related personnel. The DPJ was charged with coordinating and carrying out policy decisions both from the upper levels of the ministry itself and from ONDEPJOV; these included physical remodeling, restructuring community organizations along approved lines, distributing land titles, and any other similar tasks.

Several reasons make it worthwhile to examine the DPJ. In the first place, it had the most intimate continual contact with the pobladores. The DPJ's personnel were therefore the primary recipients of demand-making, petitioning, and complaining by the pobladores. At the time, the DPJ maintained only one locale in all of Lima for any poblador or for any squatter settlement wishing to conduct business of whatever description with the Ministry of Housing or with ONDEPJOV.[6] And finally, poblador-DPJ contacts represented at the time the archetypal instance of the demand-making mode identified in chapter 6. Analyzing how the pobladores approached the DPJ and interacted with its personnel will not only describe demand-making, it will also help to explain why later policies by the Revolutionary Government that changed procedures met with such resistance and created so much difficulty for both the poor and the government.

Probing into the established "rules of the game" for the pobladores in dealing with the DPJ will permit an analysis of how (operating within these rules) a poblador can bring pressures to bear or at least attempt to make the personnel of the office aware of his problems or desires.[7] Bureaucratic rules and operations in the DPJ (as in most Peruvian governmental agencies) follow certain set, rigid, almost ritualistic patterns. The success or failure of a bureaucratic undertaking frequently hinges on an individual's being able to either circumvent or break down these conventions. In fact, of course, it can be argued that the whole Peruvian bureaucracy has traditionally operated on a system of bypassing the written rules of the game and that people who cannot (for lack of money or connections) establish a particularistic tie with certain strategic members within a bureaucracy are doomed to interminable delays and minimally satisfactory results.

Perhaps the most fundamental rule of behavior in approaching the DPJ is simply not to break any rules—or to appear not to be breaking them. Thus, coming to the DPJ either through his own initiative or in response to a request, the individual presents himself as retiring (in the sense of not being pushy or impatient), as willing to listen and to please, and as thankful for the opportunity to come to the office. Such attitudes are especially apparent when the matter to be discussed is a new one; if the poblador, on the other hand, appears because of ongoing discussions, then he may display a certain businesslike attitude. But any show of belligerence or hostility would normally be considered not only bad form but also prejudicial and harmful. The basic attitude, then, is one compounded of respect for authority (probably real) and of attentiveness and a willingness to cooperate (perhaps less real).

It must be remembered that the poblador perceives himself (correctly) as being in a relatively weak position for demanding service from the DPJ. The inhabitants of any settlement—especially a recently founded invasion site—know full well that their situation is precarious and that a display of uncooperativeness will lead to delays of one sort or another. The remarks of a long-time leader are appropriate here; in discussing conflict present within his community, he said:

Here in 28 de Julio there isn't much trouble, except when someone gets drunk and breaks up a bar or starts beating his wife—and then the neighbors try to calm things down if they can. Most people try to maintain tranquillity here because there are lots of kids. And besides, we don't want the authorities to think badly of us, because then we won't get any help from them. When I go see someone at the mayor's office or at the Pueblos Jóvenes office, I always want to be able to tell them that our community doesn't cause trouble.

These remarks illustrate a consistent desire on the part of a poblador: to present himself and his community as law-abiding and peaceful. This attitude is based in large part on three considerations: first, that such an attitude will convince the DPJ of the community's good intentions; second, that the assistance the DPJ can offer is important to the solving of the community's problems; and third, that any attitude that can be interpreted as hostile might possibly jeopardize the gains that the pobladors and their community have made. The pobladores, after all, do operate in a very high-risk position in which their occupancy and tenancy are, at least at first, illegal. Many of them have risked a great deal to establish themselves, and they are in no way willing to gamble what they have gained across time. Therefore, attitudes that might in some way alienate the DPJ and its staff will normally be suppressed, and overt hostility is perceived as a negative strategy in demand-making.

That the DPJ does exist, that it is charged with carrying out the policies of the ministry and of ONDEPJOV, and that the pobladores are aware of this responsibility further reinforces strict adherence to rules and to convention. In sharp contrast to their willingness to participate in a land invasion,[8] most pobladores show great hesitancy to become involved in anything resembling an illegal act, and many admit that undertaking the invasion produced considerable fear of retaliation. The major motive for invasion participation—to become a landowner or homeowner—could not be met in any other way. However, since an institutional arrangement to ask for assistance does indeed exist, the pobladores appear willing to accommodate themselves to the patterns and rules of working within that framework. The desire for legality and, more broadly, for acceptance, along with a very low risk-taking potential, promotes high levels of observance of rules and procedures.

Contact can be initiated either by the community or by the DPJ. But regardless of who first makes the contact, the interaction that takes place, and the strategies employed by the pobladores in efforts to bring about a favorable resolution of a problem or an action on the part of the DPJ, remain largely the same. Exploring these strategies necessitates examining bureaucratic as well as poblador behavior.[9] The personnel of the DPJ are public servants and are immune to electoral political pressures. In addition, indirect pressures—demonstrations that might protest against the administrator, for instance—are largely unattractive due to the risk involved. Thus the question for the pobladore is, How can I act in such a way as to adhere to formal rules of behavior and yet still make the DPJ favorable to my cause?

First, in dealing with DPJ personnel, most pueblo joven representatives are more than willing to demonstrate potential cooperation by offering the services of their communities in the form of manual labor (especially) and also through organizational efforts to contribute to whatever the project might be—ditchdigging for water or sewerage pipes, in the case of an undertaking requiring extensive physical labor, or simply promising to arrange within the community for facilities to be ready and the word passed if a DPJ representative or team plans to come to the community and speak at an *asamblea.* Such offers may often be accompanied by references to past efforts, during which the community and its leaders supposedly demonstrated all manner of collaboration and cooperation. Such references not only serve to indicate the community's willingness to assist, they also act to present the community leaders as responsible, serious workers, able to mobilize their communities when called on to do so.

A community spokesman will make every effort to develop and maintain a high, visible presence in front of the DPJ personnel he encounters. One way of so doing has already been mentioned: references to previous contacts, exchanges, and undertakings. Another technique involves frequent, repeated visits, either to initiate a project (or express a need) or to push along one already in the works. The size of the DPJ (approximately 120 employees) and the very large number of projects and responsibilities it maintains at any given moment force community leaders to do anything they can to call attention to themselves and their needs. Repeated contacts and visits, then, are an attempt to fix the problems of a specific community in the minds of DPJ personnel, and to prod along a project for the settlement. Along with this goes an unwritten rule for most community leaders: "Never leave the DPJ office without setting a date for another visit." Such an act commits the DPJ to seeing the community spokesman once again (whether or not any progress has been made) and allows him to report back to his community that he has visited the DPJ, discussed the matter, and obtained another meeting to continue the discussion.

Such visits may also permit a poblador to establish the most useful of contacts: a close relationship with a DPJ member, one that can develop to the point where a DPJ planner or an architect or a social worker will concentrate more fully on his problem. This arrangement, of course, is highly valued and valuable, and something to be nurtured (but not overplayed or pushed too hard).

The techniques mentioned thus far concern the poblador spokesman and the DPJ in more or less general terms; that is, they are practical maneuvers that might reasonably be employed by any individual. But what possible means of creating pressure or of forcing the pace exist for the poblador, especially when strict adherence to rules and decorum must be observed? Can he, in any indirect way, place a demand in such a way as to threaten the DPJ? These questions call for some discussion of what the DPJ would perceive as a threat or at least as a situation to be avoided.

Within the DPJ, perhaps the strongest desire for the personnel is that work flow roughly according to schedule, with the fewest possible interruptions or surprises. The work load and available time for completing work are mapped out in blocks of a month or several months at a time; the upper levels of the Ministry of Housing expect projects to be carried out in the time allotted. Thus, when the massive push for the distribution of land titles began in 1971, the very substantial amounts of preparation that titles require placed a heavy burden on the DPJ to keep up to date and to cope with unforeseen developments as quickly as possible.

The Pamplona Invasion

In May of 1971, one of the largest and most publicized land invasions of a decade occurred on land to the south of downtown Lima, near a settlement called Pamplona. At its height, an estimated twenty-five to thirty thousand people occupied public and private lands on both sides of the Pan American Highway. Although the national political repercussions of the Pamplona invasion occupied most of the public's attention, the pressures that this event placed on the DPJ strained its facilities and personnel severely. The ministry did not allow the invaders to remain on the site, but did make available state lands further south in an area christened Villa El Salvador. Some fifty thousand lots were hurriedly surveyed and opened to the invaders, and the task of arranging for the distribution of these lots, and for checking each applicant for possession of land elsewhere in Lima, fell to the DPJ. Furthermore, due to the high salience given the invasion by the press and other media, the government took great pains to insure that its policy was carried out promptly. A bureau head in the ministry responsible for processing the applications for the official lots in Villa El Salvador incurred the personal wrath of President Velasco, who, on visiting the agency and finding waiting lines of up to three city blocks, summarily fired the hapless bureaucrat for inefficiency (see figure 4).

Although the Pamplona invasion represents an unusual, even unique event,

Plate 11. This partial view, taken about two weeks after the initial invasion, shows new lots being laid out on a hillside; some of the 35,000-40,000 invaders' huts spread out below.

Plate 12. In an effort to gain support and head off eviction, one section named itself after General Armando Artola, then Minister of the Interior and head of Peru's Civil Guard police.

FIGURE 4

OIGA, 9, no. 425 (*May 28, 1971*), p. 15.

it offered the pobladores more than one way to apply some pressures to DPJ personnel. First, the total (and unexpected) dedication of DPJ facilities to coping with the invasion brought about an abrupt halt to almost all other activity; plans and programs were put to one side while ministry energies focused on the opening of the new lands for the invaders. Quite naturally, those areas in which work was underway or expected became bitter. The same leader cited earlier stated,

> We've been after assistance from the DPJ for almost two years, and we've gone through all the red tape and the channels that we're supposed to—and now these invaders who've been there two weeks get everything that they ask for: land and titles and even street lights, while we've been waiting for twenty years for that. It's not right. [Cf. Michl, 1973: 162]

Few community spokesmen felt any hesitation about stating such feelings to the DPJ personnel, who in turn had little to say except that they had been following orders from above. The Pamplona invasion thus allowed the pobladores to criticize the DPJ with no fear of recrimination. The technique most commonly used involved four different stages: commiserating with DPJ personnel on the added work; complaining about the injustice (mentioned above); hurriedly reassuring the office that the reasons for such injustice were understandable and that the blame actually lay elsewhere; and, finally, intimating that if the lost time and injustice were not made up, the community they represented might become, in some way, unmanageable.

This last stage constituted a veiled threat, and became possible only under certain conditions; the large-scale Pamplona invasion was ideal. Normally, all efforts are made to maintain the appearance of wanting to work only within the legal and customary structures of the DPJ. But if a poblador can make some sort of threat, he will make it, thereby maximizing his chances for a favorable response. The Pamplona invasion allowed what both the pobladores and many DPJ personnel saw as a legitimate complaint—and, beyond that, permitted the pobladores relatively solid ground for further demand-making.

Just how was the Pamplona invasion utilized? Perhaps the phrase that best sums it up would be "confessed impotence" on the part of a poblador leader in reference to his own position in the community. That is, he could claim (whether truthfully or not) that his community contained large numbers of people who were upset over the preferential treatment shown the recent invaders and who might manifest their discontent through some sort of action—for example, through trying to circumvent working through the office, by going to the minister directly or to some other highly placed official, or (whether seriously proposed or not) by going to the president. Such a move, if ever carried out, might reflect on the DPJ staff and thus constitute a threat to their jobs. As was mentioned above, the invasion very nicely permitted such a strategy; however, a poblador could use this technique at other times as well, when circumstances allowed a reasonable case for community dissatisfaction.

Tied directly to the Pamplona invasion, of course, was the possibility of specifically informing the DPJ that some individual or group in the community was threatening to promote another land invasion elsewhere in the city. Discussing such conditions voluntarily (again, whether true or not) gave the spokesman a double advantage: first, by "revealing" such a possibility, he could demonstrate his loyalty to the DPJ and the government, thus creating an image of himself and his community (except for a few renegade members) as willing to cooperate. Although he could minimize the potential disruptive ability of these discontented pobladores, the poblador leader would also admit that if his request were not acted upon soon, he might not be able to control his group, and thus—despite all of his good intentions—another invasion might possibly take place, *and it would in effect be the fault of the DPJ if it did.* The DPJ had been warned, community desires had been stated, and the community spokesman had done all he possibly could. If trouble occurred, the DPJ would have no one to blame but itself.

I heard just such a strategy employed more than once at the DPJ in the weeks immediately subsequent to the invasion; during each of these occasions, the community leader in effect protested to the DPJ that the possible trouble-makers in his community were not members of his association, that they had caused difficulties before, and that, insofar as he was concerned,

It's a pity that everyone in the community can't wait and be patient like me and the members of my association. But these other people have always caused trouble, and if there are any more delays, they may be able to get some more support, because everybody really is upset.

Such reasoning thus removed the spokesman from a position of personally threatening the DPJ and yet placed the DPJ in the position of being threatened, either through disruption within a community or through the possibility of circumventing the DPJ. Pleading personal allegiance to a preference for operating in the "right" way, the poblador spokesman was nevertheless able to manufacture some edge for manipulating the system at minimal risk to himself or his community.

Although the desire to work within the rules of the game usually dominates most action choices among poblador spokesmen, occasionally the relationships between a community and the DPJ deteriorate or stagnate to such a point that the community may feel compelled to look elsewhere for a redress of wrongs, by writing letters either to other high-ranking officials or to the president (see chapter 6).

The option of going outside the normal rules is always present, but the difficulties involved do not make it a commonly employed alternative. It is, for one thing, a tedious, time-consuming, and expensive process, generally involving repeated visits to the ministry, along with obtaining the advice of a lawyer, who must be paid. Furthermore, approaching the minister (or some other, equivalent authority) involves, for the poblador, introducing a substantial element of chance into his calculations, in that the ministry and the minister constitute unfamiliar actors and a totally new arena. Office personnel are reasonably accessible, whereas the minister is a figure to whom a petition is submitted, after which it is beyond any sort of control or manipulation. All things considered, therefore, most community leaders would probably agree with a Pampa de Arena community leader who said:

> It takes a long time to work things out at the DPJ; everywhere there's so much red tape [*papeleo*], and we have to keep going back over and over again, which takes a lot of time as well. But after a while they get to know you there; I know who is supposed to be working on the remodeling project, and I go right to him or to Engineer Fulano to see what's been done since I was there last. You've got to be patient, though, and keep on. Little by little things start to happen, but I have to keep on top of it all the time.

A Case Study: The Consolidation of Primero de Enero

Although this account of the DPJ and its clientele helps to describe some of the rules and behaviors that influence demand-making, it only hints at the complexities and reciprocal give-and-take that inevitably occur. To overcome this lack of specific detail, it is instructive to consider what Primero de Enero, the invasion-formed young neighborhood, went through in order to become regularized. Since it was formed less than a year prior to the military's assumption of power, Primero de Enero is an especially useful example of bureaucrat-client interactions.

The district of Santiago de la Cruz, eight miles outside of downtown Lima, is a zone that until 1958 was almost totally uninhabited. Since that time, most of the reasonably flat land has been invaded by successive waves of squatters, until the population of the district today approaches 250,000. On each side of Santiago de la Cruz exist two similar districts: Alpamayo and Manchaca.

Primero de Enero lies within the physical boundaries of Santiago de la Cruz; however, most of the original inhabitants of that settlement came from Manchaca.

In mid-1967, some 300 families living in the Fifth Zone of Manchaca obtained the support of Guillermo Pérez, the mayor of Santiago de la Cruz, to invade and settle a piece of unoccupied land in his district. Pérez, a member of a party in opposition to President Fernando Belaúnde's Acción Popular Party, promised these 300 *excedentes* ("overflow" families living in Manchaca without land of their own, generally with friends or relatives) that they would be allowed to move onto a piece of land in Santiago de la Cruz. The mayor claimed the land belonged to the district and that, as mayor, he could dispose of it as he saw fit.

Whether or not the 300 families fully believed Pérez and his claims on the land, plans soon materialized to take advantage of his offer. The organizers of the invasion hired half a dozen outsiders—social workers, engineers, a city planner—to prepare a plan for the invasion and to survey the invasion site in such a way that it would meet all of the legal and technical requirements of the Junta Nacional de la Vivienda (the JNV, or National Housing Board) insofar as specifications (i.e., lot size, open spaces, width of streets) were concerned. The invaders hoped that the JNV would adopt this plan once the invasion had occurred and that they would thus be able to begin construction of their houses as quickly as possible. The invasion took place on January 1, 1968, and the resulting settlement was named accordingly—Primero de Enero (First of January). About 200 families made the initial move in the early hours of the morning. The police appeared shortly after dawn, and although heated discussions took place, with the police ordering the invaders to leave, the settlers never faced a truly serious attempt to dislodge them.

The claim by Mayor Pérez that the land was under his jurisdiction quickly proved to be false. The invasion site was owned by a Sra. Valdivia Quintana, who, in fact, owned not only the invaded land but an adjoining tract as well, which had been sold to a group of cooperatives that planned to build on the site. Immediately, therefore, a tangle of land problems arose. The invasion group (hereafter referred to as the Asociación de Primero de Enero, or the Association) and the cooperatives each paid Sra. Valdivia S/150,000 (about $3,500) for a fifty-acre tract of land that lies close to the major highway linking the area with Lima. The invasion occurred on land that had *not* been purchased, however, and was a clear-cut case of squatting.

The fundamental problem for the invaders and their leaders did not center on the question of whether they would be allowed to remain on the land: the survival of the settlement was assured, shortly after the invasion, with its recognition by the government as an official pueblo joven. Rather, their difficulties revolved around the allocation of officially recognized lots to individual settlers. Briefly, the actors involved in disputes over this question were the Association, the cooperatives, Sra. Valdivia, and the Junta Nacional de la Vivienda (which, after the military's coup in October of 1968, became the DPJ of the Ministry of Housing). The relationships among these actors were complicated by a number of factors, including (1) the insistence by the Association that its members be allowed to occupy 300 lots on the land that had been legally purchased; (2) the insistence by the cooperatives that the invaders were illegal and that they therefore had no claim on the land; (3) the lack of any development plan for the invasion site, since the JNV had refused to adopt the invaders' plan; (4) uncertainty regarding the amount due to Sra. Valdivia for the invaded land, to be determined by the outcome of a dispute as to whether the land had ever been cultivated; and (5) bitterness between the Association and the cooperatives, which reached the point where neither would meet with the other.

The Association made several attempts to break the impasse. Prior to the military takeover in October of 1968, at least one public threat was made to march on Congress and demand a resolution of the dispute. The Association also tried to gain the support of opposition party leaders to push through special legislation in Congress to deal with the situation. Petitions for assistance were submitted to JNV officials as well. The JNV and Sra. Valdivia went to court to obtain a determination of the value of the land. However, the military coup changed the direction of the Association's struggles almost completely. For one thing, attempts to work out a *political* solution—e.g., through congressional intervention—became irrelevant, since Congress was suspended, as was all political party activity. The government bureaucracy, therefore, became the focal point for the Association's demand-making attempts.

The DPJ of the Ministry of Housing made an effort during 1969-1970 to provide definitive lots for the settlement. The invasion site was subdivided into four *barrios;* two of these zones were not contested by the cooperatives, and a DPJ engineer arrived to survey lots in them. The engineer worked in the barrios for eight months, during which time some 800 (out of a total of 2,100) lots were surveyed and distributed. The community claimed that this was far too little, arguing that a privately hired engineer had calculated that the whole site could be surveyed in ten weeks. Matters finally came to a head when the DPJ engineer simply stopped coming, the community having made it clear that he would not be welcomed if he did.

It was at this time that the Association took the rather unusual step of going outside of prescribed community-DPJ relations by appealing directly to the

Minister of Housing for resolution of the problem. However, this move did not mean that the Association had ceased to negotiate with the DPJ altogether. On the contrary, the Association took every opportunity to mention its petition to the minister, in effect confronting the DPJ personnel with the indirect threat of sanctions if and when the appeal ever reached the Minister of Housing (a somewhat problematic assumption at best).

The Association reached the position in early 1971 that the community would not cooperate with the DPJ until official agreement was reached on the dispute between the invaders and the cooperatives and until 300 lots were released to the Association. At this point, the national government, through ONDEPJOV and the Ministry of Housing, announced its massive and rapid program for the distribution of full, legal, and definitive land titles throughout Lima. The implementation of this program became the responsibility of the DPJ. Thus the DPJ found itself faced with demands not only from the Association—which they might be able to ignore—but with pressures from the highest level of government. It therefore could no longer act as the passive recipient of petitions from Primero de Enero. It was forced to approach the Association and actively work out some solution to the land situation, since the directives from ONDEPJOV and from the Minister of Housing stated that the northern sector of Lima (which includes Santiago de la Cruz) would be the first region to receive titles. Furthermore, ONDEPJOV did not take into account the peculiarities or idiosyncracies that the DPJ might encounter in a particular settlement. It simply set up a working schedule and included Primero de Enero within its calculations, giving the DPJ staff a fixed amount of time to perform its work.

Therefore, a new social worker was attached to Primero de Enero, the once-defunct surveying office in the community was reopened, and discussions with the Association took on new life and purpose. In a series of meetings with Association leaders, the new engineer and social worker in charge of Primero de Enero admitted openly that the DPJ had committed several errors in the past, that it had been unfortunate that misunderstandings and bitterness had resulted, and that the DPJ was willing to put all of these troubles aside and go ahead with remodeling the zone, surveying and distributing lots and eventually titles to the land. The engineer stressed that the Association had to make a decision as to whether they would cooperate with the DPJ (such cooperation being a requirement for DPJ work to proceed). The work schedule allowed only three weeks for Primero de Enero, and if the Association would not agree to cooperate at this time, the DPJ would make no promises as to when negotiations might be reopened. Thus the DPJ was pressured from above and was also perhaps concerned by the pending appeal to the Minister of Housing, and the Association was faced with deciding whether and how to accommodate itself to a combined offer and threat from the DPJ.

Community assemblies in Primero de Enero, sessions among the DPJ staff, and three lengthy meetings between the DPJ and the Association finally culminated in a five-point agreement, in which the DPJ promised to seek a resolution of the Association-cooperative conflict and obtain "insofar as possible" the 300 lots in the disputed zone. Furthermore, the DPJ agreed to initiate surveying and remodeling of the invasion site and to return the S/150,000 paid for the disputed land, with the understanding that the Association would in turn repay all costs involved in the remodeling, as well as the cost of whatever land in the disputed zone they might occupy in the future. For their part, the Association promised to cooperate fully with the DPJ and to effect the changes in housing sites that might become necessary due to surveying. Finally, the Association and the DPJ agreed on a fixed date for the completion of the project. In the end, the first four of these were obeyed in the spirit (if not the letter) of the accord; the fifth was never a serious target date for either side. The invaded site was surveyed, and the settlers who found themselves forced to move their houses and possessions complied, generally with good grace.

By the end of 1971, Primero de Enero had been remodeled, lots had been distributed, and the issuance of land titles was imminent. At the termination of the DPJ's field work, Primero de Enero was still a settlement consisting almost entirely of housing constructed of *estera* matting and other temporary materials. Installation of water and sewerage facilities was still far off, although electricity was a more likely possibility. But the distribution of lots finally gave the community a sense of security it had lacked from its inception, and provided additional incentives for investment in permanent housing construction.

The activities and strategies of the settlers of Primero de Enero deserve some elaboration. In the first place, the leadership of the community consistently had wide support. Not only was the area new, and not only had it been formed through a single, massive invasion that engendered a collective sense of belongingness, but also the early, badly bungled efforts by the DPJ to regularize the land situation had created strong "we-they" feelings throughout the area.

Second, Primero de Enero's leaders kept themselves well up on DPJ affairs and work schedules and were fully cognizant of the pressures that DPJ personnel faced. The pobladores were not the only party interested in seeing Primero de Enero's problems resolved; the DPJ likewise was anxious that such hurdles be overcome. The poblador spokesmen knew this, and bargained accordingly.

Moreover, the Association established and maintained a close relationship with the DPJ; its petitions were invariably phrased in polite and indeed flatteringly cooperative language, however much the actual situation was mired in bitterness; and any attempts to ressure the DPJ—e.g., through reference to the ministerial petition—were made when the leaders of the Association knew that such moves would not bring negative sanctions of one kind or another.

Demand-making through bureaucratic channels requires a variety of factors: time, patience, a knowledge of government policies and the internal workings of bureaucratic affairs, and a sophisticated appreciation of the nuances of risk-taking. Primero de Enero's leaders had such characteristics and abilities going for them in their workings with the DPJ, and used considerable skill to gain an agreement that was clearly favorable to them.

Poblador Perceptions of Success

These case studies describe demand-making strategies that are consistently non-disruptive, conventional, and legal. One reason why such behavior is so common may lie in how the pobladores perceived the DPJ and other such agencies. Since all of the squatter neighborhoods had the DPJ in common, we can ask what sorts of positive, concrete benefits the six research areas derived from petitioning the DPJ with the sorts of strategies analyzed above. Table 20 summarizes the results of community-government interactions, and demonstrates that conventional bureaucratic demand-making did bear fruit. Nor were these five sites atypical; interviews with leaders and inhabitants in other areas of Lima showed similar results.

Although it may not always be clear whether the community or the government initiated the effort, the kinds of calculations and techniques used by the pobladores are still important. And although the list of accomplishments in table 20 may appear extensive, it should be recalled that all of the neighborhoods (with the exception of Santiago) still required many basic services. Ineffective leadership, conflict within a community, delays by the government, or any number of other reasons can explain why a neighborhood lacked something; what is more impressive is that each neighborhood can point to some essential gains.

In addition, and perhaps more important, those pobladores who participated in nationally directed demand-making had favorable views of how they were treated and of how their petitions were received (see table 21). More than four out of five pobladores felt that they were reasonably well received, and two-thirds said their demands were either answered or still pending. Thus the pobladores saw the DPJ (and presumably other government agencies) as open and responsive, thus reinforcing tendencies to go through conventional channels.

These data, along with the accounts of poblador interrelationships with the DPJ, provide convincing evidence that the DPJ as an access point functioned successfully, *according to the perceptions of the pobladores*. The pobladores

TABLE 20

OUTCOMES OF DEMAND-MAKING EFFORTS AMONG SQUATTERS, BY COMMUNITY

Primero de Enero	Pampa de Arena	Santiago	28 de Julio
Introduction of bus service to Central Lima	Grading of streets	Installation of potable water system and sewerage system	Paving of main street
Construction and staffing of primary school	Construction of daycare center for children	Installation of regular electricity supply	Expropriation of adjoining land for resettlement of some residents to facilitate urban renewal
Acquisition of electric generator for community	Expropriation of invaded land occupied by community	Paving of main street	Construction of primary school
Initiation of free breakfast program for pre-school children	Construction and staffing of health care center	Initiation of regular garbage collection service	Partial installation of water and sewerage systems
Regularization (legalization) of 1/3 of lots in community	Construction of two primary schools	Construction of three primary schools, one secondary school	Partial installation of electricity and street lighting
Expropriation of invaded land occupied by community		Construction of police station	
		Installation of street lighting	
		Installation of public and private telephones	

TABLE 21

TREATMENT RECEIVED AND EXPECTED FROM NATIONAL POLITICAL AUTHORITIES

1. Are you acquainted with the DPJ/ONDEPJOV office near
   Unidad Vecinal No. 3? **(If yes)** Have you ever gone there?
   (If yes) How do you think you were treated there?

   Better or same as anyone else 89.0%

   (N=154)

2. Have you ever personally, alone or with other residents of
   (Name of site), gone to speak with some official of
   ONDEPJOV about some problem or need? **(If yes)** What
   kind of treatment did you receive?

   Much or some attention paid to request . . . 93.8%

   And how did it turn out?

   Success 34.4

   Still pending 33.6

   Failure 32.0

   (N=125)

3. If you were to go to an office of the government—for
   example, the Ministry of Health—would you say that
   they would treat you better, the same, or worse than
   somebody else?

   Better or same 94.8

   And if you tried to explain your problem to the people
   in that office, do you think that they would pay a
   great deal of attention, only a little bit of attention, or
   would they ignore you?

   Much attention 39.1

   A little attention 46.0

   Ignore you 14.9

   (N=376)

are a clientele with some sophisticated knowledge of the political system. Community leaders did not perceive the flow of influence as exclusively one-way. Although many initiatives of course came from the DPJ down to the pobladores, neighborhood leaders also took the lead in contacting the DPJ and felt the DPJ to be receptive to such initiatives.

In addition, the pobladores did not expect the DPJ to act immediately in response to their demands, a fact that helps to explain why modest strategies and gains satisfied the pobladores. They saw their problems as solvable, either through their own efforts, through governmental assistance, or through a combination of both, and they remained firmly convinced that the government would eventually honor its responsibilities. Pobladores with frequent DPJ contacts certainly had an informed and realistic cynicism about how fast their requests or demands would be answered, and everyone had stories about interminable delays. However, this cynicism was clearly limited; widespread alienation, apathy, and frustration are noticeably absent among the pobladores in their relations with the DPJ, or, for that matter, in their overall perceptions and interactions with the government in more general terms.

Finally, table 22 indicates that the six neighborhoods had divergent opinions about the government's performance in supplying communal needs. Primero de Enero had the harshest views; no more than a third of this community ranked the government as doing well on any item. Zone B of 28 de Julio, the overcrowded area that has done so much for itself, had the most favorable. Santiago's residents reflected their concern about the lack of paved streets and sidewalks, and the people in Sendas Frutales revealed bitter dissatisfaction with the landlords' performances.

Nevertheless, demand-making in all six neighborhoods consistently followed the patterns described here. Those areas with the greatest objective needs (namely, Primero de Enero and Sendas Frutales) were also, not surprisingly, those that had taken some of the more unusual steps—i.e., petitioning a minister directly, and contacting Msgr. Bambarén. But despite these instances, and despite the relatively unfavorable rating given the government by some communities, several factors still worked to promote non-disruptive behavior: low risk-taking propensities in general terms; expectations of governmental assistance; an acceptance of bureaucratic delays and procedures and directives; and an overall belief or faith that the DPJ could and would, in time, act on its responsibilities. These conditions maintained highly predictable patterns of behavior, and kept demand-making of an aggressive or (from the DPJ's point of view) unmanageable nature at a minimum. For the DPJ and its personnel, this state of affairs was both desirable and vital; for the pobladores it was a situation that worked. The potential loss in delays or postponement of aid for disruptive

TABLE 22

EVALUATION OF GOVERNMENTAL PERFORMANCE IN SUPPLYING COMMUNAL NEEDS BY COMMUNITY

	Primero de Enero (N=93)	Pampa de Arena (N=111)	Santiago (N=104)	28 de Julio Zone A (N=55)	Zone B (N=59)	Sendas Frutales (N=105)
Evaluation of government* as "very good" in supplying:						
1. Water	13.8%	36.1%	48.0%	62.1%	87.3%	21.0%
2. Electricity	14.8	33.3	84.3	49.1	94.5	8.6
3. Sewerage	20.9	30.8	65.7	47.5	87.3	15.2
4. Sidewalks	21.8	32.7	12.9	50.0	61.8	2.9
5. Paved streets	27.9	31.8	13.9	49.2	63.6	7.4
6. Police protection	21.8	36.8	42.2	67.8	74.5	56.3
7. Land titles	25.3	42.3	53.1	37.3	67.3	–
8. Educational facilities	32.2	45.8	45.5	77.6	87.3	71.2
9. Employment opportunities	20.5	40.4	29.0	35.7	50.0	41.9
Overall evaluation						
Very favorable to favorable	21.6	40.1	55.9	59.2	78.2	7.7
Mixed	8.0	1.9	8.8	8.5	3.6	36.5
Poor to very poor	70.5	57.9	35.4	32.2	18.2	55.8

*For Sendas Frutales, substitute "landlord" for "government" for the first four items.

All differences by community are significant to .001 level or beyond, x^2 test.

behavior far outweighed any gain.

Conclusion

Having surveyed bureaucratically-directed demand-making by the pobladores, we need to answer one final question: Why are the contents of poblador
demands as modest, conventional, and acceptable to the government as they
are?   Since probably a third of Lima lives in the pueblos jóvenes, and since the
Revolutionary Government has made such strong overtures to them, the situation would appear to be ripe for increased demands or for some sort of city-
wide solidarity.

Part of the answer is that the pobladores approach the government because
they very much want and need help, not simply because they are obliged to contact an agency. They want assistance and they are quite specific about the type
of assistance they need. This being the case, the pobladores not only behave in
ways calculated to increase the probability of favorable response, they also ask
for those goods or services that have the greatest likelihood of actually being
delivered. The pobladores request only the assistance that they know a governmental office can in fact supply. They do not want to antagonize an agency
with wild or unreasonable requests, thereby jeopardizing their chances of success; and they do not want to waste their own time and political resources in
making unrealistic demands. The pobladores are very much aware that demands the government considers *outré* will either be ignored (a considerable
cost in itself) or will gain the community a reputation as a troublemaker.

Moreover, the pobladores recognize that the government operates under
restrictions of its own and that it is unable to satisfy all needs of all groups in
Peruvian society simultaneously. The government also has a recognizable patience threshold, which the pobladores approach but do not cross. Coupled
with these realizations is another limitation, already mentioned, that the pobladores themselves impose: some strongly felt needs do not become politicized.
Either by preference or distrust, the pobladores do not want government assistance—or what they might call interference—in house construction, since such
aid would doubtless carry with it financial constraints that the pobladores want
to avoid. Certain types of demands do not occur, therefore, because the pobladores know that to make them would be foolish or risky, or both; other are
not made because the pobladores do not want the assistance the government
might offer.

Another mediating influence on the content of demands has to do with the
individual who most frequently articulates that demand. The activist poblador
—he who is most apt to participate in community affairs, and most likely to

confront the government in the course of presenting a demand—is, as seen in chapter 6, precisely that individual who values his investment in his community most keenly and who has made the most intense commitment to his neighborhood. He also is disposed to give the established system of demand-making, including its formalisms and its incremental nature, credit for functioning reasonably well. In other words, the poblador most likely to create and present demands is in many ways least likely to question the system and his place in it; indeed, as chapter 6 concluded, the activists represent the sort of pobladores with whom the government would prefer to interact.

Thus the pobladores articulate only certain types of demands, and they present them in certain institutionalized ways. Throughout the analysis, few signs emerge that the pobladores are anything but willing to play by the rules; when and if they exert pressure, it is carefully and incrementally done so as to maximize potential gains while guarding against any possible backlash.

Finally, the inhabitants of a specific pueblo joven see government help as in scarce supply. This does not apply to material goods (few of which are actually offered) as much as it does to services, technical and legal assistance, and the scarcest and therefore most valuable commodity of all, time. Obtaining the attention of agency personnel is the major task of any community spokesman. Quite correctly, community leaders see that demands on government agencies are severe, and conclude that if officials direct their attention to one community, they cannot be concerned about another. For example, the leaders of the two separate but contiguous zones of 28 de Julio both made it clear that each area had initiated its own petition for additional land to the DPJ. When that office announced that both would be treated equally and simultaneously, the leaders in each zone were faced with conflicting pulls: one, to collaborate with the other zone to advance work as fast as possible; and two, to refuse on the possibility that the other would somehow extract more from the arrangement. The two zones are literally across a street from one another, and share many common problems, yet they cooperated with one another only grudgingly. Zone A, with manifestly poorer conditions, felt it should receive priority, while Zone B claimed its demonstrated competence in partially solving its own problems through local efforts should be rewarded. Both realized that ONDEPJOV operated on a very tight schedule and budget; neither zone wished to jeopardize its chances. This mutual suspicion developed between two neighborhoods that are part of the same general area; magnify these feelings across all of Lima's pueblos jóvenes, and inter-settlement trust becomes extremely difficult, basically because each community wishes to maintain a distinct identity and each wants to have *its* problems treated separately.

In sum, the pobladores participate as they do not only because circumstances permit little else but also because they find this sort of involvement reasonably satisfactory, predictable, and useful for communal problem-solving. In a word, it is rational behavior, based on nice calculations of what a particular situation will allow. However, in 1972 the Revolutionary Government changed the whole tenor of poblador-regime relationships by introducing SINAMOS. SINA-MOS was a distinctly new factor; why it came into being, what it was supposed to do, and how the pobladores reacted to it are the concerns of chapter 8.

8. SINAMOS, the Pobladores, and Corporatist Participation

From 1968 until 1971, Lima's poor, whether slum dweller or squatter, probably experienced little drastic change under the Revolutionary Government. Although some useful ways of creating pressure under Belaúnde's civilian administration were canceled, older communities at least were accustomed to military as well as civilian rule. And although policy differences clearly occurred as regimes changed (Collier, 1976), day-to-day struggles for improvements remained much the same. Moreover, the Revolutionary Government's desire to control and to centralize affairs perhaps had some advantages that partially counterbalanced the absence of electoral politics. The military's commitment to the poor placed increasing burdens on the bureaucracies, and the poor, cognizant of their salience, took advantage of their position as best they could.

To be sure, ONDEPJOV and the Ministry of Housing did more than simply replace the old Junta Nacional de la Vivienda (National Housing Board) and the Ministry of Development. ONDEPJOV was a ministerial-level organization directly responsible to the prime minister, and its given responsibility to coordinate all governmental activities concerning the pueblos jóvenes gave policies a coherence and urgency that had previously been missing. In addition, the creation of a new ministry totally dedicated to housing problems indicated that the Revolutionary Government meant to give this sector equal billing instead of burying it in a catch-all agency.

However, the ways in which the Ministry of Housing and ONDEPJOV operated remained largely familiar and acceptable to the pobladores. The great majority of social workers, architects, engineers, and other employees stayed on their jobs; the procedures by which a community and an agency came together and worked out acceptable arrangements continued; and most important, the scope of governmental activities and operations maintained approximately the same limits, at least for the first two or three years. That is to say, the pobladores and the government knew largely what to expect from one another, outside of exceptional occurrences such as the Pamplona invasion.

The first sign of change in the status quo appeared in mid-1971, when (as was discussed in chapter 7) ONDEPJOV became a community organizer. The hierarchical arrangement by which pobladores elected block delegates, neighborhood committees, general committees, and central governing boards or executive committees quickly became required for Lima's pueblos jóvenes, and a community that balked was simply told that it would be excluded from any further assistance.

ONDEPJOV, however, was absorbed in the following year when SINAMOS (National System for the Support of Social Mobilization) came into being. SINAMOS introduced distinctly new mechanisms for linking Lima's poor with the national government, and represented a qualitative departure in its purpose, scope of operation, and salience insofar as the pobladores were concerned. By examining the structure of SINAMOS as well as its rationale, we can not only learn more about poblador-government linkages but also develop an understanding of how a reformist military regime felt the society it ruled should be organized and how it should function. This latter perspective may in turn act as a foundation for analyzing the successes and failures SINAMOS met in attempting to mobilize the urban poor.

The Creation of SINAMOS

The Revolutionary Government's concern with participation emerged from its desire to involve large numbers of people in its programs. After the first two or three years, the Revolutionary Government gave increasing attention to strategies and mechanisms for creating new opportunities for greater and greater numbers of people—especially those the government referred to as "marginal" members of society—to develop a stake in the policies of the government (Delgado, 1972; Franco, 1975; Moreira, 1974).

The goal of mobilization was, of course, not unique to Peru; Weiner notes that

> ... transformative elites ... need public support to carry out their goals. Indeed, their object is typically to transform the attitudes and behavior of their citizens. Therefore most of the authoritarian elites governing the developing areas seek active rather than passive support and view some forms of political participation as desirable. Such governing elites often try to find new forms of political participation of the sort that will encourage or even mobilize citizens to support the regime and its goals. [1971: 197]

Early moves in this direction by the Revolutionary Government occurred in 1970 and 1971, when workers in industry and then in mining and fishing received a share of the profits and a voice in the management of their companies. But although these reforms and the *comunidades* (communities) they created within their respective economic sectors represented potentially significant innovations, two points should be made: first, workers in these sectors had been organized previously, and second, these reforms were sectoral-specific within the economic, and not the social, sphere of Peru. In other words, these reforms did not constitute a broad-range attempt at mobilizing those people who had historically made up the masses of Peru, namely, the unorganized and the poor, whether rural or urban.

On June 22, 1971, the Revolutionary Government proceeded to take the first large step to close this gap, through the promulgation of the Law of Social Mobilization. This law and SINAMOS, its implementing agency, appeared at least partially in response to the spontaneous emergence of Committees for the Defense of the Revolution, which developed largely in Lima/Callao and the coastal regions of Peru (Palmer, 1973: 85-88). The government praised the idea of such pro-government support, but soon took steps to coopt these committees, ostensibly to prevent their use by partisan groups (Palmer, 1973; Woy-Hazelton, 1979). However, a more fundamental reason lay in the government's determination to initiate, organize, and control any sort of grass-roots organization.

SINAMOS differed from ONDEPJOV in a variety of ways. It received enormous publicity and generous funding; it absorbed ONDEPJOV and its ideas, policies, and staff wholesale; it included among its tasks participation in the government's agrarian reform; and it was almost instantly the subject of intense public debate and controversy.

Insofar as the urban poor and especially the squatters were concerned, SINAMOS quickly became an aggressive, visible force in local affairs. SINAMOS moved vigorously to penetrate poblador daily life; it also moved (tentatively) into the slum areas of Lima, a step never contemplated by ONDEPJOV. Its penetration and organizational efforts in this setting were much less successful, since rental slum areas are inherently less well structured for mobilization and cooperation (see chapter 3). SINAMOS therefore paralleled ONDEPJOV in that they both concentrated on the more easily identifiable and reachable concentrations of the urban poor. SINAMOS's greatest efforts were for at least two or three years concentrated in Villa El Salvador, the immense (250,000 population) "planned squatter settlement" south of Lima that was formed following the Pamplona invasion.

SINAMOS: Ideology and Structure

SINAMOS existed, according to its spokesman, to achieve the conscious and active participation of the population in the tasks of social and economic development. To this end, it

> ... stimulates and supports the organization of the people; it informs the basic social groupings about the meaning of the social transformations [of the government] and their relationships with Revolutionary Theory, with present-day society, and with the model for social organizations proposed by the Revolution; it channels popular demands toward the Government and also carries to the basic levels [of organization] the executive acts that stimulate and support free and democratic popular participation. [Delgado, 1973: 16][1]

According to Delgado, the process of social mobilization necessarily included participation, and did not mean simply the organizing of people for public demonstrations or marches, but "more directly and . . . with greater realism, undertaking *a historical process . . . to change the structure of power* of [Peruvian] society" (1973: 14). To this end, Delgado laid out two complementary and equally essential paths: structural reforms, to alter in substantial fashion the relations of power and property within the economy; and popular participation, to assist in the realization of economic and structural reforms and, in general, in the concrete tasks of the revolutionary construction of a new society in Peru (1973: 14; Malloy, 1974).

The absence of meaningful mechanisms for participation among the lower levels of society explained in large part why formal democracy had always maintained an elitist and discriminatory character in Peru, and why it had always had something of a foreign character about it: it failed to relate to the experiences and lives of the lower sectors (the majority) of society. To rectify this failure, Delgado called for the creation of a web of participatory infrastructure to integrate all organizations the population itself had created throughout all spheres of activity. These could become genuinely autonomous organizations, subject only to the decisions of their members (1973: 16). Experience gained in developing these institutions would thus serve as a means of moving from the local to the national level and would allow policy decisions to be translated into coherent actions that would be authentically democratic. Delgado acknowledged that these goals could appear to be utopian and abstract, and therefore went into a lengthy discussion of the philosophy, definition, operation, and organization of SINAMOS.

Three alternatives existed for the Revolutionary Government after its take-over in 1968: the creation of an official political party; the utilization of one or more traditional parties; or (the route chosen) the rejection of all previous assumptions about the basis of political action and participation, and a redefinition of what constitutes political activity (1973: 16; see also Woy-Hazelton, 1979: 9-15). This last involved, for the government, a fundamental recasting of politics to include micro decision-making as well as the "great national issues."

> Politics refers to the things that affect the real, concrete future of human beings on a smaller scale, but of very real [*indesdeñable*] significance. It [is] not a question, therefore, of reducing the meaningful universe of politics, but of enlarging it to guarantee that it [will] faithfully articulate the lives of those who make up society. [Delgado, 1973: 17]

Attaining this end called for the development of an organizational structure that could simultaneously permit a massive broadening of participation *horizontally* throughout previously marginal sectors and permit needs, desires, and decisions to move *vertically* from micro, local levels up to the "superstructural levels of politics" (1973: 18). Thus a three-tiered organization emerged, incorporating some eight state organizations, each of which tapped into large segments of Peru's population. These eight included:

1. National Fund for Economic Development, State Development Corporations, and Public Works Boards created by special legislation
2. National Office for the Development of the Pueblos Jóvenes
3. National Office for Community Development
4. National Office for Cooperative Development
5. General Agency for Community Development (previously called Cooperación Popular)
6. Agency for Peasant Organizations
7. Agency for Peasant Communities
8. Agency for Promotion and Diffusion of the Agrarian Reform [1973: 19]

On the highest level, the National Office of Support for Social Mobilization (ONAMS) was charged with coordinating SINAMOS activities in six basic areas: cultural and professional organizations; economic organizations of "social interest" (cooperatives, etcetera); labor; youth; rural areas; and the pueblos jóvenes, together with areas labeled "internal urban underdevelopment," or central slums. An intermediate level of eleven Regional Offices of Support for

Social Mobilization (ORAMS) had responsibility for one to five of Peru's *departamentos* (states).[2] Below this came a projected seventy-five Zonal Offices (OZAMS), which constituted the level with the most direct contact with the local population. The most critical section in a Zonal Office was the "Unit for Promotion of Base-Line Organizations," made up of teams of promoters who worked directly with the people. These Zonal Offices, according to Delgado,

> . . . guarantee the direct presence of the population itself in the planning of local development actions. Here is made concrete the decisive focus of basic planning, through which the development of each locale and region will result from joint action by the State and the representative entities of the population. In this way, the actions of SINAMOS will be increasingly those decided by the participatory base-line organizations themselves. [Delgado, 1973: 23]

On absorbing ONDEPJOV, SINAMOS continued many existing policies, such as the distribution of land titles. However, the community organizer role that ONDEPJOV had begun immediately became a major thrust for SINAMOS. For a community to receive land titles, meeting the various criteria of recognition and remodeling was no longer sufficient. Instead, the whole basis of a neighborhood's internal structure had to be approved by (which meant organized by) SINAMOS.

SINAMOS personnel also undertook numerous other activities in the pueblos jóvenes, including the promotion of electricity and potable water systems, self-help housing, and the like. Such projects, it should be emphasized, were *promoted* by—but not actually accomplished through—SINAMOS. SINAMOS thus became the arranger or broker who brought together the pobladores (who provided the manual labor and the guarantee to repay a loan) and (for instance) a public utility that did the actual installation. In Villa El Salvador, the local Secretary of Economy reported that with the assistance of SINAMOS

> . . . we are grouping together the shoemakers, carpenters, bricklayers, electricians, tailors, cooks, bakers, and everyone else, in order to achieve a truly cooperative undertaking. But not an undertaking which exploits us, but one where all are members. [SINAMOS, *Informa* (1971: 30)]

The principal raison d'etre for SINAMOS, shown in ideological writings and pronouncements as well as in the actions of the field promoters, came from the Revolutionary Government's determination to *organize* the whole of Peruvian society. "SINAMOS is a school for participation," according to General Leónidas Rodríguez Figueroa, its first director; the individual citizen was thus the

student, and SINAMOS the instructor. Mechanisms of participation such as
the organization of local associations in the pueblos jóvenes were designed to
involve the individual citizen, *as long as he was willing to work within the
approved structures.* The Committees for the Defense of the Revolution,
mentioned above, were from all accounts a truly spontaneous grass-roots phenomenon. Their very spontaneity, however, caused their cooptation, eventual
demise, and replacement by SINAMOS.

Although the goals, structures, and policies of SINAMOS and its hierarchical organization were always fairly clear, one further question raised many
doubts: how was SINAMOS envisioned in the future? Was it a permanent or
temporary fixture of the Revolutionary Government?

In his essay, Delgado declared repeatedly and emphatically that SINAMOS
was *not* a political party, that it did *not* inject itself into other organizations
to direct or manipulate them, that it was *not* meant to act as spokesman for
a specific class or sector of society, and that (most important)

> . . . it is not intended to be a permanent institution in [Peru]. Contrary to
> all such assertions, SINAMOS can be defined as an institution for support,
> *and one of transitory life,* that stimulates the growth of popular organiza-
> tions, so that, progressively, the decision-making power in all spheres of
> life . . . can be transferred to such organizations. [1973: 18, emphasis mine]

Thus SINAMOS, it was claimed, would gradually disappear as the *instituciones
del pueblo* became capable of assuming the functions and responsibilities in the
hands of state agencies. But, as Palmer observes,

> . . . [although SINAMOS] takes the important step of formalizing the com-
> mitment of the military government to the gradual turning over of respon-
> sibility for decision-making to organized citizens, . . . it is also apparent that
> the military government feels that the time has not yet come to relax its own
> final control over the participation stimulation process . . . The tension over
> freedom at the base and control from the center remains. [1973: 99-100]

Public Reception of SINAMOS

As might be inferred from its goals, policies, and methods, SINAMOS became the focus of extremely heated debates. A pamphlet issued in 1973 by
SINAMOS itself was titled *Why Is SINAMOS Attacked?* It stated that "few
times in the recent history of Peru has an organization been more violently attacked by traditional groups of all descriptions than the National System for
Support of Social Mobilization." Capitalists, the old oligarchs, ultra-leftists,

political parties and their leaders, administrators, and bureaucrats—all, the pamphlet acknowledged, bitterly assailed SINAMOS, and for a variety of reasons. The pamphlet listed (and responded to) nine main reasons for attack: that SINAMOS was, or would become, an official party; that it was an octopus-like structure involved everywhere throughout Peruvian society; that it was a hotbed of radicals of various types; that it manipulated grass-roots organizations; that it wished to take over labor unions; that it intended to become a new labor confederation; that it wanted to control peasant organizations; that it was a corporatist and/or fascist entity; and that it retarded a "true" workers' revolution. Opposition came from a variety of written and oral sources across the entire ideological spectrum; responses from SINAMOS and the government ranged from written replies to, at times, deportation. One of the severest, and yet most reasoned, criticisms of SINAMOS and the military generally appeared in the magazine *Sociedad y Política* (available in Cotler, 1975); after four issues, the journal was confiscated and its editors, Aníbal Quijano and Julio Cotler, deported to Buenos Aires.

Data of any sort on SINAMOS-poblador relationships, or on poblador opinions of SINAMOS, are exceedingly scarce.[3] But it is logical to expect that evaluations vary from community to community. On the one hand, SINAMOS, according to numerous reports, achieved considerable success in some newer settlements and invasion areas. In 1972, for example, promoters organized a group of families in a community and helped them form their own savings cooperative. By December 1973, this group then moved and took over a sizeable portion of empty adjoining land and put up its collected savings as a "down payment" for the land. SINAMOS then helped acquire the land titles (Ligon, 1973: 28-29). Presumably, in a community that literally owes its existence to SINAMOS's collaboration and guidance, opinions of SINAMOS would be quite high.

In addition, many pobladores very likely had little to do with SINAMOS except to be registered, to receive their identification cards, and (perhaps) to vote in community elections. In 1975, many pobladores said either that SINAMOS had made no difference to them one way or the other or that they had nothing to do with SINAMOS (or with the community, for that matter). SINAMOS promoters likewise acknowledged that they, like community organizers and developers everywhere, found considerable disinterest if not rejection in many pueblos jóvenes, especially older and more developed communities, a pattern much in keeping with the declining participation rates discussed in chapters 5 and 6.

On the other hand, many activist pobladores showed intense dislike for the wholesale restructuring of local associations. An ex-president of Zone B in 28 de Julio, a man of crucial importance in the successes of his community, claimed that his hostility lay not in the fact that he and his colleagues were no longer in power but rather that SINAMOS promoters had treated him (and by extension, the settlement as a whole) as people who had never been able to do anything for themselves until SINAMOS arrived on the scene. He resented this intimation very strongly.

SINAMOS in fact, frequently displayed such an attitude, as seen in the following statement from a SINAMOS publication:

> The pueblos jóvenes have, in the past, been a favorite spot for "criollo" politicians, for dealers who prey on want [*necesidad popular*], for the eternal promise-makers. In the pueblos jóvenes literal "mafias" have grown up, intermediaries who prosper (as individuals or groups) by offering solutions to common problems in exchange for personal gain and influence over the pobladores. This situation of exploitation has resulted in a great number of the pobladores becoming accustomed to the idea that the Central Government or other authorities were going to resolve their problems, always in exchange for votes or other favors to the government. *This attitude, of waiting for everything from above* instead of attending a meeting or voting or creating public pressure *must give way to a new sense of individual responsibility, with the pobladores confronting problems themselves* and increasing their capacity for decision-making by learning and practicing that capacity. [SINAMOS, *Informa*, 1972: 14-15, emphasis mine]

This extraordinarily insensitive statement went against the grain of twenty years of work by both Peruvian and foreign observers, who have emphasized repeatedly that one of the most remarkable aspects of the pueblos jóvenes has been their ability to provide for themselves despite the lack of governmental assistance. Indeed, "individual responsibility" might well be said to characterize the whole squatter phenomenon. The ex-president of Zone B in 28 de Julio, when shown this statement, remarked in the bitterest way that it was only typical of SINAMOS and its workers.

SINAMOS and the War on Poverty. The United States' experience with its War on Poverty offers some striking similarities (and, admittedly, strong differences) as an illuminating case comparison. The War on Poverty made many attempts both to encourage and to force representatives from among the poor to participate on the local governing boards of community action agencies, based on the "maximum feasible participation" clause of the Economic Opportunities Act. In a study of the War on Poverty done in the Los Angeles area, Dale Marshall (1971) concludes that participation of the poor is not equal to their actually having *power:* rather, "while the poor are formally equal

participants and in fact do participate actively in the discussions and work of
. . . policy-making boards, they have not gained power on [them]." Instead,
in Marshall's interpretation, there exists an almost classic case of cooptation,
by which the community representatives have been absorbed into the leadership or policy-making structure of the organization so as to avert any possible
threat to the stability or existence of the organization itself (Marshall, 1971:
144). In Peru, the actions of the government toward the original Committees
for the Defense of the Revolution went well beyond mere cooptation, of
course; the CDRs totally disappeared. But the moves by SINAMOS to make
community restructuring a prerequisite for land titles paralleled the EOA's
policies that, while providing access to resources for the poor, also discouraged
and disarmed any other competing autonomous groups, thereby maintaining
OEO in a position of superiority (Warren et al., 1974). Cloward's conclusion
about the involvement of the U.S. poor on local action boards may have relevance for Peru:

> Membership on policy-making bodies may confer a little prestige on the
> poor persons who participate, but . . . having been granted representation
> on . . . antipoverty councils, they now seem vaguely uneasy about their
> victory. They [may] begin to sense that they have been victorious on the
> wrong battlefield, or a relatively non-strategic one. [1965: 56]

SINAMOS and Politicization. The control aspect of SINAMOS constitutes
only one facet of its views on participation. Another side of the matter needs
further exploration. For those individuals who become active in these innovations—i.e., the SINAMOS-inspired local community organizations—could
such involvement have a basic politicizing effect beyond the life of the institution itself? A study among Mexican-Americans who became involved as members of CAA boards in Los Angeles reveals that these council members developed a higher propensity to try to affect government, a greater capability in
knowledge of the government and its workings, higher skills and techniques
for creating pressure, and greater overall political participatory behavior. Experience as council members thus "took"; politicization among members remained significantly higher than among non-members, even after the structures
and institutions of the War on Poverty were dismantled (Ambrecht, 1976, chapter 7).

Comparable data among the pobladores are not available. But if SINAMOS
did achieve its stated goal of mobilizing large numbers of people, the result
could be a sharp rise in the numbers of pobladores who are familiar with the
system, who know how to operate within it, and who may become increasingly

difficult to satisfy. The initial problem of stimulating participation may fade over the long run, to be replaced by that of trying to fulfill pledges of independent, autonomous decision-making and to provide the resources needed to meet material needs.

Indeed, the diffculty of attempting to contain such forces had surfaced by the mid-1970s. Villa El Salvador, which had become a high priority target for SINAMOS, was flooded with field promoters who organized the area into hundreds of local committees, both on a block as well as an occupational basis (Jordan, 1979). The object was to create what was touted as the world's first "self-managing urban community" *(comunidad urbana autogestionaria)*. Large open spaces were to be occupied by factories and industrial parks, making the area (with a potential population total of half a million) self-sustaining. By 1976, however, unemployment was reportedly hovering near 30 percent (Stepan, 1978, chapter 5), and the government continued to relocate people from all parts of Lima in Villa El Salvador as renewal projects, highways, and new construction eradicated slum housing.

In April of 1976, some 10,000 pobladores from Villa El Salvador began a march on downtown Lima to demand answers to a list of problems that had been submitted to the government but had been ignored. The march was forcibly broken up by the police *(Latin America,* 27 May 1976). From all available accounts, it appears that SINAMOS promoters were responsible not only for organizing Villa El Salvador but also for creating expectations that could not be fulfilled, for politicizing the area generally, and even for suggesting and encouraging the march on Lima. The Revolutionary Government, faced with the demonstration, found itself in an impossible situation. To permit the march would condone mass-based demonstrative behavior and thus risk a repeat of the February 1975 riots that terrorized much of central Lima; to halt the march would strike out against a sector of society that the government had assiduously courted.

The march from Villa El Salvador thus placed the basic contradiction between encouraging and controlling autonomous participation in the sharpest possible terms. Any nation-state that attempts in novel ways to incorporate large numbers of people into the political system runs the danger of creating a mobilized group that is every bit as capable of opposing the government as of supporting it. If opposition does surface, and if the political system under question is a military regime, the tendency toward repression instead of accommodation is very strong. The Revolutionary Government was one of the least repressive military regimes in Latin America; indeed, President Velasco apparently felt closer and more comfortable with Chile's Marxist President Salvador Allende than with General Pinochet, his successor. Nevertheless, when sectors of the work force went out on strike or otherwise engaged in demonstrative behavior, the government showed its willingness and ability to repress what it considered counter-revolutionary activities.

SINAMOS as a Clientelist Participatory Mechanism

SINAMOS and its purposefully structured hierarchy used both carrot and stick to channel, control, and defuse demand-making among the pobladores rather than to encourage it in any autonomous sense. Prior to SINAMOS, ONDEPJOV had also undertaken selective pueblo joven reorganization as noted; Michl concluded in 1973 that by "helping pobladores provide for their own physical development needs, and by creating and controlling organization within the settlements, the government may hope to confine demand-making to the institutional channels it has set up" (1973: 172). Despite ONDEPJOV's bureaucratic absorbtion, this tendency became even more pronounced under SINAMOS.

But the nature of the relationship between poblador and government needs more exploration. To begin, when pobladores petitioned the DPJ as described in chapter 7, they acted largely as clients. It may be true that within this framework the pobladores had room to maneuver and to maintain a flexibility that was of considerable value. Nonetheless, they were clients in that they had no formal access to decision-making regarding the size of the pie (outputs)—only its distribution (outcomes).[4]

Delgado and other spokesmen claimed that SINAMOS would inject a new element into this client-bureaucrat relationship and that the eventual transfer of decision-making power to the pobladores would transform hat-in-hand petitioning into bargaining between equals; in more formal terms, truly meaningful participation in actual output decision-making would supercede superficial petitioning over outcomes (Delgado, 1972, 1975; Franco, 1975). In this way, the pobladores were supposedly to gain meaningful power in that their claims would eventually be incorporated as the basis for *policy* by government decision-makers. The pobladores would thus attain the "attentive interest" of relevant authorities and, in Scoble's (1968) terms, gain "access to politics."

Clientelism. The descriptive data available suggest that SINAMOS promulgated a patron-cliente relationship modified and expanded into a clientelistic system within a corporatist state.[5] Although the basic characteristics of a patron-client pattern—unequal status, reciprocity, and proximity—still hold, a clientele *system* also requires the presence of "mediators" or "brokers" to provide a linkage between the local and national social systems (Powell, 1970). Within such a state, loyalties that hold the ruled to the rulers come to depend increasingly on material incentives and rewards (Roth, 1968: 196).

Lemarchand and Legg (1972) correctly point out that clientelism is not necessarily confined to traditional societies or to small groups. Instead, they argue that this pattern easily fits within the framework of formal, legal-rational institutions. The crucial element is provided through intermediary middlemen or brokers:

> As the state structures become more and more differentiated and complex, as individual interests change and are transformed into collective interests, brokerage functions tend to be performed not only by nation-oriented influentials, but by national institutions, parties, and pressure groups. . . . Along with this change in the extensiveness of clientage networks, there occur substantial shifts in the type and source of resources available to these "middlemen" . . . [who] are now in a position where they can use state resources (usually in the form of policy outputs) to exert new forms of control and manipulation over their clients. At this point the forms of control . . . [become] a far more encompassing network of relationships, directly dependent upon the volume and allocation of resources from the center. [1973: 154, 158-159]

What SINAMOS did, despite all official disclaimers, was to perpetuate much of the existing pattern of poblador-government relationships, but at the same time to excise those aspects of flexibility and initiative most valuable to the pobladores. Under SINAMOS, the government not only played the role of initiating improvements, it also decided what resources would be made available, thereby deciding de facto what improvements would in fact be carried out. Such a state of affairs was far removed from the SINAMOS goals of encouraging the pobladores to take control of the micro-level daily decisions that directly affected their lives and their immediate surroundings.

As was shown in chapter 7, the pobladores found the traditional system of bureaucratic petitioning to be pragmatically effective. They were reasonably content to play the role of clients, and in fact may have found that role comfortable. The pobladores perhaps never expected, or even wanted, to be treated as "equals," due to their high-risk positions, the hierarchical nature of Peruvian society, and the traditional place of the poor in the Peruvian political system. Being clients, therefore, was probably not the major source of frustration for the pobladores. Rather, SINAMOS's centralization and control of procedures by which the poor could obtain access to government resources left the pobladores with all of the disadvantages of being clients and with none of the previously available benefits.

Despite repeated protestations that it was merely a transitory, catalytic institution, SINAMOS came almost immediately to act as a broker or middle-man for the pobladores; its uniqueness lay in the fact that this broker was created, sponsored, supported, and imposed by the national government. In Weingrod's view, two critical factors characterize nation-states in which the clientelist-broker system emerges. The first is relatively severe isolation between various communities or regions; the second is centralized political power that only occasionally reaches into these communities or regions (Weingrod, 1968: 382). In Lima, no autonomous federation or association of all the pueblos jóvenes ever existed prior to 1968; in fact, as was noted in chapter 6, any intercommunity collaboration is rare. In addition, most regimes have paid attention to the pobladores only because they might be seen as threats to security or as a possible source of votes and support. In a word, the pobladores and their communities were segmented from one another and were only partially integrated into national political life at best. According to Weingrod, "It is within this context of relative segmentation that a category of 'mediators' arise who may act to bridge the different . . . levels" (1968: 382). SINAMOS thus moved to fill the gaps within the system by occupying previously vacant political space (Stepan, 1978, chapter 5). Not only did SINAMOS channel aid and resources to the pueblos jóvenes, thus creating and maintaining a dependent relationship; it also, through its reorganization of the settlements, replaced any grass-roots, independent, or indigenous local association.

Peru in some ways contradicts Weiner's (1971: 197) contention that authoritarian transformative elites concerned with mobilization may seek support without allowing demands. SINAMOS in fact facilitated the presentation of many poblador demands to government ministries and agencies, and the Revolutionary Government did not try to avoid these demands. Indeed, the bureaucratic reshuffling that created SINAMOS and ONDEPJOV allowed demands to be articulated. Moreover, the government has made limited resources available to answer them (see below). But SINAMOS only encouraged "approved" demand-making that used "approved" channels for "approved" goods and available resources. Demand-making and participation in general, therefore, to a large extent became controlled, predictable, and manipulable, just as the Revolutionary Government preferred to have them. In sum, the Revolutionary Government attempted to make the pobladores assume the role of mobilized, participatory clients looking for patronage. SINAMOS, as their broker, therefore sought to control the content of these demands, to manage their articulation, to co-opt and/or prohibit other demand-making groups that might start to form, and (through all of these roles) to stimulate support for the Revolutionary Government's policies and ideologies.

SINAMOS thus followed the steps Huntington and Nelson (1976) describe as necessary for promoting autonomous political participation: "sharpening the cleavages in society, hardening the social structure, encouraging residential segregation, restricting horizontal and vertical mobility, intensifying group consciousness, and stimulating lower-class organizations" (103).

But although SINAMOS might have done virtually all of these things (consciously or not), if truly *autonomous* participation was not its major goal, or if it was at best a rhetorical goal, then it is no surprise that SINAMOS found itself enmeshed in self-contradictory attempts to stimulate and control participatory activities.

Clientelism, Participation, and Corporatist Authoritarianism

SINAMOS, by its ideology, structure, and activities, was an archetypal example of a corporatist political organization. Many observers, both Peruvian and foreign, have characterized post-1968 Peru as corporatist (e.g., Cotler, 1973; Chaplin, ed., 1976; Stepan, 1978), and this label is nothing new. Yet this detailed discussion illustrates how closely SINAMOS came to fulfilling all of the conditions generally posited as distinctive of corporatism. Schmitter's (1974) definition, cited in chapter 1, contains four major characteristics: (1) constituent units of representation are organized into a limited number of singular, compulsory, non-competitive, hierarchically-ordered, and functionally predetermined categories, which are (2) certified or licensed (if not created) by the state and (3) granted a deliberate representational monopoly in their respective categories, (4) in exchange for observing certain governmentally imposed controls on leader selection and demands articulation (1974: 94).

Although Schmitter's definition refers to an ideal-type regime, his structural components and roles parallel almost precisely the most important elements and functions of SINAMOS's relations to the national government and to the pobladores. All those features of SINAMOS that have been described—its sponsorship by the government, its hierarchical nature, and its efforts toward monopolization—provide close empirical approximations to Schmitter's description.

Most analysts (Schmitter, 1974; Linz, 1970, 1975; Morse, 1974; Newton, 1970, 1974) view pluralism as an essential element of corporatism. These scholars all recognize the inevitability of structural differentiation and interest diversities in a modern state; the difference, according to Schmitter, occurs when pluralism "suggests numerical proliferation, horizontal extension and competitive interaction" to meet such changes, whereas corporatism "advocates quantitative contraction, vertical stratification and complementary interdependence" (Schmitter, 1974: 97). As Linz puts it, corporatism purposely *limits* pluralism through institutionalizing political participation in a limited number of groups and encouraging their emergence and growth. In addition, the co-optation of leaders is a constant process through which individuals or groups can become participants, or can at least be represented in the system (Linz, 1970: 225-256; also Linz, 1975). The way in which SINAMOS was created, in which it took instant and full life by absorbing several on-going organizations at the national level, and in which it quickly became concerned with leadership selection, all provide clear instances of the limited, controlled pluralism to which Linz and Schmitter refer.

As SINAMOS became increasingly important (and controversial) during the 1972-1975 period, President Velasco's attempts at populism could not ameliorate the miscalculations, excesses, and backlash that the mobilization agency produced.[6] Its inherent paternalism, co-optive (and at times coercive) tactics, clientelist structure, and severe limitations on pluralism were not necessarily new to the urban poor; certain corporatist group dynamics and political structure existed in Peru prior to 1968 (Malloy, 1974: 84). Rather, two things made SINAMOS a significant departure. First, these elements (paternalism, co-optation, clientelism, limited pluralism) reinforced one another, intensifying each one separately and all four together. Second, SINAMOS (unlike ONDEPJOV) was exclusively a product of the Revolutionary Government; it had few roots with and (ideologically speaking) less familiarity for the poor. These two facts, along with SINAMOS's high profile, its excessively wide-ranging jurisdiction, and its importance in the Revolutionary Government's scheme of things, made its success for the government absolutely essential, but its accomplishment virtually impossible.

SINAMOS: Poblador and Governmental Perspectives

What were the results of the Revolutionary Government's efforts to organize and control politically relevant activities in the pueblos jóvenes? Throughout this chapter, we have mentioned various incidents and have also related individual poblador opinions and feelings. However, it is now appropriate to come to some general conclusions about SINAMOS and the effect it had on the pobladores and on the government as well. The latter is at least as important as the former: SINAMOS might have been a governmentally created agency, but its effect was presumably not everything that its originators hoped.

By and large, SINAMOS achieved at least some of its major stated and unstated goals. In the first place, SINAMOS was most effective in penetrating the squatter population and setting up approved community structures. Stepan (1978, chapter 5) reports that by late 1972, two-thirds of the total blocks throughout Lima's pueblos jóvenes had been structured according to SINAMOS standards. Second, by making land title distribution and all other assistance dependent on approved organizational structures, SINAMOS moved beyond co-opting of existing community organizations to replacing them completely. By allowing only officially recognized organizations exclusive access to government resources, SINAMOS made counter- or anti-regime organizing very difficult. Simultaneously controlling leadership selection, organizational structure, and access to resources obviously placed SINAMOS in an extraordinarily advantageous position to manipulate communal political activity, both as to how demands are placed and as to what is demanded.

SINAMOS and the Revolutionary Government

These achievements, however significant they may be, created problems for both SINAMOS and the Revolutionary Government. Perhaps one of the most serious has already been touched on: the possibility that its widespread, intensive mobilizational campaign may have incorporated and politicized previously quiescent groups too successfully. Any government that by rhetoric and organization gives a group a sense of inclusion or of power runs the risk of having that group act in ways that were not originally envisioned. Changing the status quo—or claiming to want to change it—cannot take place in a vacuum, and mobilization cannot be easily contained and channeled by those who start it. A democratic pluralist system can cope with spillover mobilization through elections or the creation of pressure groups, although (as the civil rights movement in the United States abundantly illustrated) uncontrollable demonstrative and violent behavior can clearly occur. In a relatively non-mobilized society such as Peru (Palmer, 1973: 5-9), however, limiting participation to officially recognized and sponsored structures may backfire if the mobilization and subsequent new patterns of politicization take unanticipated directions. Given the monopoly of force that military rule possesses, and given the predilection to use that force when threatened, a military regime may (as it did in Peru when confronted by the Villa El Salvador march) resort to means that are antithetical to its ideological commitment to foster autonomous decision-making.

Another problem occurred because SINAMOS concentrated its efforts in Lima on those sectors of the urban poor that are the most easily reached— namely, the squatters. Cotler (1975) labels such distribution *segmentary,* and argues that "the benefits have been directed selectively at the best organized or potentially most politically troublesome groups within any given social sector" (64). Lima's squatter population has been noticed and courted and cajoled for thirty years or more. But the "hard-core" poor—the unemployed and unemployable, the truly marginal and destitute—do not live in the pueblos jóvenes, but rather inhabit tugurios such as Sendas Frutales. These rental slum areas contain the city's major social and economic problems, and were virtually untouched by the Revolutionary Government. No urban reform law attempted in a comprehensive fashion to control real estate speculation, over-development through tract lots and housing, rents, landlord abuses, multiple ownership of dwellings, or the maintenance of basic services in the slums. Compared with the pueblos jóvenes, the slums present enormous difficulties socially, economically and occupationally, and almost nothing was done.[7]

In the pueblos jóvenes, ONDEPJOV and then SINAMOS proceeded to distribute land titles and to supply a few other infrastructural needs. Land titles were a pressing concern for the pobladores; however, they constituted a one-time good that the government could supply at virtually no cost to itself (Stepan, 1978: 167-169).[8] But purchasing good will in this fashion may have raised expectations that more goods and services would be forthcoming, when in fact physical (as opposed to legal) improvements were far off. For example, when questioned as to whether the increased distribution of land titles was not an improvement, one long-time resident of Pampa de Arena answered:

> Sure, I have my title—finally—and that's good. Now I can improve my house, but that doesn't give me or any of my neighbors running water or electricity. Anyhow, I've been waiting for that title for years. The way I see it, that's no great gift from the government; they *owe* us titles. Who else would be here if we weren't? And who else would have built these houses?

Seen from this perspective, land titles were not a privilege but a right—something that should have been made available years before, as was so often promised. Although they were appreciated, and were frequently looked on as vindicating much hard work and effort, they in no way cured other problems. Granting titles also legally incorporated the pobladores into state-sponsored organizations, as Stepan suggests (1978, chapter 5). When the state then failed to supply other salient needs, its non-responsiveness or incapacity produced distrust, an unwillingness to become further involved in other projects, frustrated expectations, and diminished legitimacy for the government. Edelman (1971: 7) has argued that "political actions chiefly arouse or satisfy people not by granting or withholding their stable, substantive demands, but rather by changing the demands and the expectations."

But Edelman may have missed the most important point, for both the poor and the political system: whereas not granting a demand simply maintains the status quo, *granting any stable, substantive need will and must change expectations and hence demands.* If the poor have been ignored, repressed, or simply placed in bureaucratic holding patterns for an extended period of time, a new regime can break these patterns by providing what may appear to be a minor good. But, as was seen above, land titles (a partly symbolic, partly tangible government output) can, among the poor, frequently provoke changes in the content and intensity of demands as well as expectations. If outputs do not become increasingly tangible, but instead remain symbolic or become regulatory (Hanna, Niculescu, Silver, 1977: 155), as was often the case with SINAMOS, then the poor and their government will suffer.

Compounding these problems was another difficulty within SINAMOS itself. SINAMOS as an organization came into existence very quickly; it was given the broadest (and, at times, vaguest) mandate, and was accompanied by a great deal of fanfare. However, any bureaucracy that attempts to do as much as SINAMOS as quickly as it was supposed to, inevitably runs into trouble. By absorbing some eight large agencies, many internal bureaucratic responsibilities became blurred, while externally a number of officials (up to ministerial levels) expressed concern that SINAMOS was infringing on their jurisdictional territories. In addition, the promises and commitments that accompanied SINAMOS, especially in the early days, simply went beyond the agency's capacities to deliver. SINAMOS could make land titles available relatively quickly, but since supplying (for example) a potable water system involved coordinating many public, semi-autonomous agencies outside of SINAMOS, bureaucratic delays became enormous (Dietz and Palmer, 1976, 1978).

Poblador-SINAMOS relationships also became a concern. The local-level field promoters who had the greatest day-to-day contact with the pobladores were also responsible for gaining acceptance from the communities, a task that proved difficult. Not only did existing organizational leaders frequently protest the dismantling of their associations, many promoters also felt that the pobladores responded to SINAMOS overtures, pleas, and demands for cooperation only when it was instrumentally beneficial for them to do so. That is, if the pobladores perceived it was rational—i.e., in their own best interests—to become involved, they would do so, but not otherwise. Mobilization and participation as ends in themselves had, unsurprisingly, no appeal.

The importance of this "discovery" by SINAMOS personnel only repeated what many community developers and academic observers have found (Portes and Ferguson, 1977: 98, 99). If the poor feel that they are being asked (or forced) to cooperate or to participate in activities whose results are preestablished, then involvement will inevitably be grudging at best. But when the poor are urged to participate for what they see to be incorrect or irrelevant ends, two things can happen: resounding apathy or strident opposition, or both. Although SINAMOS workers were at times sensitive to local communal needs,

they frequently had to follow orders from superiors to concentrate on organization and surveillance rather than problem-solving.

SINAMOS and the Pobladores

Insofar as the pobladores are concerned, SINAMOS appears to have been at
best a mixed success. As was suggested earlier, many pueblo joven inhabitants
probably had little to do with SINAMOS; they were included within the SINA-
MOS census and registration, they voted when called on to do so, and they contributed in some form to community projects. But beyond such cursory involvement, perhaps a majority of the pobladores did not think much or care
much about SINAMOS.

Nevertheless, it is also obvious that the poor had complaints about SINA-
MOS. Its success in incorporating virtually all of the squatter population led
many pobladores to question whether the benefits to be derived from SINA-
MOS-imposed conditions balanced out the loss of the maneuverability they
formerly had. A number of long-time activists and leaders expressed the feeling that the mobilization demanded by SINAMOS called on the pobladores to
give in to the government, whereas the government in turn did not supply anything new in the way of goods or services.

Many pobladores also objected to the constant urging by SINAMOS promoters to attend the frequent meetings, assemblies, and seminars that SINA-
MOS held on community organization. The pobladores, especially the male
heads of household, have relatively little spare time to devote to community
political affairs, and they resented being pressured into what they saw as non-
productive activities.

The paternalism of SINAMOS, already mentioned, was a closely related grievance. "Talking down" to the pobladores, or treating them as uneducated peasants in the city, caused more than one SINAMOS employee considerable trouble.
At a meeting in Santiago (the most highly developed of all the research sites),
a SINAMOS promoter assigned to the neighborhood began very badly by say-
ing that he felt he could help a great deal since he had spent two years in the
southern sierra organizing peasant cooperatives. This remark was not well received.

In addition, the SINAMOS regulations concerning who could be elected as
block delegates or community committee members frequently excluded previous community leaders. SINAMOS employees defended this as a move to
overcome the tendency for some local associations to cement their members
into office permanently. Although such re-elections had clearly occurred in
many areas, the wholesale demolition of indigenous organization alienated the
activist citizen identified in chapter 6. This individual, with his commitment

to his neighborhood and his strong preference for (and success with) intra-community efforts, may have found SINAMOS participation most unappealing. If so, then the result could have been the loss of a valuable asset to both the community and the government.

Regardless of individual responses to SINAMOS, it became clear that it had not won any genuine, broad acceptance within the pueblos jóvenes, nor had it penetrated the slum population. Indeed, a land invasion in 1972 along the Rímac River produced a violent SINAMOS-poblador confrontation.[9] SINA-MOS tried to coerce the invaders to move to Villa El Salvador by withholding assistance. Not only did this attempt fail, but also the pobladores became virulently opposed to SINAMOS and stormed its local headquarters and burned it. As *Latin America* (1973: 7, no. 9, p. 66) aptly put it: "In effect, [the pobladores] are telling SINAMOS that they do not need outsiders' support to get them mobilized."

Conclusion

Perhaps the fundamental reason why SINAMOS brought about so much controversy and bitterness lies in the differences in goals between SINAMOS and the pobladores. The Pamplona invasion played a major role in creating SINA-mos; from all accounts, Pamplona was totally unexpected, and the government became determined that it would not happen again. The most logical preventative was to penetrate and incorporate the squatter areas. Thus any SINAMOS promotion of local-level autonomous decision-making was from the outset implemented by coercive installation rather than by nurturing already existing tendencies and structures. As a result, what constituted a success for SINA-MOS and the government was in general perceived as irrelevant, interfering, or counterproductive by the poor.

The poor, of course, were well aware of the co-optive nature of SINAMOS and its plans, and adapted as well as possible. Such adjustment usually took the form of minimal acquiescence to demands in order to obtain desired goods and services (Leeds and Leeds, 1976: 222). But SINAMOS's attitudes toward the poor, its endless talk of participation as an end in itself, and its lack of sensitivity at times backfired badly, and it is doubtful that many of the poor miss SINAMOS since its disappearance.

SINAMOS's insistence in organizing communities as it saw best, along with its attempts to close the informal but highly useful avenues of demand-making described in chapter 7, deprived the pueblos jóvenes of their separate identities as communities and quite possibly robbed them of effective, independent leadership. Bryan Roberts noted the same phenomenon in Guatemala City:

> . . . the more formally organized the neighborhood becomes the more likely
> are leaders to be perceived as unrepresentative and self-interested. . . .The
> incapacity of the poor to organize effectively is due to their overintegration
> into the city and not to their isolation from its political and social processes.
> [1973: 311]

Although an outsider might have seen SINAMOS as a potentially positive contribution toward settlement improvement—representative local leaders, clear
channels for petitioning, etcetera—the pobladores viewed it as a threat, much
as they viewed political party enticements or campaign promises skeptically.
During periods of electoral politics, pobladores often and purposely do not affiliate themselves with one party, preferring the flexibility of playing off one candidate against another, without putting solid credence in any of them. A leader
who overtly aligns himself with a party, or with SINAMOS, runs the risk both
of losing legitimacy among his neighbors and of denying himself a sometimes
extraordinarily useful source of political leverage (Cornelius, 1975, chapter 6).
In effect, compelling acceptance of a formal organizational structure may des-
troy any genuine, indigenous community leadership, thus denying the settlement and the government an invaluable resource.

SINAMOS, for the pobladores, constituted an intrusion. The bureaucratic,
clientelistic relationships between a community and ONDEPJOV, though subject to unpredictableness, inefficiency, and perhaps abuse, functioned in many
ways vital to the pobladores. They produced, for the most part, the sorts of
goods and services the pobladores wanted from, and for which they were dependent on, the government. These goods and services frequently had significant costs in time, money, and energy, but not in daily governmental interference in the community itself. Neither the pobladores nor the government
would argue that the pre-SINAMOS arrangement was ideal; however, the government determination to improve the situation resulted in just the opposite.
Poblador-government relationships prior to SINAMOS were confined to certain
specified areas. SINAMOS attempted to increase the dependence of the pobladores on the government without any concomitant material benefits.

> In this respect, formalization of organization, however desirable from [an
> outsider's] view of participation and decision making, is inappropriate in
> environments where there is not the context of trust, public or private, to
> maintain it. [Roberts, 1973: 337]

Greenstone and Peterson (1973) note a mistake from the War on Poverty
that also occurred in SINAMOS policy. In both the United States and Peru,

the government tried to move participation and politics from instrumental, distributive concerns to ideological ones, supposedly based on widely shared role or class interests (9). Portes and Ferguson (1977: 99) describe the result in Latin America:

> Whereas [government promoters] spoke of value changes and the need for an abstract integration into society, [the poor] spoke of strategies for job hunting and resource sharing, legal codes affecting land tenure, the means of manipulating local politics for personal and collective advantage, and the techniques for securing water and electricity when not legally available.
>
> Those to be promoted often turned out to be far more adept at dealing with urban life than their promoters.

SINAMOS and the poor did not share, for the most part, common ideologies, goals, or means. As controversy both within and surrounding SINAMOS mounted in the mid-1970s, and as severe macro-level economic troubles made any capital expenditures on the poor increasingly rare, SINAMOS became increasingly involved with regulation, surveillance, and control. And as SINAMOS's ability to facilitate the extraction of tangible resources diminished, the poor viewed it as little more than another bureaucratic hurdle. The experiment in mobilization doubtless made an impact, but in ways neither its creators, opponents, nor clients had envisaged.

Conclusion

This study began with the notion that the confluence of rapid urbanization and military rule in Latin America deserves scrutiny. Although these two phenomena have coincided in many countries since the early 1960s, mere frequency is not by itself the most important reason for the examination. Rather, the question that in the end makes the topic justifiable is whether authoritarian military rule makes any difference for the urban poor.

The Revolutionary Government of the Armed Forces (1968-1975) was by consensus unprecedented, both for Peru and for Latin America. In Peru, no parallel exists (Lowenthal, 1975; Collier, 1976); certainly since World War II, only Cuba since 1959 or perhaps Chile during Allende's regime (1970-1973) offers comparable instances of widespread attempts at reform.[1] So, although the Revolutionary Government was unique, those aspects that made it so— military, transformational, mobilizational, quasi-populist—also make it an exemplar of reformist rule.[2] In other words, could this regime, given all of its apparent strengths and good intentions, produce significant, positive changes for the urban poor?

One seemingly basic difference that would distinguish an authoritarian regime from an electoral would be the closure of participatory options for the masses. Yet chapter 7 illustrated how the elimination of electoral demand-making strategies was not especially stifling to Lima's poor. Intra-community activities continued as always, while bureaucratic demand-making (Perlman's "administrative participation" [1975]) simply assumed greater salience. An apparent limitation thus became a way of obtaining more direct access to the political system. At the same time, the Revolutionary Government's desire for legitimacy and support led the regime to do away with old ways and means of political involvement by widespread mobilization toward the creation of *una democracia social de plena participación* ("a social democracy of full participation"). Such publicly announced goals gave the poor another indirect means of pressuring the state apparatus: a bureaucracy and its personnel could now feel pressure from above—i.e., from a military determined to change Peru—as well as from below—i.e., from the masses who had been promised a major role in those changes. The real source of potential power for the poor therefore emerged from their realization of that role and their expectations that the government would initiate some new policies or would better conditions materially. It should be emphasized that President Velasco and his closest advisors had not made only a rhetorical commitment to Peru's masses; most observers feel that Velasco especially had a personal empathy toward the poor (Villanueva, 1969, 1972, 1973; Einaudi, 1973a; Moreira, 1974; also Velasco, 1973) and a determination to make things both different and better.

The decision, then, to transform the structures, purposes, and levels of participation emerged in part from the government's desires for improvement and change. But the state's equally pressing determination to control and channel participation also led to what can be called the *politicization of participation* (Edelman, 1977, chapter 7).[3] Edelman argues that defining any issue as appropriate for public (i.e., state) decision-making politicizes that issue, thereby denying people the right to act autonomously and privately (1977: 120). Politicizing an issue—labeling it as requiring public policies or public attention—can be done in two basic ways. On the one hand, elites can for a variety of reasons designate substantive or policy area as public; on the other hand, the poor (or masses) through collective action can (minimally) call attention to a need or (maximally) force elites to address an issue.

Regardless of whether the initiation is from top or bottom, politicizing an issue generally involves a call for increased participation by the poor in solving their problems (Moynihan, 1969; Delgado, 1972, 1973). However, for the poor, a fundamental dilemma may arise when *elites turn participation itself into a politicized issue.* Politicizing the act of participation means that, for the poor, the choice as to whether to become involved at all, or the choice as to what issues merit their becoming involved, are no longer autonomous options. Instead, politicized participation becomes coercive, not voluntary; ritualistic and formal, not influential; acquiescent and symbolic, not substantive.

From this perspective, considerable evidence exists that the Revolutionary Government did in fact politicize participation, making the act of involvement itself more salient than the goals or reasons for involvement. The state, which was determined to stimulate, control, and limit participation, could achieve these inevitably contradictory goals only by removing participation from its previously quasi-autonomous state. Prior to SINAMOS, but after the military *golpe* in 1968, Lima's squatters had not occupied a high-profile position for the government, ONDEPJOV and bureaucratic reshuffling notwithstanding. But the Pamplona land invasion of 1971, along with other crises in Peru, forced the government to do something to avoid confrontation again with the poor under circumstances not of the government's own making (Collier, 1976: 104-111; Dietz and Palmer, 1976).

SINAMOS was proclaimed as a new device, a new initiative to demonstrate the Revolutionary Government's concern for the poor. The poor, therefore, were expected to participate in SINAMOS because it existed for their own benefit and good; not participating would run against one's own self-interest.

The poor, however, did not see things in the same way. Politicizing the *needs* of the squatter communities (or slums) of Lima—that is, making them vulnerable to public (non-local) decision-making—might have gained support from the poor if resources (technical assistance, money, credit) had been forthcoming. Instead, under SINAMOS, politicizing the needs shifted quickly to politicizing the means through which the poor could become involved. Unless a community organized itself in a specified form, and unless demands or petitions were channeled through approved structures, its needs were apt to go unattended insofar as external assistance was concerned.[4] SINAMOS and the poor both realized that those who can exercise influence *outside* the context of formal structures can wield real power. Military rule in general negated many potential sources of outside influence; SINAMOS abetted the process of closure by politicization and by its penetration ever more deeply into community and individual lives. Selznick's conclusion (1964: 14) regarding cooptation politics applies nicely: "The forms of participation are emphasized [so that] action is channeled . . . to fulfill administrative functions while preserving the locus of significant decision in the hands of the initiating group."

All this having been said, it is apparent that a partial, first-level response to the question of whether authoritarian military rule changes anything for the poor must be clearly affirmative. Government policies do shape and affect the poor; the poor also influence the government, through sheer weight of numbers, massive political action (the Pamplona invasion), or reaction to policy initiatives. Whether, however, the poor approve of changes so introduced, whether government policies are congruent with the expectations or needs of the poor, and whether the poor will react as the elites plan or hope are very different questions. Answers vary enormously within a nation-state (due to the inherent heterogeneity of the poor) and across military regimes in different nations. But regardless of the answers, military rule has an impact—of some sort.

Change versus Progress

A more far-reaching interpretation of the question of change is possible,

however. Can a reformist military regime in a Third World country undertake
any action or implement any policy that will bring about fundamental betterment and basic changes in the conditions of the poor? Can any of the root
causes of aggregate urban poverty be challenged or partly reversed?

There are at least a couple of ways of answering these questions. The first
one, commonly adopted by highly-placed spokesmen and decision-makers in
the government, asserts that the regime has put into practice all that needs to
be done to correct deeply seated inequities—that what must be done is to fine-
tune the structures and organizations the regime has created. In an article that
appeared in 1975, Helan Jaworski, who was for a period of time the highest-
ranking civilian in SINAMOS, admitted that a variety of shortcomings existed.

1. The majority of society has been subordinated to a reduced number of
   technocrats who formulate and propose decisions that affect the direction of Peruvian society.
2. Lack of coordination among diverse sectors concerning their regional
   boundaries creates confusion among the masses.
3. In the decision-making process, especially in defining policies, decentral-
   ized organisms have no power; their intervention is limited to the execut-
   ing phase of the plan.
4. Local governmental participation in development planning is nonexistent.
   Furthermore, local governments still have no incorporated representatives
   of the organized masses.
5. The non-participation of the population in the planning process itself
   makes it difficult to include their wishes *post hoc.*
6. Regional and sectoral plans are often carried out on too abstract a level,
   thereby inhibiting their concrete realization on a local level.
7. This situation leads to the conclusion that at the present time (the end
   of the 1973-74 biennium) planning in Peru is still not based on an appropriate footing and that it ignores the basic necessities of the majority of
   the country. [Jaworski, 1975: 11]

Jaworski thus both implied and assumed that what was needed was further
tinkering with the organizations and policy goals set down by the Revolutionary Government. But Jaworski did not seem to consider the possibility that the
government's concentration on participatory exercises that have no immediate
payoff was itself miscast. The "successes" by which the Revolutionary Government might have judged its mobilizational efforts—e.g., the absence of any anti-
regime organizational groups in the pueblos jóvenes—are meaningless to the poor
themselves. Stepan (1978, chapter 5) notes that governmental policies in the

squatter settlements successfully stifled alternative structures of interest articulation. Although that is true, the urban poor might well feel that this is a totally irrelevant point. A more germane question would ask whether government policies prevented or sidetracked demand-making emanating from the poor.

If this "fine-tuning" answer seems inapposite, there is another, less sanguine possibility: that a reformist regime, whether military or civilian, cannot change conditions in any fundamental way, and that in fact it can do nothing more than cope with problems of urban poverty, not ameliorate (let alone solve) them. Chapters 5, 6, and 7 have spelled out the ways and the several reasons why the poor cope and are often satisfied to do so. However, the elites also had to content themselves with coping, all talk of revolution aside. To do otherwise would have invited self-destruction (given the power and resource redistribution required), necessitated capital and technical skills far beyond the nation's capacities, and perhaps demanded severe repression and regimentation, all conditions the Peruvian military would not accept.[5]

The interactions and dealings with the urban poor in particular highlighted many of the inherent paradoxes, contradictions, and tensions that confronted the military. Reformist rhetoric called for new mechanisms of participation. as did the military's own desires for support; yet the new was not demonstrably better than the old, and became increasingly unproductive and confining for the poor. Old personalistic and clientelistic politics were attacked as inefficient, corrupt, and unjust; yet the poor found the new were equally clientelistic, much more rigid, and far more limiting. The intra-national analogues of external dependency (e.g., center-periphery assymmetry) did not disappear or diminish. Ironically, the politicization of participation exacerbated (in some ways voluntarily, in others not) poblador dependence on the nation-state instead of permitting autonomous local-level decision-making.

Perhaps the underlying flaw for the military lay in its equating national security with national development. From one point of view, the whole mobilization/participation aspect of the Revolutionary Government sprang logically from this equivalency. The nation can only be secure if social, political, and economic development takes place; it can only develop if orderly and stable relationships exist among the nation's social forces (Palmer and Rodríguez, 1972; Middlebrook and Palmer, 1975: 12). The two are, therefore, inseparable and reciprocal.

But implementing such a construct uncovered a perhaps fatal contradiction: development requires change, security requires control. To resolve this basic tension, the Revolutionary Government moved toward the idea of controlled change—change initiated from the top to benefit the masses. Such a concept, however, is essentially unstable. If mobilization begins to outpace control, then a military government (or, probably, any government) will inevitably respond with measures designed minimally to restore equilibrium. But given the military's fear of "chaos latent in the mass" (Bonilla, 1970: 127, cited in Fagen and Tuohy, 1972: 163), its inevitable yearning for efficiency and predictability, and its determination to govern (as opposed to simply responding to pressures), control will take precedence over change if a choice must be made. Thus participation—actual autonomous, influential involvement in decision-making—became relegated to the status of a long-term ideal. As the 1971-1975 National Development Plan explains:

> [Our] people are relatively untrained and incapable of assuming fully and in the short run [their] responsibilities [under the new plan]. Therefore it is the responsibility of the State to stimulate, channel, and consolidate popular participation. [Middlebrook and Palmer, 1975: 51, note 17]

A final reason that an authoritarian, corporatist regime may be forced to emphasize control over change is economic. Redistributive change is extremely costly, especially if the elites are unwilling to redistribute existing wealth (see note 4). Wealthy nations have the option of large-scale welfare programs, as a way of increasing (or at least maintaining) a minimal standard of living as well as maintaining control over an acquiescent poor (Piven and Cloward, 1971). But an underdeveloped nation-state whose economy is dependent on external, international conditions beyond its control may not only be poor; it will also face far more uncertainties and have more fragilities than a wealthy country (Caiden and Wildavsky, 1974, chapter 2). Frederick Pike (1978) concludes that

> in . . . Peru, the production of wealth cannot procede rapidly enough to permit attainment of social harmony based on society-wide gratification of individualistic, acquisitive instincts, [Its] national leaders have properly perceived this; and so they have exalted collectivism, only to discover that among the masses values of individualism have been making headway. [261]

If in such a nation a reformist regime (civilian or military) decides that it will not or cannot ignore massive societal poverty, and simultaneously discovers that the basic needs of the poor require material assistance and capital investment, then the masses and the rulers will unavoidably collide over the reasons and means for political participation.

Appendices

Appendices

APPENDIX A

THE COLLECTION OF DATA

THE SURVEY AND SURVEY TECHNIQUES

I decided from the start that I would try to gather different types of data through a variety of techniques. Once the research communities had been selected and the questionnaire developed (see below), I spent the great bulk of my own time in being in the neighborhoods as much as possible. I became involved in everything from soccer games and birthday parties to attending community meetings at night, working on construction projects, and going to fiestas and fund-raising parties, along with other such individual, family, and community activities. I also developed some close personal ties with the lower-echelon social workers, architects, and engineers in ONDEPJOV who were in daily contact with the five squatter settlements. No equivalent agency exists for the slum areas.

The questionnaire took shape slowly, despite the fact that I had Wayne Cornelius's interview schedule from his work in Mexico City (Cornelius, 1975). His questionnaire and mine were purposely similar to allow a rigorously comparable study. Nevertheless, writing and translating and verifying and rechecking the questionnaire took many hours, and I had been in Lima for almost half a year before actual pretesting could begin.

Although my questionnaire was nowhere near the size of Cornelius's instrument, average completion time was still close to two hours. This length flies in the face of accepted practice, which generally assumes that neither the interviewer nor the respondent can maintain sufficient interest for a prolonged period of time and that respondent fatigue can become a major problem. However, it is my impression, gathered from personal experience and from extensive debriefing of the interviewers, that this is not necessarily the case. A good deal of research using interviews has been carried out in the pueblos jóvenes, and I had some preliminary feelings that the pobladores might be tired of being questioned. However, I have seen almost all of these questionnaires, and the great majority treated the pobladores only as a means of gaining information of a dry and impersonal nature. My own questionnaire pertained almost exclusively to the life history of the individual in question, and to *his* opinions, *his* attitudes, and *his* beliefs, values, and patterns of behavior. "Todo el mundo quiere opinar"—everyone wants to express his opinion. Again and again, in debriefing the interviewers, I found that the respondents had taken considerable pleasure and interest in being asked what they felt about Peru, their communities, their neighbors, and—above all—*themselves*. One poblador summed up the feeling of many when he remarked to me, "No one ever asked me what I thought about. The only other time I ever talk about politics is on Sunday afternoons." I had hoped from the beginning that the willingness of the pobladores to enter into the interviewing fully would offset the length of the questionnaire. Few pobladores became tired or bored with the questions, and sample mortality due to incompletion was virtually nil (see Cornelius, 1975: 277, for similar results in Mexico).

Anthony Leeds (1970) has argued that "the method of applying questionnaires is itself totally foreign to the life experiences of (lower class urban) informants . . . so that unnatural, conventionalized, or misinterpreted responses —thought by the informant to be appropriate to the question asked—are elicited" (270). Most respondents were, on the contrary, accustomed to answering survey questions; what surprised and pleased them were the *types* of information solicited.

Leeds has also identified some possible pitfalls that survey work can encounter in an environment such as the pueblos jóvenes, and warns that "no adequate questionnaire can be made up without prior extensive and intensive ethnographic participation and observation" (270). I agree fully, and tried in my field work to obtain the best of both qualitative and quantitative data-collecting techniques.

During this process of questionnaire preparation, I spent a good deal of time deciding what sort of interviewers to hire: professionals from a social science research agency of some sort, or university students. I had in mind some remarks by Cornelius, who had strongly suggested the need to employ professionals with previous experience.

However, for a number of reasons I decided to use university students, and I have no reason to regret this choice. I made contact with a group of girls (largely) who were advanced fourth and fifth year students at Ricardo Palma University in the School of Social Work. All of them without exception had had previous interviewing experience among the urban poor, some in the same districts in which I hoped to work. Thus all of them were acquainted (some very thoroughly) with the populations under investigation. I would not have hired individuals without these basic qualifications.

Three lengthy meetings were held *en masse* prior to any field work. These meetings consisted of an introductory session in which the intentions of the study were explained, copies of the questionnaire were handed out, and basic information about each potential interviewer was ascertained. A week later, a long (3-4 hours) training session was held with those who returned; there was no effort made to persuade reluctant candidates to participate, and anyone who claimed interest but who asked to miss the meeting was told that the training sessions were absolutely essential and that to miss one would be grounds for being dropped. This second session consisted of going through the questionnaire item by item, explaining each one and its reason for inclusion in the study. I found this to be a good strategy, since it was possible to demonstrate to the students just what it was we were after and to answer any questions that had developed (they were numerous). A third session then provided the opportunity to clear up further points and to distribute two questionnaires as pre-tests. The interviewers were told to go to the areas in which they were to work, to complete the pretests within a week, and then to return for another training session. At this meeting, the questionnaires were again discussed from beginning to end, and any difficulties, misunderstandings, peculiarities, and unexpected problems were ironed out. Some further changes in the wording of questionnaire items were also made as a result of these pretests.

Thereafter, each interviewer was on his or her own. Each was given five interviews at a time; when these were completed, the interviewer came to my office and handed in the completed questionnaires. This manner of running the actual survey allowed each interviewer to work at his own pace; I placed no quota or minimum for work. Furthermore, it allowed me to keep in constant and frequent contact with the interviewers, to head off any potential problems as they developed, to answer any questions, and to talk with each interviewer while field impressions were still fresh. It also permitted me to review the questionnaires as they came in and to note any mistakes or clarify any vague or inadequate responses. I feel that treating each interviewer as an individual generated a good deal of enthusiasm, since they came to realize that they were playing an important and specific role in the study. This maintenance of morale was, to my way of thinking, extremely important. It was also time-consuming, but I saw no other way of maintaining sufficient control as the field work progressed. As might be expected, the rate of work varied widely; a few interviewers did as few as four or five interviews; the majority did somewhere around fifteen or twenty, and four or five did more than fifty. The interviewing was done at a fortunate time: it was begun about the first of March and was completed by the end of May. During this period the academic year ended, and the interviewers were able to work full time (or as fully as they wished).

An informally developed strategy of having the girls (especially) work in pairs or teams proved particularly valuable. The Ricardo Palma students were all members of the same class and all knew one another; moreover, some were close friends and had worked together in field situations. Many of them spoke of the advisability of having a friend along to reinforce one another when difficulties arose and to assist one another in various ways. In areas such as 28 de Julio, the environment made interviewing difficult at best, and the boldest interviewer might well have second (or third) thoughts about entering into some of the streets and alleyways in such a neighborhood. The presence of a friend and a fellow worker thus became highly desirable.

I was well pleased with the work of the students. The questionnaire was not a simple instrument to administer, and certain sections needed careful explanation to the respondents. Nevertheless, all of the interviewers showed themselves capable of handling the questionnaire and the respondents. Since the universe investigated was composed exclusively of male heads of households, interviewing became difficult because there were only certain hours during which the majority of respondents were at home. All interviewers, however, showed little hesitation in traveling to the communities during early evening hours and staying until 9 or 10 at night—a sometimes difficult job when there is no illumination and when the area is unfamiliar. The bulk of the interviewing, therefore, was done on weekends, and that presented its own set of problems, since Saturday and Sunday afternoons (the latter especially) are the traditional times for men to get together for some serious drinking. The girls, therefore, made efforts to arrive in the communities early Sunday morning, and were on the whole successful.

Another bit of strategy that proved worthwhile was that of locating the house specified for interviewing and then having a brief chat with whoever happened to be at home at the time. Such a talk served several purposes: it permitted the family to know that a study was underway; it allowed the interviewer to make certain that the house did in fact contain a male head of family; and it allowed the interviewer to find out when the head of the family was normally at home and to make an appointment to see him. Admittedly, this technique involved more time on the part of the interviewer, but it also allowed the interview to take place at a time convenient to the respondent, thereby generally allowing completion of the questionnaire in a single session, thus saving time on repeated callbacks. I was keenly aware that the pobladores have been interviewed before, and although I felt that my study would produce data of a somewhat different nature, I determined from the start to make every effort not to intrude unreasonably into the respondents' free time. The insistence on making appointments arose partly from this determination.

All interviewers in the field had certain means of introduction and identification. A covering letter was attached to the interview itself, and was read or shown to the respondent as necessary. This letter carried both my own signature as supervisor and the name of the head of the Academic Program of the Social Science Research Institute at Catholic University. Moreover, Catholic University agreed to have its name used in conjunction with the study—a useful connection that was more than once instrumental in securing access to communities and their leaders. I was also able to provide each interviewer with an identification card, signed and sealed by the head of the Institute. These ID cards were essential in many instances when a respondent asked for some proof con-

concerning the legitimacy of the interview.

Sampling Procedures

Sampling was, for the most part, straightforward, since I made no effort to stratify the communities and drew instead a random sample. I knew, however, that occasionally vacant lots would be discovered, that repeated callbacks would prove fruitless, and that refusals would from time to time occur. I therefore drew two complete samples for each community so as to give the interviewers an alternative if the first sample proved impossible. In addition, I encountered problems that were unique to each community.

Primero de Enero. This was certainly the most difficult area to work in as far as sample selection was concerned. Of the 2,080 families listed in the Association rosters, about 800 had fixed lots at the time of interviewing. I obtained this list and drew a random sample from it by taking every sixteenth name, starting with a random number. There was no way to obtain a lot map or plan, since the area was constantly shifting and in a state of flux. The names selected were written on the questionnaire, along with an address; these presented relatively little difficulty. But where there were no assigned or legal lots, sample selection became much more difficult. I finally decided to draw a random selection of names from the Association's membership list, to determine from this list in what approximate part of Primero de Enero the individual supposedly lived, and then simply to track him down by knocking on doors. The crude lot map that the community had was some eighteen months out of date—which is to say that it was useless. I found it possible to locate most individuals selected in the manner described; however, it was a time-consuming procedure.

Pampa de Arena, all four sections. Sampling procedures in the four districts of Pampa de Arena were for the most part the same. Lot maps obtained from ONDEPJOV were checked out and found to be reasonably accurate; these were used as the basis for selection of approximately thirty lots per district, giving a total of 120 interviews. In two small sectors, all of the blocks were used, and lots selected from them. In the two larger ones, however, a two-stage sampling technique was used, whereby first blocks were selected and then lots within them. The interviewers were given sketch maps and questionnaires with names and addresses.

28 de Julio, Zones A and B. I originally attempted to use the most recent maps that ONDEPJOV had in its possession. However, even the briefest try to correlate the maps with reality showed that numerous and fundamental physical changes had occurred since the maps were made up. I was able to obtain from the field director of ONDEPJOV copies of the most recent *empadronamiento* (censal registration of all families) carried out in the two zones. Included in this effort were the full names and addresses of all the inhabitants. I therefore drew a random sample from these lists of pobladores, and the

interviewers were given questionnaires with full names and addresses, as well
as copies of maps of the areas, brought up to date.

Santiago. All of Santiago was chosen for the sample, meaning an area of
some 83 blocks and almost 1,700 lots. The same technique used in the larger
sectors of Pampa de Arena was employed in Santiago: that is, some 26 blocks
were selected, and then five lots within each block, for a total of 130 lots.
Sketch maps of separate blocks were then provided. A further note: Santiago
was the only seriously contaminated area in which I worked, in that the interviewers encountered severe refusal rates in one part of the community. After
some digging to see what the problem was, I discovered that approximately
eight months prior to my own work, somebody had run a "survey," informing the inhabitants that there was a certain sum that had to be paid to "participate" in the survey. Furthermore, several incidents had apparently
occurred when the interviewers (all men) tried to enter the house, using the
interview as an excuse. Such an experience naturally placed any legitimate survey at a great disadvantage, and the few male interviewers working for me reported an almost 80 percent refusal rate in certain blocks. Female interviewers
were sent back in an effort to recover some of the lost interviews, and they
were successful to a point. Nevertheless, sample mortality was higher in Santiago than in any other settlement.

San José. I had no other way but to walk the entire neighborhood and
make a complete map of all of the alleyways and the number of dwellings in
each. There were almost five hundred dwelling units, and I drew a probability
sample of slightly more than one hundred.

Completion rates throughout were very good; outright refusals were less
than 6 percent. I ascribe this not only to the hard work, persistence, and skill
of the interviewers, but also to the patience and willingness of several hundred
people to be interviewed at considerable length. I felt (and still feel) myself
to be extremely fortunate that the study went as well as it did. About 550
completed interviews were eventually turned in and accepted. In an effort to
spread the coding tasks as narrowly as possible, my wife and I did all the coding. She also accompanied me frequently to all six research communities, and
was from the start an overworked and extraordinarily underpaid principal asso-
ciate of the whole project.

APPENDIX B

ENGLISH-LANGUAGE VERSION OF QUESTIONNAIRE

VARIABLE NAME
CASE NUMBER OF RESPONDENT
LOCATION
MIGRATORY STATUS

1. Is your wife living with you at the present time?
2. (IF YES:) Are you married by civil ceremony, by the Church, or by civil and Church ceremony? (IF NONE OF THE ABOVE:) Are you living in free union?
   (IF NO:) Are you single, widowed, separated, or divorced?
   IF THE RESPONDENT IS MARRIED:
3. How long have you been married?
4. How many children do you have?
IF THE RESPONDENT HAS CHILDREN:
5. How many of your children live with you in this house?
TO ALL THE RESPONDENTS:
6. In total, how many persons live in this house, including yourself?
7. Who are they? That is, how many are sons and daughters, brothers and sisters, parents, etc.?
8. Where were you born?
   a. SIZE OF LOCALITY
   b. DEPARTMENT
   c. REGION
IF THE RESPONDENT WAS BORN IN LIMA, GO TO QUESTION NO. 94.
9. Where did you live when you were 15 years old?
   a. SIZE OF LOCALITY
   b. DEPARTMENT
   c. REGION

      d. PROVINCE WHERE RESPONDENT SPENT THE MAJORITY OF HIS LIFE BEFORE HE WAS 15 YEARS OLD.

      e. SOCIO-ECONOMIC STATUS OF PROVINCE WHERE RESPONDENT SPENT THE MAJORITY OF HIS LIFE BEFORE HE WAS 15 YEARS OLD.

      f. MIGRANT/NON-MIGRANT STATUS.

10. How old were you when you left (INSERT PLACE MENTIONED IN QUESTION 9; IF THE RESPONDENT ANSWERS LIMA IN QUESTION 9, INSERT THE NAME OF HIS BIRTHPLACE, QUESTION 8)?

10a. How old were you when you left (PLACE MENTIONED IN QUESTION 9)? CODED ACCORDING TO AGE GROUP.

11. When you left (PLACE MENTIONED IN QUESTION 9; IF THE RESPONDENT ANSWERS LIMA IN QUESTION 9, INSERT THE NAME OF HIS BIRTHPLACE), how would you describe your hometown? Would you say it was a small town, a medium-sized town, a small city, or what?

12. Did you live downtown or outside of town?

13. Did you leave (PLACE USED IN QUESTIONS 10 AND 11) alone, with other family members, or with friends?

14. Who made the decision to leave (PLACE USED IN QUESTIONS 10 AND 11 ABOVE)? You alone, and independently, other members of the family, or who?

15. Birthplace.

16. Amount of time spent in birthplace.

17. Employment in birthplace.

17a. EMPLOYMENT IN BIRTHPLACE CODED ACCORDING TO OCCUPATIONAL LEVEL.

18. Reasons for leaving birthplace.

19. Department of first migration site after birthplace (IF NOT LIMA).

20. Number of years spent at first migration site.

21. Employment at first migration site.

21a. Occupation level at first migration site.

22. Reason for leaving first migration site.

REPEAT QUESTIONS 19-22 FOR UP TO THREE MORE MIGRATION SITES PRIOR TO ARRIVAL IN LIMA, USING NUMBERS 23-34 AS NECESSARY.

35. How old were you when you came to live in Lima?

35a. How old were you when you came to live in Lima? (CODED ACCORDING TO AGE GROUP)

36. Had you visited Lima before you came to live in Lima?

37. (IF YES:) When was the first time you visited Lima?

DIRECT OR INDIRECT MIGRANT (DRAWS ON QUESTIONS 15, 19, 23, 27, 31)

AMOUNT OF EDUCATION RECEIVED OUTSIDE OF LIMA BY RESPONDENT (DRAWS ON QUESTIONS 17, 21, 25, 29, 33)

AMOUNT OF TIME SPENT IN ANOTHER CITY BESIDES LIMA (DRAWS

ON QUESTIONS 15, 19, 23, 27, 31)
TO ALL THE RESPONDENTS:
38. Did you come to Lima alone, with other members of the family, or with friends?
38a.Were you the first member of your family to come to live in Lima?
IF NO:
39. Who was the first?
40. Why did (PERSON MENTIONED IN QUESTION 39) come to Lima to live?
41. Did you have any relatives or friends who helped you come to Lima?
42. IF YES: Who were they?
43. What did they do to help you?
TO ALL THE RESPONDENTS:
44. Did you come to Lima as the result of a personal decision, or a decision that other persons made? (IF OTHERS MADE THE DECISION) Who made the decision for you?
45. What reason did you have/the persons who made the decision have for leaving the place where you lived and moving to Lima?
46. Before you came to Lima, did you ever think of going to some other place to live?
IF YES:
47. Where?
47a.MIGRATION TO MAJOR CITY BESIDES LIMA.
48. Why did you think about going to (PLACE MENTIONED IN QUESTION 47)?
49. Why did you decide to come to Lima and not to (PLACE MENTIONED IN QUESTION 47)?
TO ALL THE RESPONDENTS:
50. Why did you decide to stay in Lima permanently?
51. Was it more difficult or less difficult to live in Lima than you had expected?
IF THE RESPONDENT ANSWERS "MORE DIFFICULT" OR "LESS DIF-FICULT":
52. In what way was it more/less difficult?
TO ALL THE RESPONDENTS:
53. When you came to Lima did you have a job ready and waiting for you, or did you have to look for a job after you arrived?
54. What was you first job here in Lima?
54a. What was your first job here in Lima?   (CODED ACCORDING TO OCCUPATIONAL LEVEL)
IF HE HAD TO LOOK FOR WORK:
55. Would you say that you had much, little, or no difficulty in getting your first job in Lima?
56. How long did it take you to get that first job in Lima?

TO ALL THE RESPONDENTS:
57. Where did you live immediately upon your arrival in Lima?
58. What type of housing was it?   (IF NECESSARY:) A private house, an apartment, a quinta or callejón, a turgurio, or what?
59. Did you live with a relative or friend at this location?
60. Did you receive any assistance from a relative or friend to establish yourself in Lima?
IF YES:
61. Who helped you?
62. What type of help did they give you?
TO ALL THE RESPONDENTS:
63. How much money did you have with you when you came to Lima?
WHERE RESPONDENT LIVED AND IN WHAT TYPE OF HOUSING
64-65. (SUMMARY FROM QUESTIONS 57,58).
66. First residence in Lima.
67. Time spent at first residence in Lima.
68. Employment at first residence in Lima.
68a. Employment at first residence in Lima (CODED ACCORDING TO OCCUPATIONAL LEVEL)
69. Type of dwelling in first residence in Lima.
70. With whom did you live?
71. Reason for leaving first residence in Lima.
REPEAT QUESTIONS 66-71 FOR UP TO THREE MORE RESIDENCES IN LIMA PRIOR TO ARRIVAL IN PRESENT SITE IN A SQUATTER SETTLEMENT, USING NUMBERS 72-77 AS NECESSARY.
78. Present residence in Lima.
79. Amount of time at present residence in Lima.
80. Employment at present residence in Lima.
80a. Employment at present residence in Lima. (CODED ACCORDING TO OCCUPATIONAL LEVEL)
81. Type of dwelling at present residence in Lima.
82. With whom do you live at the present time?
83. (SUMMARY FROM QUESTIONS 66-81).
INTRACITY RESIDENTIAL MOBILITY: NUMBER OF PLACES LIVED IN LIMA.
INTRACITY RESIDENTIAL MOBILITY: AVERAGE INTERVAL OF TIME SEPARATING INTRACITY MOVES.
INTRACITY RESIDENTIAL MOBILITY: TOTAL TIME OF RESIDENCE IN CALLEJONES.
84. Are you satisfied with having come to Lima, or would you have preferred to stay in (NAME OF BIRTHPLACE)?
IF RESPONDENT ANSWERS HE "WOULD HAVE PREFERRED TO STAY IN HIS BIRTHPLACE":
85. Why haven't you gone back to your birthplace?

TO ALL THE RESPONDENTS:

86. In what ways would you say living in Lima is better than living in (HOME TOWN)?

87. And in what ways would you say living in Lima is worse than living in (HOME TOWN)?

88. Have you returned to (HOME TOWN) since you arrived in Lima?

IF YES:

89. How many times have you returned?

90. Why did you return?

TO ALL THE RESPONDENTS:

91. If you had the chance would you go back to live in (NAME OF HOME TOWN)?

92. Do you now consider yourself more a *provinciano* or a *limeño*?

93. Why do you feel that way?

94. What do you like most about Lima?

95. And what do you like least about Lima?

96. Would you say that your present house is much better, better, the same, worse, or much worse compared with the first place you lived in Lima?

ONLY TO MIGRANTS:

97. And is your present house better, the same, or worse compared with the house where you lived in (NAME OF HOME TOWN)?

TO ALL THE RESPONDENTS:

98. Do you know any people or have any friends who have left Lima to go back to the provinces?

IF HE KNOWS SOMEONE:

99. Do you know why they left?

100. Keeping everything in mind, would you say that people are more satisfied in the city or in the country?

101. Do you think it is more difficult for a *provinciano* to get ahead in Lima than for someone born and raised here, or do you think it doesn't make any difference?

IF HE ANSWERS "MORE DIFFICULT FOR A PROVINCIANO" OR "MORE DIFFICULT FOR A PERSON BORN IN LIMA":

102. In what ways do you think it is more difficult?

TO ALL THE RESPONDENTS:

103. If it were up to you to decide, would you be in favor of allowing all the people who are able to come to live in this city, or would you be in favor of stopping people from coming here?

104. Why do you feel that way?

105. Would you help people who wanted to migrate to Lima to live?

And now some questions about your job.

106. What is your present job or work?

106a. What is your present job or work? (ACCORDING TO OCCUPATIONAL LEVEL)

106b. What is your present job or work?   (ACCORDING TO ECONOMIC
ACTIVITY).

IF THE RESPONDENT HAS WORK, ASK QUESTION 107; IF HE DOES
NOT HAVE WORK, GO TO QUESTION 109.

107. How many hours a day do you work at this job?

108. And how many days a week do you work at this job?

IF THE RESPONDENT DOES NOT HAVE WORK.

109. How long has it been since you've been out of work?

110. Why aren't you working at present?

TO ALL THE RESPONDENTS WITH JOBS:

111. Where do you work at present?

FACTORY EMPLOYED OR NOT. (SUMMARY FROM QUESTIONS 106,
111)

112. How long have you worked as (PRESENT JOB)?

113. How long have you worked at (PRESENT JOB SITE)?

IF THE WORK SITE IS A LONG WAY AWAY OR OUTSIDE OF THE COM-
MUNITY:

114. How long does it take you to get to work each day?

115. Talking about your principal job, how satisfied are you with your present work? Would you say you are very satisfied, somewhat satisfied,
only a little satisfied, or not satisfied at all?

116. Why do you feel that way?

117. Do you think that your job offers you opportunities to get ahead and
to better your economic situation?

118. Why do you feel that way?

119. What type of job do you think you will have 5 years from now?

119a. What type of job do you think you will have 5 years from now? (AC-
CORDING TO OCCUPATIONAL LEVEL)

MOBILITY EXPECTATIONS: DIFFERENCE BETWEEN LEVEL OF MAIN
OCCUPATION CURRENTLY HELD AND OCCUPATION EXPECTED FIVE
YEARS FROM NOW (SUMMARY FROM QUESTIONS 106, 119)

120. If you could choose any job, what kind of job would you pick?

120a. If you could choose any job, what kind of job would you pick? (AC-
CORDING TO OCCUPATIONAL LEVEL)

MOBILITY ASPIRATIONS: DIFFERENCE BETWEEN LEVEL OF MAIN
OCCUPATION CURRENTLY HELD AND PREFERRED OCCUPATION.

121. Can you tell me anything about the new Industrial Community Law?

IF YES:

122. Do you think this law will affect your job?

IF YES:

123. In what way will it affect it?

MIGRANTS ONLY:

124. What was the last job you had before coming to Lima?

124a. What was the last job you had before coming to Lima?   (ACCORDING
TO OCCUPATIONAL LEVEL)
IF THE JOB IS RELATED TO AGRICULTURE:
125. Were you a land owner, a *campesino* with your own land, a peon, or
what?
MOBILITY PATTERN: LAST OCCUPATION BEFORE LIMA COMPARED
TO FIRST OCCUPATION AFTER ARRIVAL.
MOBILITY PATTERN: DIFFERENCE BETWEEN FIRST POST-MIGRATION
OCCUPATION AND CURRENT MAIN OCCUPATION.
IF RESPONDENT IS 45 YEARS OLD OR OLDER: OVERALL PATTERN
OF OCCUPATIONAL MOBILITY.
TO ALL THE RESPONDENTS:
126. What was the principal job your father had?
126a. What was the principal job your father had?   (ACCORDING TO OCCU-
PATIONAL LEVEL)
DIFFERENCE BETWEEN RESPONDENT'S OCCUPATIONAL LEVEL AND
OCCUPATIONAL LEVEL OF RESPONDENT'S FATHER.
Now I have a few questions about education.
127. How many years of schooling did you have?
128. Would you have liked to have had more schooling?
IF YES:
129. What was the principal reason that you didn't study more than you did?
130. Do you think you would have a better job if you had more education?
131. How many years of schooling would you like your oldest son to have?
132. Would you say that you would have more respect for the mayor of a big
city, the rector of a university, or the owner of a large business?
133. How many years of schooling do you think your oldest son will have?
ASPIRATION/ACHIEVEMENT DIFFERENCES IN EDUCATION FOR OLD-
EST SON.
COMPARISON OF RESPONDENT'S EDUCATIONAL LEVEL WITH LEVEL
OF EDUCATION DESIRED FOR OLDEST SON.
COMPARISON OF RESPONDENT'S EDUCATIONAL LEVEL WITH LEVEL
OF EDUCATION EXPECTED FOR OLDEST SON.
134. If there are facilities available, such as teachers and school buildings, how
many years of schooling do you think the sons of a person like yourself
should have?
DIFFERENCE BETWEEN RESPONDENT'S PERSONAL ASPIRATION FOR
HIS ELDEST SON AND RESPONDENT'S GENERAL ASPIRATION FOR
SONS OF OTHERS IN THE SAME CLASS.
135. Some people say that if a man works hard, saves his money, and has am-
bition, he will get ahead in life. Do you think that such a thing happens
frequently in Peru? Would you say that it happens very frequently, not
so frequently, very infrequently, or never?

Now I have another kind of question. Here's a picture of a ladder. Let's suppose that the top of the ladder represents the best possible life for you, and that the bottom represents the worst possible life for you.

136. Where on the ladder do you feel you personally stand at the present time?
137. Where do you think you were 5 years ago?
138. Where do you think you will be on the ladder 5 years from now?

LIMEÑOS ONLY: MOBILITY ACHIEVEMENT.

MIGRANTS ONLY:

139. Where were you when you first arrived in Lima?
140. And where on the ladder more or less would you be if you had stayed in (PLACE MENTIONED IN QUESTION 9; IF THE RESPONDENT ANSWERS LIMA IN QUESTION 9, INSERT THE NAME OF HIS BIRTH-PLACE)

MIGRANTS ONLY: MOBILITY ACHIEVEMENT BETWEEN PRESENT, FIVE YEARS AGO, FIVE YEARS HENCE, FIRST ARRIVAL IN LIMA, AND HOME TOWN.

MIGRANTS ONLY: MOBILITY ACHIEVEMENT BETWEEN PRESENT POSITION ON LADDER AND POSITION IF RESPONDENT HAD REMAINED IN HIS HOME TOWN.

TO ALL THE RESPONDENTS:

141. Do you think that most people would try to take advantage of you if they had the chance or would they try to be fair?
142. What do you think are the principal causes of poverty?
143. Do you think that your children will have a life that is better than, more or less the same as, or worse than yours?
144. What are your principal reasons for believing this?
145. Do you think that your children will have better, more or less the same, or worse opportunities to get ahead in comparison with other young people in Lima?
146. What do you think are the principal reasons for the differences between the opportunities for your children and the children of other people?

Here's the picture of the ladder. Imagine that the ladder represents the social levels of everyone in the country. This means that the top of the ladder is occupied by the people of the highest social position; in the middle are those people who occupy the middle social position; and on the bottom of the ladder are those who have a lower social position.

147. On what part of the ladder are people in the same social position as yourself?
148. And where do you think your children will be when they are grown?

DIFFERENCE BETWEEN RESPONDENT'S SOCIAL POSITION AND THAT OF HIS SON.

Sometimes one hears the term social class as in "middle class," "upper class," "working class," etc.

149. What term would you say is most applicable to you and your family?
150. Would you say that it is very difficult, only a little difficult, or easy to move from a lower social class to a higher one?
151. Why do you feel that way?
152. What social class do you think your children will belong to?
DIFFERENCE BETWEEN RESPONDENT'S SOCIAL CLASS AND EXPECTED SOCIAL CLASS OF CHILDREN.
Here are some statements about different aspects of life and work. I am going to read a pair of statements. We would like to know which statement you believe is the more acceptable, or truer, of the two. In some cases, you may feel that both statements are acceptable; in other cases, you may think that neither of the two statements is true or acceptable. But for each pair of statements we want you to choose (without thinking about it too much) the statement which seems to you to be the more acceptable of the two.
(READ EACH PAIR OF STATEMENTS CLEARLY; REPEAT IF NECESSARY)
153. (1) The only important thing is to work hard—that is the only way to progress in life.
     (2) Getting ahead in life is mostly a matter of having better luck than others.
154. (1) People with wild and strange opinions should not be allowed to speak in public in this country.
     (2) Anyone with something to say should be allowed to speak out, regardless of what ideas or point of view he may have.
155. (1) You sometimes can't help wondering whether life is worthwhile anymore.
     (2) Life is often hard and unfair, but one must always make the best of what one has.
156. (1) In the long run, we ourselves are responsible for having bad government.
     (2) Someone like me doesn't have any say about what the government does.
157. (1) Nowadays a person has to live pretty much for today and let tomorrow take care of itself.
     (2) It is necessary to prepare ourselves for the future and make plans for it.
158. (1) The best job to have is one where you are part of a group all working together.
     (2) It is better to work alone and achieve your own goals than to work with other people and have to depend on them.
159. (1) Listening to all the different points of view on something is very confusing; it's better to hear just one point of view from somebody who is informed.
     (2) Before making a decision, it's good to consider the opinions of as many different people as possible.

160. (1) One of the major causes of wars is that people do not take enough interest in what is happening in the world.
     (2) However I might try, I feel more and more helpless in the face of what is happening in the world today.
161. (1) A person should strive to be successful even if it means he will lose friends and others will be jealous of him.
     (2) In the long run, it is more important to be liked and respected by one's friends and neighbors than to become successful in life.
162. (1) Any leader should be very strict with the people under him in order to gain their respect.
     (2) Being respected as a leader comes only from treating one's followers well.
163. (1) I usually feel that I'm very much a part of the things going on around here.
     (2) These days I get a feeling that I'm just not a part of things.
164. (1) It is essential for effective work that our bosses tell us just what is to be done and exactly how to do it.
     (2) We can usually get the job done just as well without any instructions from our bosses.
165. (1) Sometimes politics and government seem so complicated that a person like me can't really understand what's going on.
     (2) If a person just pays attention to what is going on in politics and government, he should be able to understand what is happening.
166. (1) No matter how hard some people try, it's difficult for them to get ahead in life.
     (2) Most people who don't get ahead just don't have enough will power.
167. (1) It is best to make plans for the things you want in life.
     (2) It is best to leave things to fate.
168. (1) It's hardly fair to bring a child into the world, the way things look for the future.
     (2) No matter how bad things may look at times, we should always have hope for what the future may bring.
169. (1) It's useless to kill yourself working, if you have little time left for anything else.
     (2) The job should come first, even if it means sacrificing time from recreation or from one's family.
170. (1) What young people need most of all is strict discipline by their parents.
     (2) Young people today should have more freedom and independence from their families.
171. (1) You can always count on someone to help you out when things get bad enough.
     (2) When you get right down to it, no one is going to care much about what happens to you.

172. (1) The secret of happiness is not to expect a lot and to be content with what comes your way.
   (2) One should make any sacrifice in order to succeed in life.
173. (1) What we need most is a strong leader to tell us what to do.
   (2) We are better off trying to figure out what we should do by ourselves than listening to some leader who claims to know what's best for us.
174. (1) A person can pretty well make whatever he wants out of his life.
   (2) No matter how much a person tries, it is hard to change the way things are going to turn out.
175. (1) Everything is so uncertain these days that it almost seems as though anything could happen.
   (2) In spite of everything, it's really not hard for a person to know where he stands from one day to the next.
Now I would like to ask you some questions about your house.
176. Are you the owner of this house or do you rent it?
177. IF HE IS THE OWNER: Did you build it yourself?
178. IF YES: Did you build all of it or only some parts?
179. How much time have you devoted to the construction?
180. How much money have you spent on construction?
TO ALL THE RESPONDENTS:
181. How did you get the land?
IF THE RESPONDENT ANSWERS "BY INVASION" IN WHATEVER MANNER, ASK QUESTIONS 182 THROUGH 192; IF HE ANSWERS IN ANOTHER MANNER, SKIP TO QUESTION 192.
182. Did you participate in the original invasion of the land here in (NAME OF SITE)?
183. How did you find out about the plans to invade this land?
184. Altogether, how many families participated in the invasion?
185. What was the most important reason for participating in the invasion?
186. Did you help in some way with the organization of the invasion?
187. (IF YES:) What did you do specifically?
TO ALL THOSE WHO PARTICIPATED IN THE INVASION:
188. Could you tell me something about your feelings while you were participating in the invasion of this land?
189. At the time that you took possession of the land, did you think that you would not have serious difficulty in holding it, or did you think it would be necessary to fight to retain possession?
190. Did you have difficulties in retaining possession?
191. (IF YES:) Could you tell me something about these difficulties?
TO ALL THE RESPONDENTS:
192. Do you have title to this land?
IF THEY ALREADY HAVE TITLE:

193. How much did you have to pay for the title?   That is, not per square
     meter, but in total in order to get the title?
IF RESPONDENT DOES NOT HAVE TITLE YET:
194. Why don't you have title yet?
TO ALL THE RESPONDENTS:
195. Is it very, somewhat, or not at all important to you to have title to this
     land?
196. Are you paying for this land?
197. (IF HE IS PAYING:) How much do you pay monthly for this land?
TO ALL THE RESPONDENTS:
198. Is there a housing cooperative here in (NAME OF SITE)?
IF THERE IS A HOUSING COOPERATIVE:
199. Are you a member of this cooperative?
IF THE RESPONDENT IS A MEMBER OF THE COOPERATIVE:
200. How many members are there, more or less?
TO ALL RESPONDENTS WHO RENT THE HOUSE:
201. Where does the owner of this house live?
202. How much do you pay monthly for rent?
TO ALL THE RESPONDENTS:
203. Were you evicted from your previous house, that is, from the house you
     were living in before coming here to (NAME OF SITE)?
IF YES:
203a. Why were you evicted?
204. Who evicted you?
205. How did you feel when you were evicted?
206. How do you feel about your present situation as regards your house and
     land—do you think that your possession is secure?
207. What would you do if someone tried to evict you or relocate you some-
     where else?   For example, in a housing project built by the government?
208. Do you have any specific plans to improve your house or land?
IF THE RESPONDENT HAS PLANS TO IMPROVE THE HOUSE:
209. Could you tell me something about them briefly?
IF THE RESPONDENT HAS NO PLANS TO CHANGE HIS HOUSE:
210. Would you say that the house is finished?
TO ALL THE RESPONDENTS:
211. In general, how do you like (NAME OF SITE) as a place to live?
212. What do you like most about living here in (NAME OF SITE)?
213. What do you like least about living here?
214. Would you say that (NAME OF SITE) is progressing?   Do you think it
     is progressing rapidly, slowly, not progressing at all, or getting worse?
215. Do you think that relative to the rest of Lima (NAME OF SITE) is very
     much forgotten, more or less forgotten, not very forgotten, or not at all
     forgotten?

216. As far as you know now, do you intend to stay here permanently or do you have plans to move?

217. Do you think that (NAME OF SITE) has changed since you arrived here?

IF RESPONDENT ANSWERS THAT IT HAS CHANGED:

218. What have been the most important changes?

219. (IN REGARD TO THE FIRST CHANGE:) Who was/is the most responsible for this change?

220. (IN REGARD TO THE SECOND CHANGE:) Who was/is the most responsible for this change?

221. Can you recall any event, incident, or experience that may have occurred here in (NAME OF SITE) since you arrived that is something you consider very important or about which you feel very strongly? (IF NECESSARY) Something which made you feel very upset or very happy?

222. (IF YES:) What was the incident?

223. Why did this make you angry/make you unhappy?

TO ALL THE RESPONDENTS:

224. How do you think (NAME OF SITE) will be five years from now?   In what ways do you think it will be different?

IF THE RESPONDENT SAYS "IS NOT GOING TO CHANGE" OR "IS GO-
ING TO STAY THE SAME":

225. Why do you think (NAME OF SITE) is not going to change?

TO ALL THE RESPONDENTS:

226. You probably have many friends here in (NAME OF SITE). Thinking about your neighbors, would you say that all are friends, some are friends, or none are friends?

227. Why do you feel that way about your neighbors?

228. In what area or district do your three best friends live?   Here in (NAME OF SITE) or outside?

229. Do you think the people here in (NAME OF SITE) are very united, more or less united, only a little united, or not united?

230. Have you collaborated with other inhabitants of (NAME OF SITE) in any sort of community work? (IF NECESSARY) For example, in building a community center or a medical post or sidewalks or something like that?

IF THE RESPONDENT HAS COLLABORATED IN COMMUNITY WORK:

231. What type of collaboration or help?

232. How many times (more or less) have you collaborated in this manner?

TO ALL THE RESPONDENTS:

233. In many places there are groups that are opposed to each other. Think-ing about (NAME OF SITE), would you say that there are such groups —ones with differences of opinion?

IF YES:

234. What are the principal groups that oppose each other here?

235. Do you think that such differences of opinion are good or bad for (NAME OF SITE)?

TO ALL THE RESPONDENTS:

236. In your opinion who are the three people who have the most influence here in (NAME OF SITE)?   That is, the three people who are most successful in getting their way and getting things done?

237. What type of occupation or job do these people have?   (CODED ACCORDING TO OCCUPATIONAL LEVEL)

238. Why do these people have influence here in (NAME OF SITE)?

239. When you meet someone for the first time here in (NAME OF SITE), should you:

–Trust him until he proves to be unworthy of that trust;

–Be cautious about trusting him until you know him better;

–Not trust him because he may take advantage of you?

240. Do you think what you say applies only to people who live here in (NAME OF SITE), or does it apply to people in general?

IF THE RESPONDENT ANSWERS THAT THE PREVIOUS QUESTION APPLIES ONLY TO PEOPLE HERE:

241. In what way is there a difference between people around here and others elsewhere?

TO ALL THE RESPONDENTS:

242. Some people are inclined to help others; other people tend to look out only for themselves. Which do you think is more applicable to people here in (NAME OF SITE):

–Most people here are helpful to others; or

–Most people here look out only for themselves?

243. Why do you say this?   Can you remember any incident or experience that illustrates this?

244. There are some people who say that violence should never be used to settle personal quarrels or disputes–that is, those involving relatives, friends, neighbors, co-workers, and so forth. Others say that in some cases it may be necessary to use violent means to settle a dispute. How do you feel about this?   Should violence never be used to settle personal questions, or may it be justified in some situations?

IF RESPONDENT ANSWERS THAT VIOLENCE MAY BE USED IN CERTAIN SITUATIONS:

245. In what type of situation?   Could you give me an example of when violence would be justified?

TO ALL THE RESPONDENTS:

246. How about political questions or disputes?   Do you think that violence should never be used to settle this type of dispute, or may it be justified on certain occasions?

IF RESPONDENT ANSWERS THAT VIOLENCE MAY BE USED IN CERTAIN SITUATIONS:

247. In what type of situation?

TO ALL THE RESPONDENTS:

248. Did you go to the rally in the Plaza de Armas last October?
249. Do you have friends who went?
250. Do you know if there was a delegation from (NAME OF SITE) at the rally?
251. Suppose that something happened to your family—for example, a case of serious illness or an accident, the loss of your job, etc. Is there some person or group or agency you could rely on to help out in such circumstances?
252. IF THE RESPONDENT SAYS THERE IS A PERSON OR GROUP: Who are/is they/he?
253. In your opinion what are the most urgent or serious problems and necessities here in (NAME OF SITE)?
254. Which of the problems or necessities is the most important for you?
255. Would you say that many of the other people here in (NAME OF SITE) are also worried about these problems, or not?
256. Do you think that these problems mentioned can be resolved by the people here in (NAME OF SITE), or would help be needed from outside?

IF RESPONDENT SAYS "OUTSIDE AID WILL BE NECESSARY":

257. Who might be able to provide such assistance to resolve these problems?

TO ALL THE RESPONDENTS:

258. Do you think that there are persons or groups within (NAME OF SITE) who can help to resolve such problems?
259. IF YES: Who are these groups?
260. In general, which is most important for improving the conditions of life here in (NAME OF SITE): (1) the hard work of the residents, (2) God's help, (3) the government's help, or (4) good luck?

Here's the picture of the ladder. Suppose that the person or group who contributes most to the welfare of the people here in (NAME OF SITE) is on the top part of the ladder, and that the person or group who does least or nothing for the wellbeing of (NAME OF SITE) is at the bottom.

261. Now, then, where would newspapermen be in terms of their contribution to the welfare of the people here? Near the group or person who contributes most or the person or group who contributes least to your welfare? NOTE THE NUMBER ON THE LADDER AND REPEAT THE QUESTION FOR EACH GROUP OR PERSON ON THE LIST BELOW, NOTING THE RATING FOR EACH ONE.
262. Priests?
263. President of the Republic?
264. Schoolteachers?
265. Police or Guardia Civil?
266. Member of the Municipal Council of (NAME OF SITE)?
267. Mayor of the city of Lima?

268. Private entities?
269. Leaders of the local associations?
SUMMARY VARIABLE: IF ONE PERSON OR GROUP IS RANKED HIGHER
THAN ALL THE OTHERS, WHICH ONE? (SUMMARY FROM QUESTIONS
261-269)
270. Are you acquainted with the National Office of Pueblos Jóvenes near
     Unidad Vecinal No. 3?
271. IF YES: Have you ever gone there?
272. Why did you go there?
273. How do you think that you were treated there—better than other people
     who go there, the same as others, or worse than others?
TO ALL THE RESPONDENTS:
274. Have you ever seen any official of the Office of Pueblos Jóvenes come
     here to (NAME OF SITE)?
275. IF THE RESPONDENT HAS SEEN SUCH AN OFFICIAL: Do you know
     why this person came here?
ASK QUESTIONS 276 TO 281 ONLY IN PAMPA DE ARENA:
276. Have you ever heard of Acción Comunitaria?
277. IF THE RESPONDENT KNOWS ABOUT ACCIÓN: Could you tell me
     something about the work of Acción here in Pampa de Arena? For instance,
     do you think that Acción contributes to the welfare of the people here?
278. IF THE RESPONDENT SAYS THAT IT CONTRIBUTES TO THE WEL-
     FARE: How does it contribute?
279. Have you or some member of your family benefited in some way from
     the activities of Acción?
280. Have you contributed in some way to the construction of the branch of
     the Hospital de Empleados here? (IF NECESSARY) I mean the medical
     post along the side of El Milagro?
281. IF THE RESPONDENT HAS CONTRIBUTED: In what way did you
     contribute?
TO ALL THE RESPONDENTS:
282. Are you a delegate from your block?
283. IF THE RESPONDENT IS A DELEGATE: Why did you decide to be
     a delegate?
284. Would you say that the government is acting very well, not so well, or
     badly in fulfilling its responsibility in supplying potable water?
285. Supplying electricity?
286. Supplying sewerage facilities?
287. Supplying sidewalks?
288. Paving streets?
289. Supplying police protection?
290. Handing out property titles?
291. Supplying schools and teachers?
292. Giving work to those who need it?

SUMMARY VARIABLE: EVALUATION OF GOVERNMENT RESPONSI-
BILITY (SUMMARY FROM QUESTIONS 284-292).

293. Last November, there was a census of the people in the pueblos jóvenes.
Did a person come to your house to include you in this census?

294. Why do you think this census was conducted?

295. Have you ever worked or cooperated with other residents of (NAME OF
SITE) to try to solve some problem or meet some need of (NAME OF
SITE)?

IF THE RESPONDENT HAS COLLABORATED:

296. When did you do this?

297. With what type of problem or necessity were you concerned?

298. What did you try to do about it?

299. What were the results of your efforts?

TO ALL THE RESPONDENTS:

300. Thinking now about the problems of Peru: In your opinion, what are
the most important problems of the country?

301. The present Revolutionary Government is trying to do a great deal. Can
you tell me about the principal ideas or goals of the government? (LOOK
FOR A SPECIFIC ANSWER)

302. Of all the persons you know or have heard or read about, alive or dead,
whom do you admire the most?

303. What did/does this person do that was/is outstanding?

304. What do you think a person should do to be a good Peruvian?

305. Do you know who Luis Bambarén is? (LOOK FOR SPECIFIC
IDENTIFICATION, SUCH AS: THE BISHOP OF THE PUEBLOS
JÓVENES)

306. And can you tell me the name of the mayor of the district of (NAME
OF DISTRICT WHERE PLACE IS LOCATED)?

307. What is the name of the President of the Republic? (JUAN VELASCO
ALVARADO)

308. How often do you listen to the radio or watch television for national
and international news?

309. And how often do you read national and international news in the newspapers?

ONLY TO MIGRANTS:

310. Since you left your home town, have you become any more or any less
interested in politics and public affairs?

TO ALL THE RESPONDENTS:

311. How much effect does the national government and its activities have on
your daily life? Much, some, little, or no effect?

312. IF THE RESPONDENT SAYS "MUCH" OR "SOME" EFFECT: In what
way does it principally affect you?

313. And how much effect does the district government—that is, the municipal
council of (NAME OF DISTRICT WHERE SITE IS LOCATED)—have on

your daily life?

314. IF THE RESPONDENT SAYS "MUCH" OR "SOME" EFFECT: In what way does it affect you?

315. In general how often do you discuss politics and public affairs with other people? Would you say that you discuss them very frequently, not so frequently, almost never, or never?

316. IF THE RESPONDENT SAYS "WITH MUCH OR SOME FREQUENCY": With whom do you discuss these matters?

317. Do you try to be informed about politics and public affairs?

318. In the last three months have you attended any meeting or assembly here in (NAME OF SITE)?

IF YES:

319. What type of meeting?

320. Do you think it is worthwhile to attend these meetings?

321. Do you feel obliged to attend or participate in such meetings?

TO ALL THE RESPONDENTS:

322. Have you ever personally, either alone or with other residents of (NAME OF SITE), gone to talk with some official of the local association about some problem or need?

IF THE RESPONDENT HAS GONE:

323. What type of problem?

324. What kind of treatment did you receive?

325. And how did it turn out?

TO ALL THE RESPONDENTS:

326. And have you ever personally, alone or with other residents of (NAME OF SITE), gone to speak with some official of the National Office of Pueblos Jóvenes about some problem or need?

IF THE RESPONDENT HAS GONE:

327. What type of problem?

328. What kind of treatment did you receive?

329. How did it turn out?

SUMMARY VARIABLE: TREATMENT BY LOCAL ASSOCIATION COMPARED WITH TREATMENT RECEIVED BY RESPONDENT AT NATIONAL OFFICE OF PUEBLOS JÓVENES. SUMMARY FROM QUESTIONS 324,328.

TO ALL THE RESPONDENTS:

330. If you were to go to an office of the government—for example, the Ministry of Health—would you say that they would treat you better than, the same as, or worse than somebody else?

331. And if you tried to explain your problem to the people in that office, do you think they would pay a great deal of attention to you, pay only a little bit of attention, or ignore you completely?

SUMMARY VARIABLE: TREATMENT ACTUALLY RECEIVED AT NATIONAL OFFICE OF PUEBLOS JÓVENES COMPARED WITH TREATMENT EXPECTED AT OTHER NATIONAL OFFICE. SUMMARY FROM

QUESTIONS 328, 331.

332. Which of the following qualifications is most important for a man to hold a position of authority? (1) Have a good background and come from a good family, (2) Stick to the old way of doing things, (3) Be the most popular with the people, or (4) Be well educated and have special skills?

333. What type of news interests you the most? (1) World and international news (2) News about Peru (3) MIGRANTS ONLY: News about your home town (4) Sports (5) Religious affairs?

334. What newspaper do you generally read?

335. Suppose you were to meet someone who has just arrived from another part of Peru, a long way off—hundreds of kilometers away—and where you have never been, do you think you could understand his way of thinking?

336. What is the most important thing for the future of Peru? (1) The work of its citizens (2) Planning by the government (3) God's help (4) Good luck?

337. Are you a member of a union where you work?

338. Are you currently a member of a religious association?

339. A social club or group?

340. A sports or recreation club?

341. A cooperative?

342. An association of families in the school?

343. A savings and loan association or mutual?

344. A regional club?

345. The local association?

SUMMARY VARIABLE: NUMBER OF AFFILIATIONS THE RESPONDENT HAS. SUMMARY FROM QUESTIONS 338-345.

Now to finish, I have a few questions about the house. Which of the following things do you own?

346. A radio?

347. A television?

348. A wrist watch?

349. A gas stove?

350. A blender?

351. A refrigerator?

352. A sewing machine?

353. A primus?

354. A car?

355. A kerosene stove?

356. A truck?

SUMMARY VARIABLE: NUMBER OF ITEMS OWNED. SUMMARY FROM QUESTIONS 346-356.

357. Do you have land or a house anywhere else?
358. Do you receive your salary daily, weekly, every fifteen days, or monthly?
359. Can you tell me how much you receive?
360. Are you currently saving money?
361. IF RESPONDENT IS CURRENTLY SAVING MONEY: What are you saving money for?
362. Do you think that your income is sufficient to cover your most pressing needs?
363. Do you think that your present economic situation is better than, the same as, or worse than that of the majority of people in (NAME OF SITE)?
364. ONLY TO MIGRANTS: Would you say that your economic situation is better than, the same as, or worse than when you arrived in Lima?
TO ALL THE RESPONDENTS:
365. Do you have running water in the house?
366. IF THE RESPONDENT DOES NOT HAVE RUNNING WATER: How do you get your water from day to day?
367. How many people including yourself and all the children sleep regularly in this house?
368. What is your religion?
369. What do you do normally in your spare time or day off?
370. What do you normally do for July 28th?
371. How old are you?
372. What was the last year of school you completed?
373. Do you plan on having any further education?
374. Do you speak any languages besides Spanish?
375. IF YES: Which ones?
INFORMATION TO BE ASCERTAINED BY THE INTERVIEWER AFTER THE INTERVIEW—NOT TO BE ASKED.
376. Socio-economic level of respondent by observation.
377. Respondent's race by observation.
378. House construction: walls.
379. House construction: roof.
380. House construction: floor.
381. The interview began at _____o'clock _____ (DATE) and ended at _____ o'clock _____ (DATE).
382. The interview (1) was completed without long interruptions (2) was completed with one or more prolonged interruptions (3) was not completed.
IF THE INTERVIEW WAS NOT COMPLETED, EXPLAIN
383. How many times was it necessary to visit the respondent before terminating the interview?
384. The interview took place where?
385. Who besides the respondent was present during the interview?

386. The attitude of the respondent was (1) very cooperative (2) generally co-operative (3) somewhat cooperative (4) not cooperative (5) indifferent.
387. How would you classify the respondent's ability to understand and answer the questions?
388. Note the number of the questions that caused special difficulties.
389. Note words, terms, expressions, and specific passages that caused special difficulty.

SAMPLE STATUS
REASONS FOR SAMPLE MORTALITY
INTERVIEWER NAME

THE FOLLOWING QUESTIONS APPLY ONLY TO THE RESPONDENTS FROM SENDAS FRUTALES AND ARE NUMBERED SEPARATELY.

1. Have you ever thought about leaving here to go to live in some other place or part of Lima?
2. IF YES: What other part?
3. IF YES: Why did you think about going to (PLACE MENTIONED ABOVE)?
4. IF YES: And why didn't you go there?
5. Do you have friends or know people who have left Sendas Frutales to live in a barriada or pueblo joven?

IF YES:

6. Do you know why they left?
7. Do you know where or to which barriada he/they went to live?   CODED ACCORDING TO GEOGRAPHICAL AREA.
8. Do you know where or to which barriada he/they went to live?

TO ALL RESPONDENTS:

9. Why did you choose Sendas Frutales as a place to live?
10. How did you find out that houses were available for rent here in Sendas Frutales?
11. What would you do if they tried to evict you from here to relocate you somewhere else?   TAKEN FROM QUESTION 207.
12. Have you collaborated with other inhabitants of Sendas Frutales in any sort of community work?   TAKEN FROM QUESTION 230.
13. IF YES: How many times, more or less, have you collaborated in this manner?   TAKEN FROM QUESTION 232.
14. Are you acquainted with the office of the Municipality of San José? TAKEN FROM QUESTION 270.
15. Have you ever seen any official of the Municipality of San José come here to Sendas Frutales?   TAKEN FROM QUESTION 274.
16. IF YES: Do you know why this person came here?   TAKEN FROM QUESTION 275.
17. Would you say that the owner of this land/house is acting very well, not

so well, or badly in fulfilling his responsibility in supply water?   TAKEN
FROM QUESTION 284.

18. Supplying electricity?
19. Supplying sewerage facilities?
20. Supplying sidewalks?
21. Paving streets?
22. Have you ever gone personally, alone or with other residents of Sendas
    Frutales, to talk with the owner of this house about some problem or
    need?

IF YES:

23. What type of problem?
24. What did the owner say?

TO ALL THE RESPONDENTS:

25. And have you ever gone personally, alone or with other residents of Sen-
    das Frutales, to talk with some official of the Municipality of San José
    about some problem or need?   TAKEN FROM QUESTION 326.
26. IF RESPONDENT HAS GONE: What type of problem?
27. Do you have electricity in the house?
28. Is there a toilet in this callejón that works consistently?
29. Is there a shower or bath here in the callejón?
30. Do you pay for garbage collection?
31. IF YES: How much do you pay?
32. How many rooms does this house have?
33. How much rent do you pay?   CODED ACCORDING TO GENERAL
    LEVEL.
34. How much rent do you pay?

Notes

Chapter 1: Participation and Authoritarian Rule

1. The need to take extra-local agencies into account when investigating local-level political behavior has seemingly (and finally) impressed itself on scholars of both developed and underdeveloped nations (see Walton, 1979a: 164). Samuels (1978) provides a useful discussion of whether local politics is subordinate to national concerns or vice versa, and what the nature of linkages might be.

In this light, anyone familiar with Lima's poor, or with poor people anywhere, could maintain (and rightly so) that the national government is not the only source of assistance, material or otherwise. In Lima, many public, private, and religious organizations, both national and international, have worked with the city's poor; Rodríguez et al. (1973) list dozens of such associations, and each of the six sites selected for this study had had contacts in one form or another with various of these groups. Nevertheless, since the whole purpose of the investigation from the start was to examine the political behavior of the poor under an authoritarian regime, these other sources of aid were excluded from the study. Municipal governments were also considered to be tangential, since local government has for decades been an extremely weak force in Peru, especially in Lima (see chapter 3). Thus Lima is a "dependent" city, since it looks to the national socio-political system for resources to solve its problems. See Katznelson, 1976: 219.

2. The literature on dependency and underdevelopment is now voluminous and is characterized by definitional problems, by internal disagreements and contradictions, by repetition, and by controversy. Sources include Cardoso and Faletto (1968), Cohen (1973), Dos Santos (1970), Quijano (1970), Portes (1977), Chilcote (1974), Fagen (1977), O'Brien (1975), Castells (1973), Gunder Frank (1966), and many others. Critics abound; see Bath and James (1970), Kaufman et al. (1975), Sloan (1977), and Ray (1973). Some Marxist scholars reject dependency; see, as regards Peru especially, Dore and Weeks

(1977). *International Organization* (Winter 1978) devotes an entire issue to dependency.

3. This is not to say that dependency is without its critics or that I accept dependency as the new paradigm (à la Kuhn) for explaining all of Latin America's ills. But the dependency perspective does offer an explanatory leverage missing in the mainstream developmental literature found in the United States and Western Europe. See Portes (1974) for a good contrast of the two approaches; see also Walton (1976, 1977). In addition, whether the reader finds the dependency argument congenial or not, its persuasiveness among Peruvian technocrats, planners, and academics (e.g., Delgado, 1972) means that policies were often formulated with dependency and clientelism as givens. The ultimate irony of the Peruvian military's use of dependency may lie in the claim of many *dependentistas* that capitalist modernization increases the possibility for authoritarian political solutions that (despite all altruistic efforts to the contrary) will not diminish societal poverty (Cardoso and Faletto, 1969: 135).

4. Friedgut (1979) puts forth this argument and makes a strong case for investigating the presence and structure of political participation in the U.S.S.R. If the political system is in fact little more than the extension of an individual leader, then that individual (and hence the "system") might conceivably eliminate or severely reduce the collective activities referred to above (e.g., François Duvalier in Haiti, Idi Amin in Uganda). If, though, the political system has any life beyond the existence of such a leader, then participation by definition would have to be present, even if in severely truncated terms. This diminution of participatory opportunities, however, might intensify the efforts of individuals and groups to gain access to the system; it might also encourage the growth of anti-system involvement in activities such as demonstrations, insurgency, or guerrilla operations.

5. The necessity of including data collected on individual, community, and macro-systemic levels is inextricably linked to the whole area of concern surrounding the individualistic and the ecological fallacies in social research. Briefly stated, data gathered at the level of the individual (e.g., through surveys) tell nothing about group behavior; contrariwise, aggregate data (e.g., census statistics) say nothing about the behavior of a single individual. Eulau (1969(, Dogan and Rokkan (1969) and Dzudnowski (1976) treat this problem area in general; Kaufman (1970) develops a typology for urban research based on micro and macro criteria.

6. However, the type of economic system in operation in a society may play a major role in determining how many individuals are (relatively speaking) poor and the degree to which they are poor (compared with the wealthy). Income and material deprivation in a socialist economy may be considerably less than in a capitalist; indeed, Leeds (1969) argues that the whole urban squatter phenomenon occurs primarily in dependent capitalist economies (see chapter 2 as well for more elaboration). The economic system of a country influences both the concept and magnitude of poverty, whereas the political

system plays much less of a role in affecting poverty.

7. These communal needs are what Mancur Olson (1965) and others associated with rational choice theory (e.g., Rogowski, 1977; Frolich, Oppenheimer, and Young, 1971) label collective or public goods. Such a good is usually defined as any that cannot be withheld from any member of a specified group once it is supplied to one member of that group. Booth and Seligson (1978, 1979) use the notion of communal goods as well.

8. Other studies of political participation, such as Verba and Nie (1972) and Milbrath (1965), among others, also exclude violent or extralegal activities. These authors have been criticized for this stance, the complaint being that disruptive or violent political activities, especially during the 1960s in the United States, cannot be left out of any treatment of politics that claims to be complete (Rusk, 1976). Although I agree with this criticism, it does not alter my focus on conventional techniques in Lima, for a variety of reasons. First, violence as a strategy for communal problem-solving is highly exceptional, for reasons discussed at length in chapters 5, 6, and 7. The conventional patterns described in chapter 7 still constitute the norm. Second, the nature of the research environment obviated any use of items on a standardized questionnaire that probed into an individual's approval of violence or his participation in it. Although I experienced few difficulties in administering the questionnaire (see Appendix A), I had no intention of asking questions that could have jeopardized the research, and items directly or indirectly referring to violence as a means of expressing anti-regime sentiments clearly trod on dangerous ground. I therefore depend on informal techniques for discussing demonstrations (see chapters 6 and 8). Cornelius (1975) and Fagen and Tuohy (1972) follow this same strategy.

It should, nevertheless, be noted that since 1975 the squatters of Lima have shown what many have found to be surprisingly leftist sympathies, at least in their voting patterns. See chapters 8 and 9.

9. I should indicate here my agreement with other scholars who, in their studies of the poor (especially peasants in Third World nations), have put forward a political economy perspective. In his persuasive study of the peasantry in Vietnam, Popkin (1979) bases his analysis on a "rational actor" political economy model. He argues that a peasant acts after evaluating each outcome in accordance with his own subjective estimate of the likelihood of the outcome, and then makes a decision that he believes will maximize his expected utility. Rationality, according to Popkin, "implies that individuals evaluate the possible outcomes associated with their choices in accordance with their preferences and values" (Popkin, 1979: 30-31; also Portes and Walton, 1975: 72).

Whether the political economy model represents a new paradigm, as Walton (1979b) claims, remains to be seen. But although I do not base the entire study on a political economy model, many of my analyses and conclusions are congenial with this perspective. The decision to migrate first to Lima and then to a squatter settlement (chapter 5), the decision to invest in long-term construction projects (chapters 3 and 4), the sorts of participation undertaken (chapter 6), the decision-making process leading to national-level demand-making (chapter 7), and the resistance to structured, co-optive mobilization (chapter 8) can all be understood through this concept of rational behavior found in the political economy model.

My use of this model is aligned with Popkin's (1979) formulation in that both are concerned with how the *individual* poor person makes his decisions. Walton (1979b: 12-14), on the other hand, calls for investigating the macro-level political economy, i.e., urbanization in socialist and state capitalist countries, and the role of cities in the world economic system. Although I fully subscribe to such formulations, my emphasis is on how individuals act and on what rationality is for the poor in a Third World dependent capitalist nation-state.

10. The term *pueblo joven* (plural, *pueblos jóvenes*) first came into public use about 1967, and was coined by Bishop Luis Bambarén, who had at that time been named Bishop to Lima's squatter populace. The Revolutionary Government adopted the name in 1968, when it created ONDEPJOV (National Office for the Development of the Pueblos Jóvenes; see chapters 2 and 7). The label caught on and quickly replaced the earlier, more pejorative term *barriada*. The pobladores themselves prefer the term, and the mass media now use pueblo joven exclusively. Rather than translate it each time as "young town" or use some neologism such as "squatment" (Leeds and Leeds, 1976), I shall simply use the term itself generically, as I use *poblador* and *pobladores* to refer to the inhabitants of these communities.

Chapter 2: The Velasco Administration

1. No single study in Spanish or English covers the Belaúnde years comprehensively. Marrett (1969), Bourricaud (1970a), and Pike (1967) all include descriptions of the period; Kuczynski (1977) is a first-hand account of economic and financial problems as they related to politics; Webb (1977) compares economic and fiscal policies of Belaúnde and Velasco. The annulment of the 1962 election receives detailed treatment in Payne (1968). Belaúnde's election received considerable attention internationally; he was touted as the ideal Alliance for Progress executive when he appeared on the cover of *Time* (25 March 1965). The background to his overthrow in 1968 receives excellent treatment in Nunn (1979) and Philip (1978).

2. Analyses and (especially) criticisms of the Velasco period are now legion; Pease (1977) contains a bibliography with 1,100 citations. The best chronological account of the 1968-1975 period is Pease and Verve (1974, 1977).

3. This is the name the military adopted on its assumption of power, and I shall use it as well. Statements throughout the book that contrast the Velasco reformist efforts with other regimes exclude the Cuban experience from the comparison. Cuba is inevitably *the* exception in Latin America; from all

accounts, its efforts at producing socio-political mobilization and widespread participation have been broadly successful. For an early assessment, see Fagen (1969); see also Butterworth (1974) and Harnecker (1975). Perhaps the major difference between the two regimes lies in Castro's determination to remake Cuban society, to eliminate whole sectors of the old society by force if necessary, and to redistribute both existing and new resources to the whole population. Velasco, even during his most radical period, never made such goals part of his effort. Cuba more closely approximates a revolutionary system, whereas Peru was clearly reformist. Alberts and Brundenius (1979) provide a preliminary examination of development policies in Brazil, Peru, and Cuba.

The similarities and differences between Peru and Mexico also deserve mention here. Many have labeled Mexico corporatist, as I label Peru under Velasco. Yet the politicial systems of the two countries clearly differ. Mexico's well-entrenched electoral traditions, its highly developed national political party (the PRI), and its largely apolitical military (apolitical in the sense of not actively intervening or seizing power from civilians) all stand in contrast to Peru. Purcell (1975) refers to Mexico as an exclusionary system, in that it relies on coercion or force to exclude mobilized groups from participation in the system. Peru, in contrast, is called an inclusionary system, in that it supposedly does not exclude by force any mobilized group (7-8).

Such a label (at least by this definition) is misleading. The Revolutionary Government was less inclusionary than mobilizational—that is, it viewed the poor as non-mobilized. In addition, certain groups and their leaders, though perhaps not "forcibly excluded" from participation, obviously operated under continual harrassment and threats. For example, the National Agrarian Society was dissolved, the National Industries Society severely weakened, and the two major labor unions (the CGTP and the CTP) confronted by a regime-backed CTRP. Thus, although Mexico and Peru do differ along a variety of dimensions, the exclusionary-inclusionary dichotomy may not be especially accurate.

4. This section of chapter 2 draws on Dietz and Palmer (1976), which was later substantially rewritten and published as Dietz and Palmer (1978). The Peruvian military has been examined by a variety of scholars and observers, both Peruvian and foreign. For a sampling of sources, see Astiz and García (1972, 1973), Bourricaud (1970a, 1970b), Chaplin (1976), Clinton (1971), Einaudi (1973a, 1973b), García (1973), Grayson (1973), Johnson (1973), Lowenthal (1975), Malloy (1974), Palmer (1973), Palmer and Middlebrook (1975), Philip (1978), Rozman (1970), Stepan (1978, especially chapter 4), Valdez Pallete (1971), Villanueva (1969, 1972), Wilson (1975). Baella (1976), Moncloa (1977), Bejar (1976), and Pease (1977) are generally critical assessments of the Velasco period written after his removal from office.

5. Defining support under no-party authoritarian rule has its problems for academicians as well as for actual rulers. Presumably ceremonial support (attending rallies, joining approved organizations, etcetera) is important. However,

with its emphasis on mobilization and involvement on the local level, the Revolutionary Government permitted elections of neighborhood leaders, union leaders, and other such local officials, especially as cooperatives and communities were being created, and encouraged broad involvement in these elections. The regime apparently felt (at least initially) that widespread member participation indicated support for the reformist structures and, hence, for the Revolution. But the results frequently went against the obvious desires of the government, as previous labor leaders and/or party-affiliated individuals (especially Apristas) showed considerable strength, especially on the northern coastal sugar plantations (see Palmer, 1971; Dietz and Palmer, 1978; Stepan, 1978, chapter 6).

6. Schoultz (1977) examines popular authoritarianism in Latin America by using Peronism in Argentina as prototypical. He notes that "popular authoritarianism melds intensive political mobilization of previously excluded social sectors within political structures which severely limited these groups' ability to affect public policy" (1,423). Schoultz concludes that a substantial rate of economic growth along with an area's working-class population helps to explain a very large percentage of the Peronist vote. He classifies the Velasco regime as popular authoritarian as well (1,424). However, no such parallel conclusion should be made for Peru, since the Velasco regime was not voted into power. Velasco, unlike Perón, faced the extremely difficult challenge of developing support *after* he assumed office. Thus he and his administration, though authoritarian in structure, tried to take on a populist image; the regime was certainly not a popular one in the electoral sense, or perhaps in any sense at all. Even at the best of times, the Velasco regime confronted widespread cynicism and was apparently unable to generate truly widespread loyalty (cf. Hammergren, 1977: 457). The 200,000 attendants at Velasco's burial on December 26, 1977 (*Latin American Political Report* 12, no. 1: 6) probably appeared as much in protest against President Morales Bermúdez as in grief at Velasco's death.

Chapter 3: Urbanization, the Urban Poor, and Poor Neighborhoods
1. Mangin (1967a, 1967b), Turner (1965, 1968), Cotler (1971), and many others point out this same pattern. Turner refers to the two types of environments as "bridgehead" (slum) and "consolidation" (squatter) settlements. Leeds (1974) draws parallels and differences between Lima and Rio de Janeiro. Brown (1972) applied Turner's Lima dichotomy to the Mexico City case but found it only partially repeated.
2. On the tugurios of Lima in general, see Delgado (1971), Mariátegui (1969), ONPU (no date), Paredes (1971), Patch (1961, 1967), Paz Soldán (1957), Rotondo et al. (1963), Millones (1978), Santos (1975), Sánchez León and Guerrero de los Rios (1979). The squatter areas are covered by a much larger literature, and the following is only suggestive: Aduriz (1969), Andrews and Phillips (1970), Becker (1965), Berckholtz Salinas (1963), Boggio (1970),

CISM (1967), Collier (1975, 1976), Córdova (1958), Deler (1975), DNEC (1966), Llontop (1970), Low (1975), Lutz (1970), Mangin (1967a, 1967b, 1973), Maruska (1972), Matos Mar (1966, 1968), Michl (1973), ONDEPJOV (1969, 1970, 1971), ONEC (1972, 1974), Riofrio (1978), Robles (1972), Rodríguez et al. (1969), Rodríguez and Jaworski (1969), Rodríguez (1973), Sánchez (1965), Turner (1963, 1965, 1968), Uchuya Reyes (1971).

3. The only example of direct national intervention into a slum neighborhood occurred in 1971, when the Ministry of Housing undertook a large-scale urban renewal project in La Victoria, Lima's second-largest district, in a complex of medium-rise (4-6 stories) buildings known as El Porvenir. This housing project, built in the early 1940s by the Prado family, perhaps the wealthiest in Peru at the time, had been notorious for overcrowding, unsanitary conditions, and high crime rates; it also served as a common first stop for low-income migrants as well as Lima's more traditional lower class. Patch's three-part study of Lima's central market area (1967) gives the flavor of the area; Paz Soldán (1957) includes descriptions of El Porvenir itself as well as other areas. The 1971 renewal was only partially completed and successful, for costs quickly outstripped all expectations. A report by the Ministerio de Vivienda (1973) presents an account of conditions in 1971. No other similar renewal project has been undertaken in Lima, with the possible exception of the UN-sponsored PREVI project in Barranca, a southern district of the city.

4. Webb's use of the term "urban traditional sector" should not be understood to be equivalent to some sort of "marginal" sector. Although chapter 5 discusses marginality in some detail, I should note here that Webb disagrees with Quijano and others who automatically extend the thesis of marginality to cover the urban traditional sector (Webb, 1975: 91-92). Webb argues that the modern and traditional urban sectors are intimately linked with one another, rather than operating in discrete spheres. That the latter is subordinate to, and dependent on, the former may well be true, although the relationship is probably much more complex than might first appear. Santos (1975) has some suggestive but incomplete insights into the simultaneous and partially overlapping functioning of these two sectors; see also Peattie (1974, 1975), Perlman (1975), Portes and Ferguson (1977: especially 96-99), Roberts (1978, chapters 5 and 7), and World Development (1978, entire issue).

5. This is not to say that informal credit arrangements for everything from food to clothing and household goods are not available; indeed, in many cases informal credit operations are extraordinarily widespread within and across poor neighborhoods, markets, and small business establishments. The nature of more formal credit structures, and their demands for regular salaries and employment, make them both unobtainable by and useless to the poor. See Leeds and Leeds (1970), Peattie (1970), Perlman (1975), Mangin (1967).

6. Cornelius (1975) uses the same three factors; he and I concluded prior to and during fieldwork that they were crucial for our studies, which were

planned in conjunction. I visited Mexico City while Cornelius was in the field, and had a chance to become acquainted with his selected communities. Other studies of urban poverty use similar, if slightly different, criteria for site selection; see Butterworth (1973), Eckstein (1977), and Perlman (1975).

Chapter 4: Six Low-Income Neighborhoods

1. These accounts of community histories, and the descriptions of the areas, come from a variety of sources. The most important, of course, were in-depth conversations and unstructured interviews with long-time residents and community leaders. I also spoke with government officials who had worked in the areas, and had the good fortune to have access to JNV, ONDEPJOV, and the Ministry of Housing files for reports written by social workers, engineers, architects, and other personnel. In the case of the more recent invasion sites, Lima's newspapers carried accounts that were occasionally useful for day-to-day events.

2. This figure as an average is somewhat misleading; the plots of land along the main street tend to be quite large (150-200 square meters), and consequently, many other plots are tiny indeed—fifteen, twelve, or even ten square meters.

3. *Barriada* is the now discarded term for the squatter settlements; thus *barriada tugurizada* means roughly "slumified" squatter settlement.

Chapter 5: Poverty, the Pobladores, and Their Neighborhoods

1. This section is a distillation of Dietz (1976), which presents a much fuller examination of the migration data of the sample. Mangin (1973), Cotler (1971), Valdivia Ponce (1970), and DNEC (1966) are common sources for Lima-directed migration data; Vandendries (1973) analyzes the DNEC data. Other major studies include Alers and Appelbaum (1968), Martínez (1968a, 1968b), Matos Mar (1966, 1968), Montoya Rojas (1967), and Vázquez and Dobyns (1963).

2. A number of respondents in the sample cited employment as both advantageous and disadvantageous—i.e., Lima was *better* than the home town because of chances to work, but *worse* when there was no work available. Unstable or seasonal laborers (for instance, construction workers) were among those who expressed such opinions.

3. Much of the relevant literature has its roots in such classic studies as Redfield (1947, 1961), Park (1928), and Handlin (1951). Many of their assumptions and conclusions have been criticized, especially in the Latin American case; Cornelius (1971) and Nelson (1969, 1971, and especially 1979) are good summaries. See also Mangin (1967a, 1967b), Turner (1963, 1965, 1968, 1970), Portes (1971, 1972), and Dietz (1969) for studies refuting the "disrupting migrant thesis."

4. Patch (1967, Part I) provides a rare description of one migrant from Puno who did not succeed. My sample, by design, excludes most such cases, as the

inhabitants of Lima's squatter neighborhoods have almost all found at least modest success. Sendas Frutales may contain a somewhat larger proportion of potential failures, since it is in fact an area where migrants may live initially while attempting to settle into an urban existence. Many other studies from Latin America find slum-squatter differences; see Cornelius (1975), Ray (1969), Perlman (1975), Andrews and Phillips (1970), Butterworth (1973), and Karst, Schwartz, and Schwartz (1973).

Whether a migrant can "succeed" (by whatever criteria) within a city of course depends on innumerable variables, many of which lie outside his control. Macro-economic factors such as recession, inflation, or unemployment will all have a direct, devastating effect on low-income groups, as noted in note 8 below.

5. The figures here are what the *head of household* reported he made; they are not *family* income, which Figueroa (1974) used in his study. Figueroa's annual income for pueblo joven families was $1,900 ($160 monthly). His figures and mine do not coincide because a large number of pueblo joven families have more than one wage-earner and/or source of income. It may also be that a tendency existed to under-report income.

6. Lewis (1973) corroborates these findings. He found "the share of employment in commerce and the services in the [pueblos jóvenes] was, at most, only slightly more than in the city as a whole" (147). He also found approximately the same percentage in marginal occupations as my sample. Santos (1975) provides a rare description and analysis of street vending in Lima; he concludes that vending is a relatively stable form of employment whose importance for Lima as a whole (and not just its poor) is considerable. See also Peattie (1975).

7. Whether or not the pobladores should be called "urban proletarians" is a matter for debate. In a non-ideological sense, the label probably applies; Leeds and Leeds (1975) use it occasionally. However, in a more doctrinaire, Marxist sense of the term, considerable doubt emerges. *Comparative Urban Research* (3, no. 3: 1975-1976) devotes an entire issue to this problem; Berg (1975-1976) sketches in the definitional and ideological problems of classifying sectors of a lesser-developed nation's urban poor as the classic lumpenproletariat, and concludes that using Marx and Engels to predict the political behavior patterns of the urban poor is risky indeed. The informal urban sector is discussed at length in *World Development* (1978, entire issue).

8. It should be kept in mind throughout that the data (and analysis) are based on conditions that existed in the early 1970s. As noted in chapter 1, note 8, and in chapters 8 and 9, circumstances have worsened. Inflation in Lima exceeded 50 percent in 1978 and 1979, prices for various basic goods and services (cooking oil, bread, rice, potatoes, bus fares) rose drastically after subsidies were abruptly discontinued, and devaluation decreased the value of the *sol* from 42 = US $1.00 in 1975 to 225 = US $1.00 in 1976 (*Latin American Political Report, Latin American Economic Report,* various issues).

Under such conditions, most reports from Lima indicate that frustration and discontent have risen to high levels and that demonstrations, marches, and other quasi-violent disruptions have occurred. Whether such disruptive techniques have been successful in actually obtaining material assistance is highly doubtful (see chapters 8 and 9), and whether they were employed through choice, through desperation due to the exhaustion of all other resources, or through externally provoked agitation (or a combination of all three) is unclear. But regardless of such changes, the data from the early 1970s argue that violence and disruption were at that time rare.

9. Portes (1977) has correctly noted that marginality in many ways was a sophisticated variant of a whole range of theories that place the blame for poverty on the poor. Although Portes convincingly argues that "ideologies of poverty" differ markedly between the United States and Latin America, *marginalidad* still bears some similarity to Oscar Lewis's "culture of poverty" (Lewis, 1966, 1968, 1969): both avoid confronting serious structural influences and causes. Lewis in recent years has been severely criticized (Leacock, 1971, especially chapters by Leeds, Peattie, and Valentine).

In Latin America, however, *marginalidad* continues to be used frequently; Nun (1969), Villar et al. (1970), and Quijano (1975) have discussed it extensively, and Lomnitz (1975, 1977) uses the term in the titles of both the Spanish and English versions of her study of a Mexican shantytown. Yet the general conclusions of the 1977 Inter-regional (Africa-Latin America) Seminar on "Marginal Human Settlement" stated unequivocally that squatter areas are neither ecologically, culturally, nor socially marginal and that "Precarious Human Settlements" is much preferred (SIAP *Correo Informativo*, 1977: 3-4). Thus the debate over definition and usage continues unresolved.

10. Alford and Scoble (1968) use a similar variable, which they call "community attachment," as one of their independent variables for explaining local political involvement.

11. Vedlitz (1974), among others, develops an index that he labels Neighborhood Social Integration; the five variables in his index parallel and in two cases duplicate items present in table 9.

12. The Peruvian data are at considerable variance with similar data from Mexico City (Cornelius, 1975) and Guayaquil, Ecuador (Moore, 1977), as seen below:

"What is most important for improving life here in ———?"

	Mexico City (N = 676)	Guayaquil (N = 347)	Lima (N = 527)
Government	40.5%	61.2%	41.7%
Hard work	28.4	20.3	53.2
God's help	17.5	16.5	3.3
Good luck	13.5	2.1	1.9

These data reveal the Peruvian pobladores to be much more self-reliant than either their Mexican or their Ecuadorian counterparts and to be far less inclined to leave matters to fate. Although the contrasts between Peru and the other two samples are really quite extraordinary, they may reflect, and rather accurately, the realities of the situation. In Mexico, for instance, the urban poor have perhaps been socialized into depending upon the government to aid them (Cornelius, 1975: 174-177); in Peru, whatever the poor have done, they have done by themselves.

Chapter 6: Modes of Participation and the Community Activist

1. This analysis treats only the squatter population (N=422). As is seen later on in this chapter, the slum sample produces somewhat different results in terms of the structure of participation. In addition, the very low levels of involvement within the slum neighborhood do not permit the same type of step-by-step analysis performed here. I am indebted to Richard J. Moore for his assistance on this chapter, especially for the path analysis.

2. A linear causal model involves constructing an oversimplified portrayal of reality so that the model will consider only a limited number of variables and relations out of the universe of social reality. Using the results of past research and current theory, the causal model is written as a set of structural equations that represent the causal processes assumed to operate among the variables under consideration (Land, 1969: 3-5). Path coefficients for the theorized model are the standardized beta (slope) coefficients for the set of regression equations (Nygreen, 1971: 37; Blalock, 1967: 130-136). As Nie, Prewitt, and Powell (1969: 810) note, "The causal properties are linked to the fact that each succeeding equation adds a new variable to the model and is described as a dependent variable 'caused' by all preceding variables in the model, but by none of the ones subsequently added. The final dependent variable . . . is the product of all other variables."

3. This finding supports a great deal of the literature on participation both in developing countries and in the developed nations (Cornelius, 1971; Goldrich, 1970; Mangin, 1970; Milbrath, 1965). Particularly significant is the support this finding renders to community action through community organizations (Carmichael and Hamilton, 1967; Mangin, 1967; Ross, 1973).

4. These two categories are of course extreme types. The pobladores can become involved in a variety of ways and on a variety of levels, as we have shown. Concentrating on the extremes allows us to distinguish the most likely opposite types. See Alford and Scoble (1968) for a similar treatment of mobilized and apathetic types of individuals.

5. Rusk (1976) suggests that Verba and Nie, in their study of political participation in the United States, slight two especially relevant areas of political involvement: interest-group activities and protest behavior. Rusk notes that "what is conspicuously lacking from the Verba-Nie typology are group participation modes that are characterized by either economic motivation or

mass demonstration methods" (584).

6. Other potential modes that might have been identified through questioning include protest behaviors, demonstrative petitioning, and the like. For instance, it might be proposed that participating in a large-scale organized land invasion would be another mode of political involvement. And although large numbers of the pobladores did in fact so participate (97 percent in Primero de Enero, 55 percent in Pampa de Arena), being a member of the invasion does not necessarily mean that the same individual will become active later on. "Invasion participant" as a variable loaded at only .23 with the other seven indicators in table 14B, and became a unique mode in the rotated solution (see Moore, 1979: 205-206).

It is likely that an individual active under a military government would also participate more frequently in party-related involvement (e.g., voting, campaigning) under an electoral regime. The reason that such modes were not pursued through further questions lies in the fragility of the research environment. Although I personally encountered no hostility or opposition to the study from any source, pre-tests and lengthy conversations with Peruvian friends convinced me that asking either about protest involvement of any sort or about past party activities might well have endangered the whole research undertaking. Indications were clear that people who had been involved in protesting were sometimes hesitant to say so, and the military's rather disdainful suspicion of civilian parties and politicians might well have produced reluctance and/or biased responses as well. Under such circumstances, the need to use survey methods in conjunction with more intensive anthropological techniques becomes imperative. For similar conclusions in Peru's rural sector, see Whyte and Alberti (1976: chapter 21), who spell out the necessity and desirability of combining methodologies.

7. Cornelius (1975) found that three percent of his sample in Mexico City's low-income neighborhoods had gone to protest or complain to a public official, and only two percent had ever participated in a protest meeting or demonstration. In Lima, truly mass demonstrations or antigovernmental protests by large numbers of squatters (or slum dwellers) historically have been rare. A threatened march of several thousand pobladores during Belaúnde's regime was a unique occurence (see Maruska, 1972), and the abortive attempt in 1976 by some ten thousand inhabitants of Villa El Salvador to march on Lima ended with the police disrupting the gathering and arresting some dozen demonstrators (see chapter 8). The poster-waving by Zone B of 28 de Julio at President Velasco's parade involved perhaps a few dozen people at most.

8. The activist poblador and the qualities that characterize him echo Inkeles (1969), who quite properly pointed out that those "qualities . . . appropriate to and expected in the citizen of a democracy . . . are equally appropriate to, and desirable in, the citizen of a one-party dictatorship" (255). Participant citizenship has little to do with the nature of the political system; theoretically, the activist poblador would be an attractive citizen under any regime.

9. Detailed accounts of political bargaining by squatter community leaders are, not surprisingly, rare. Marcia Koth de Paredes (1973, chapter 4) uses questionnaire data to describe how community leaders obtained services during the Belaúnde administration. Access to public officials constituted the most widely practiced and successful strategy. Paredes (1973) lists some eleven organizations commonly contacted; the most common of these was the National Housing Board, the direct predecessor of ONDEPJOV and SINAMOS.

Chapter 7: National-Level Political Demand-Making

1. John Turner was one of the first to perceive the squatter areas of Lima as a prime example of self-help housing built by and for the poor. Turner's work in Peru goes back to the mid-1950s; see Turner, 1963, 1968, 1970; Turner et al., 1969.

2. People also identify needs as individual (e.g., housing, employment) or communal. Each poblador might have two separate lists of needs; the first would reflect his most important personal problems, the second his perception of his community's needs. Probably some overlap would exist, in that a personal need might depend on communal action (e.g., installing potable water) to fulfill an individually felt need.

3. For a much simplified version of the same model, see Cornelius (1975: 170) and Cornelius and Dietz (1976); Nelson (1976) has a useful treatment of the problem of seeking help in general, as has Dahl (1971, especially 95-104). Nelson employs the term "authoritative help-seeking," which closely parallels the petitioning and demand-making activities reported here. Whyte and Alberti (1976) discuss similar questions and conditions in rural Peru as part of their treatment of peasant attempts to obtain valued goods. See chapter 18, especially pp. 212-213. For a discussion of participation as gaining access to welfare in the United States, see Van Til (1973).

4. Here, and for the rest of the discussion, I shall use the terms "activist" (as defined in chapter 6) and "leader" as approximately synonymous. By empirical definition, an activist poblador has participated in at least six of the seven activities used in table 13; in other words, the activist is that individual who has in fact made demands to the DPJ, attended meetings, and helped in communal projects. The activist, however, is not necessarily a community leader in the sense of occupying a formal position in the local association. But on the other hand, and not surprisingly, all formal community leaders interviewed (N=35) were activists by definition. When we speak of community leadership, therefore, we generally are referring to formal leaders who are activists. But as non-elected spokesmen frequently accompany neighborhood delegations to government agencies, the two terms can be used as approximate equivalents.

5. The six settlement types derived by the Junta are:
Type A. Those with rectangular streets and blocks, free spaces, sufficient land, and ample lots, located on flat terrain. Materials used in construction are

largely permanent.

Type B. Similar to Type A except that the settlement is located on hilly terrain.

Type C. Similar to Types A and B but with smaller lots and with limitations for expansion or remodeling.

Type D. Those in which the overall density of population is too high, where land space is finite and inflexible, and where the majority of the dwellings are of *estera* matting or other temporary material.

Type E. Similar to Type D except that the majority of houses are brick and mortar, thus hindering widespread relocation and making such a policy very expensive.

Type F. Those that the JNV felt would, at some future time, have to be eradicated for technical reasons—eminent domain, etcetera.

6. Shortly after initial field work terminated, ONDEPJOV and the Ministry of Housing opened a few branch offices in Greater Lima, and when SINAMOS absorbed ONDEPJOV, other branches appeared. However, the interplay of poblador and bureaucrat described here remained very much the same, and the account is therefore not written in the past tense.

The major point of this account is to describe the routine bureaucracy-client relationships that existed prior to SINAMOS but after the elimination of electorally-based processes. This is not to say that the interactions discussed here did not exist under civilian rule—quite to the contrary, they were common, daily occurrences. But these bureaucratically directed petitions necessarily assumed far greater importance after 1968, when the Revolutionary Government limited the ways by which the poor could gain access to the national political system.

7. The materials in this section and in the case study of Primero de Enero came from extended interviews and conversations with various parties concerned, both in the DPJ and in numerous pueblos jóvenes. Although individuals cannot be named (half a dozen open arrest warrants were still reportedly out for the leaders of the Primero de Enero invasion, for instance), I am grateful to all of those who were willing to spend time with me.

8. Either forming or participating in a land invasion in Peru is illegal. Decree-Law 14495, Article 3, states: "He who independently or as a member of a group of persons, an association, or a similar institution organizes, foments, directs, or provokes the undertaking of collective invasions on public or private lands, and he who takes part in such lands without authorization of the owner, commits the crime of disturbing the public tranquillity and will be punished in accordance with the sanctions stated in Article 283 of the Penal Code" (which in turn states that the punishment shall be no more than two years' imprisonment or a fine of three to thirty days' salary). This law (and the punishment) were prominently displayed at the main entrance to the DPJ.

9. The only other detailed studies of urban poor/bureaucrat interactions of which I am aware are by Uzzel (1972, 1974a, 1974b), who develops a lexicon

of "plays," "black boxes," and the like for his analysis. Uzzell (1974b) examines the attempts of a taxi-driver's union to deal with the Velasco regime.

Chapter 8: SINAMOS, the Pobladores, and Corporatist Participation
   1. Carlos Delgado was named in April 1972, on the formation of SINAMOS, as General Director of the National Office (ONAMS)—the second in command and the highest-ranking civilian in the organization. Delgado is a U.S.-trained sociologist/anthropologist; for a time he was head of the expropriated Lima newspaper *Expreso*, former member of the splinter left-wing APRA movement, ex-director of the National Institute of Planning, a forceful and prolific spokesman for the Revolutionary Government, and a speechwriter for President Velasco. Delgado is cited at length here for two reasons: first, his is a viewpoint from within the government; second, his lengthy essay entitled "SINAMOS: Popular Participation in the Peruvian Revolution" constitutes a coherent and integrated treatment of the subject. Many other spokesmen, especially President Velasco himself, expressed parallel ideas and thoughts; see Palmer (1973). For further writings, see Delgado (1972); see also Malloy (1974). The literature on SINAMOS is still not large, especially (of course) in English. See Franco (1975), Béjar (1976); Woy-Hazelton (1978, 1979) is the best source in English, as she combines analytic rigor with her personal experiences as a SINAMOS trainee.
   2. Strictly speaking, nine regional offices covered all of Peru, including Lima/Callao and Ica. ONDEPJOV Lima-Callao, however, became the tenth region of SINAMOS (Decree-Law No. 19352, 4 April 1972), and was concerned exclusively with the pueblos jóvenes of Lima and Callao—an indication of the perceived importance of the settlements by SINAMOS and (therefore) by the government (Collier, 1976: 107).
   3. My initial survey work, informant interviewing, and direct observation concluded August 1971, considerably before SINAMOS and its three organizational levels came into existence. Thus extensive empirical or quantifiable data are not available. Much material was collected during a summer's work in 1975. At that time, SINAMOS was going through an intensive internal restructuring as public opposition to it became increasingly apparent. Nevertheless, SINAMOS hung on until 31 August 1978, at which time its administrative programs were taken over by appropriate ministries (*Latin America Economic Report 6*, no. 12 [24 March 1978]: 95). Purposely omitted here are any discussions of SINAMOS as a bureaucracy (i.e., its high-level personnel changes) or the ideological debates that surrounded it (see Delgado, 1972; Cotler, 1975; Woy-Hazelton, 1978). Although important, these high-level personnel changes often meant relatively little to the pobladores and their daily contacts with SINAMOS.
   4. Many observers of the Third World have noted that individual and group demands frequently reach the political system *after* legislation or decrees have been passed (Scott, 1969). Riggs (1964) states: "Since the clientele is unable to organize or to exercise political influence to modify the rules, its primary

strategy involves direct pressure upon the officials concerned with policy implementation, to secure a suspension of the rules or to speed the provision of authorized services" (271).

5. Stepan (1978) distinguishes between the patron-client model and what he calls the "organic-statist" model (chapters 3-5, especially 166-167). Although I agree in large part with Stepan's description of the Velasco period, I am not as willing as he to make a sharp distinction between the two, nor am I sure that an increased rate of land title distribution is a clear indicator of diminishing clientelistic relationships (167-168). And the power asymmetry Stepan ascribes to the patron-client model is surely maintained in the organic-statist scheme.

Portes (1979), who labels the Velasco government a "populist military" administration (see chapter 2, footnote 6) argues (and I would agree) that the Velasco regime was a subtype of O'Donnell's bureaucratic-authoritarian state (see O'Donnell, 1973; Collier, 1978, especially footnotes 3 and 6, contain much bibliographic material; also Collier, 1979). While noting that O'Donnell's characterization is not perfectly generalizable to all authoritarian states, Portes seems to dismiss the corporatist label for such regimes as "premature" (1979: 3). I would argue that a populist military regime can (and readily will) employ corporatist strategies and structures in order to achieve its ends of incorporating the urban poor into new societal organizations.

6. Newton (1974) provides a useful discussion of the relationship(s) between corporatism and populism in Latin America, arguing that populism since the 1930s—manifested in Peru in APRA—produced basic changes that focused in particular on distribution of socio-economic resources. Corporatism emerged as a means of managing competing demands on production and distribution (Newton, 1974: 45). President Velasco's own populism juxtaposed with his government's corporatist strategies should not be surprising; they exemplify the inherent contradiction between simultaneously encouraging and controlling large-scale mobilization.

However the military came to formulate a corporatist structure such as SINAMOS, I disagree with the thesis that corporatism represents some sort of culturally correct or historically inevitable solution for Latin America. Wiarda has presented such an argument (Wiarda, 1973, 1978), as have others (Newton, 1970, 1974; Landy, 1979). Stepan counters such a view (1978: 52-59) with a series of telling criticisms, and concludes that corporatist solutions have emerged as responses to political crises. For the Revolutionary Government, the urban political crisis came with the Pamplona land invasion; the response was SINAMOS.

7. The lack of an urban reform policy as a parallel to the government's sweeping land reform is puzzling (Collier, 1976: 116-119). Changing land ownership laws, for instance, or enforcing existing laws would not necessarily have required large capital outlays, and the political harvest reaped might have been substantial. As in the pueblos jóvenes, any capital invested would be

repayable by the groups who benefited (see note 8, below).

The case of Sendas Frutales being declared a pueblo joven by SINAMOS officials is perhaps the exception that proves the rule. SINAMOS did not enter into the landlord-tenant imbroglio until Msgr. Bambarén intervened. In other words, SINAMOS was called in by a third party; it did not itself initiate any assistance for Sendas Frutales, nor did the community seriously consider petitioning SINAMOS.

8. The awarding of land titles involves several steps; all depend, of course, on the settlement's being officially recognized and designated as a pueblo joven. A complete census of the community is followed by the selection of those families who will be permitted to stay in the area and of those who will have to move if it is determined that the overall density is too great. For instance, those individuals with business in their homes, or those who live very close to their places of work, are given priority. The next step—remodeling—varies greatly from site to site and depends on a number of factors. If streets and lots are largely regular in size and layout, as in Primero de Enero and Pampa de Arena, then the remodeling can be quickly completed and inexpensive. If, on the other hand, many houses have to be razed, or if the area is hilly and requires heavy earth-moving equipment to put in streets and the like, as in 28 de Julio, then this phase can be lengthy and costly. Following physical renovation, lots are then handed out to the pobladores through random drawings and assignments. Again, if the zone developed originally in an orderly and planned fashion, few families are forced to move, since the office tries to accommodate itself to the existing community structures as fully as is practicable. Where extensive remodeling has taken place, however, a community may essentially be starting anew.

A good deal of legal and bureaucratic work accompanies these steps, especially if a family has an "irregular" situation—e.g., if the land has been passed on from one family member to another, or if the family has moved or has arrived in the zone during the previous stages outlined above. Such cases are postponed and the individual notified that no title can be given him until and unless he regularizes ownership. However, for those with no such difficulties, the next step involves official signing of the titles into law, done through the Ministry of Housing. The official sanction given, an autonomous state organization called EMADI (Empresa de Administración de Inmuebles, or Real Estate Administrative Board) then actually hands out the titles to the pobladores on payment of the costs involved.

The cost of a piece of land in a pueblo joven can vary enormously from one settlement to another, with the major variable being the remodeling. Officially, the government realizes no profit on the land or its work; by law, the price of state lands in the pueblos jóvenes is S/1.00 (in 1971, about US $0.025) a square meter, obviously a nominal price. But in almost every instance, added charges raise this base price. For one thing, if the land on which the settlement is located was originally private or cultivated land, then the government will expropriate this land, pay the owner, and then pass the expense along to the community. In addition, if the land is hilly or irregular, and if considerable time and expense are involved by the government in bulldozing in streets and in laying out lots, then the costs to the pobladores will increase, since all such remodeling work must be assumed by the inhabitants of the community.

9. Lima newspapers carried almost daily accounts of the invasion and subsequent events. See also Collier (1976: 113, 123), *Latin America* (7, no. 9 [1973]: 66), and Leeds and Leeds (1976: 220-221).

Conclusion

1. The major differences, of course, are that Castro established by fiat a non-electoral state that rejected capitalism entirely, and that Chile elected a socialist leader who attempted to remake the country incrementally. In Peru, the military acted by fiat (Jacquette, 1972), but purposely maintained capitalism as its economic moving force. Repression and toleration of dissent in Peru were also unique; though not as open as Allende's Chile (nor anywhere near as brutally repressive as the post-Allende regime), Peru has allowed for more diversity than Castro's Cuba.

The only other parallel might be Bolivia's 1952 revolution under Pas Estensorro's MNR. Although certain basic reforms took place, its inability to maintain any consensus among civilian political elites (or with military leaders) led to its rather muddled abandonment and a return to military rule until 1979 (Malloy, 1970).

2. The study ends its detailed consideration of the poor and the Peruvian experiment in 1975, when General Francisco Morales Bermúdez replaced President Velasco. Since that time, economic troubles of the severest kind (inflation, devaluation, unemployment and underemployment, balance of payment problems, an immense foreign debt, depleted foreign reserves) have created enormous difficulties for Peru and for its masses in particular. Not surprisingly, the material needs of Lima's poor have dropped precipitously in priority, as has the whole mobilization-participation component of the regime. With the end of SINAMOS, it is very likely that politics and participation will revert to the *status quo ante:* internal self-help and bureaucratic petitioning. When and if civilian elections are held in 1980, no doubt the squatter settlements will become the target of much political activity, especially since the far left was able to carry a plurality or (at times) an absolute majority in 1978, when national elections were held to select delegates to a constitutional assembly. Although I was unable to obtain voting data by individual community, district-level data are available. The interpretation of these data, however, is problematic. Although many observers (including the leaders of the left) were surprised by the votes but it may be premature to consider the pobladores as permanently radicalized. The results of the vote might be due to discontent with the choice of parties available (Belaúnde did not participate) or with political and economic conditions in general (see Schoultz, 1972,

Parties or Coalitions	San Juan de Miraflores (includes Pampa de Arena)	28 de Julio	Comas and Carabayllo (includes Primero de Enero)
1. APRA	23%	20%	21%
2. Leftist groups (includes FOCEP, PDC, PSR, UDP, PCP)	41	36	48
3. PPC (rightist)	19	20	10
4. All other parties/ blank ballots	17	23	21

for a parallel discussion of Colombian voting). And given the leftist success, the centrist and rightist parties will doubtless campaign much more vigorously in the squatter settlements in the future. Finally, the leftist groups may have internal trouble in producing an agreed-on candidate (e.g., Hugo Blanco) for the scheduled 1980 elections.

Apart from all such political concerns, it is likely that the poor will retain a good deal of their cynicism and "show-me" attitude toward elites, whether civilian or military, rightist or leftist. The poor have been the focus of campaign, populist, and mobilizational tactics for years; whether this attention will produce anything material for them remains open to question, since in the past it has seldom done so.

3. In chapter 1 and again in chapter 7 I use politicization in a somewhat different but still related way. There I define "politicized need" as one that the poor perceive as requiring external assistance for resolution. I stress that the poor have rather clear ideas as to what needs are and are not politicized. Edelman's use of politicization (making an issue—e.g., a need—appropriate for public decision-making) and my use both include external, non-private referents. The major difference is that in my usage, the poor decide when to politicize a need; in Edelman's usage, elites decide. Although the results might (but not necessarily will) be similar, the *reasons* for politicization can be totally distinct, and so perhaps will be the results of the politicization process.

4. SINAMOS, of course, promoted self-help solutions whenever possible. Unfortunately, its attitude of having "invented" self-help (as shown in chapter 8) created many problems.

5. This list of paths not taken illustrates why the Velasco regime was reformist, not revolutionary. In economic and social costs as well as risks, the 1968-1975 administration was unwilling (if not unable) to undertake truly revolutionary measures. Redistribution was always to involve new stock, not existing wealth and resources; worker management plans were incremental,

partial, and limited in scope; foreign and domestic private investment was always welcomed and encouraged, despite changes in how money could be invested, profit levels, repatriation, and so forth. The solutions sought for the various facets of urban poverty, whether housing, facilities, infrastructure, participation, or whatever, were almost always minimally acceptable ones that allowed the elites to hold on to their positions of dominance while simultaneously enabling the state to maintain domestic tranquility. That domestic peace was eventually interrupted by these same solutions was, of course, unforeseen. For an early but still trenchant Marxist critique along these same lines, see Quijano (1971).

Bibliography

Abrams, Charles. *Man's Struggle for Shelter in an Urbanizing World.* Cambridge, Mass.: M.I.T. Press, 1964.

_____. *Squatter Settlements: The Problem and the Opportunity.* New York: Department of Housing and Urban Development, Special Report to the U.S. Agency for International Development, 1965.

Acción Comunitaria del Perú. *Estudio económico familiar de Pamplona Alta.* Lima: Acción Comunitaria del Perú, July 1969.

Adelman, Irma, and Morris, Cynthia Taft. *Economic Growth and Social Equity in Developing Countries.* Stanford: Stanford University Press, 1973.

Aduriz, Joaquín. *Así viven y así nacen.* Cuaderno A3. Lima: DESCO, 1969.

Alberts, Tom, and Brundenius, Claes. "Growth versus Equity: The Brazilian Case in the Light of the Peruvian and Cuban Experiences." Discussion Paper 126. Lund, Sweden: Research Policy Institute, Lund University, 1979.

Alers, J. Oscar, and Appelbaum, Richard. *La migración en el Perú: Un inventario de proposiciones.* Lima: Centro de Estudios de Población y Desarrollo, 1968.

Alexander R., Alberto. *Estudio sobre la crisis de la habitación en Lima.* Lima: Imprenta Torres Aguirre, 1922.

Alford, Robert R., and Scoble, Harry M. "Sources of Local Political Involvement." *American Political Science Review* 62, no. 4 (December 1968): 1192-1206.

Almond, Gabriel, and Powell, G. Bingham. *Comparative Politics: System, Process, and Policy.* 2nd. ed. Boston: Little, Brown, 1978.

Ambrect, Biliana. *Politicizing the Poor.* New York: Praeger, 1976.

Andrews, Frank M., and Phillips, George W. "The Squatters of Lima: Who They Are and What They Want." *Journal of Developing Areas* 42 (January 1970): 211-224.

Astiz, Carlos. *Pressure Groups and Political Elites in Peruvian Politics.* Ithaca, N.Y.: Cornell University Press, 1969.

Astiz, Carlos. "The Military Establishment As a Political Elite: The Peruvian
    Case." In *Latin American Prospects for the 1970's: What Kinds of Revo-
    lutions?*, edited by David H. Pollock and Arch R. M. Ritter, pp. 203-229.
    New York: Praeger, 1973.
————, and García, José. "The Peruvian Military: Achievement Orientation,
    Training and Political Tendencies." *Western Political Quarterly* 25, no. 4
    (December 1972): 667-685.
Austin, Allan. *Estudio sobre el gobierno municipal del Perú.* Lima: Oficina
    Nacional de Racionalización y Capacitación de la Administración Pública,
    1964.
————, and Lewis, Sherman. *Urban Government for Metropolitan Lima.* New
    York: Praeger, 1970.
Baella, Alfonso. *El poder invisible.* Lima: Editorial Andina, 1976.
Balán, Jorge. "Migrant-Native Socioeconomic Differences in Latin America: A
    Structural Analysis." *Latin American Research Review* 4, no. 1 (Spring
    1969): 3-29.
————; Browning, Harley L.; and Jelin, Elizabeth. *Men in a Developing
    Society: Geographic and Social Mobility in Monterrey, Mexico.* Austin: Uni-
    versity of Texas Press, 1973.
Bamberger, Michael. "A Problem of Political Integration in Latin America: The
    Barrios of Venezuela." *International Affairs* 44, no. 4 (October 1968):
    709-719.
Banfield, Edward C. *The Unheavenly City Revisited.* Boston: Little, Brown
    and Co., 1974.
Bath, C. Richard, and James, Dilmus D. "Dependency Analysis in Latin
    America." *Latin American Research Review* 11, no. 3 (1970): 3-54.
Baylis, Thomas A. "The Faces of Participation: A Comparative Perspective."
    In *Political Participation in Latin America, Volume I: Citizen and State,*
    edited by John Booth and Mitchell Seligson, pp. 34-42. New York: Holmes
    and Meier, 1978.
Becker, Truman. "The Lima *barriada* of Leticia." *Peruvian Times* 23 (April
    1965): 8.
Béjar, Héctor. *La revolución en la trampa.* Lima: Perúgraf Editores, 1976.
Berckholtz Salinas, Pablo. *Barrios marginales: Aberración social.* Lima: n.p.,
    1963.
Berg, Elliott. "Some Problems in the Analysis of Urban Proletarian Politics in
    the Third World." *Comparative Urban Research* 3, no. 3 (1975-1975):
    46-60.
Berger, Peter, and Luckman, Thomas. *The Social Construction of Reality.*
    Garden City, N.Y.: Anchor Books, 1967.
Beyer, Glenn H., ed. *The Urban Explosion in Latin America.* Ithaca, N.Y.:
    Cornell University Press, 1967.
Blalock, Herbert. *Causal Inferences in Nonexperimental Research.* Chapel
    Hill: University of North Carolina Press, 1961.

Blalock, Herbert. "Causal Inferences, Closed Populations, and Measures of Association." *American Political Science Review* 61 (March 1967): 130-136.
————. *Causal Models in the Social Sciences.* Chicago: Aldine-Atherton, 1971.
Bloomberg, Warner, and Schmandt, Henry J., eds. *Urban Poverty: Its Social and Political Dimensions.* Beverly Hills, Cal.: Sage Publications, 1970.
Blumer, H. "Sociological Implications of the Thought of George Herbert Mead." *American Journal of Sociology* 71 (1966): 535-544.
Boggio, Klara. *Estudio del ciclo vital en Pamplona Alta.* Cuaderno A6. Lima: DESCO, 1970.
Bonilla, Frank. *The Failure of Elites.* Cambridge, Mass.: M.I.T. Press, 1970.
————, and Girling, Robert, eds. *Structure of Dependency.* East Palo Alto, Cal.: Nairobi Bookstore, 1972.
Booth, John, and Seligson, Mitchell. "Development, Political Participation, and the Poor in Latin America." In *Political Participation in Latin America,* vol. 2, *Politics and the Poor,* edited by John Booth and Mitchell Seligson, pp. 3-8. New York: Holmes and Meier, 1979.
Boudon, Raymond. "A Method of Linear Causal Analysis." *American Sociological Review* 30 (June 1965): 365-371.
Bourricaud, François. "Lima en la vida política peruana." *América Latina* 7, no. 4 (October-December 1964): 85-95.
————. *Power and Society in Contemporary Peru.* New York: Praeger, 1970a.
————. "Los militares ¿por qué y para qué?" *Aportes* 16 (April 1970): 13-55.
————. "Voluntarismo y experimentación. Los militares peruanos: Manos a la obra." *Mundo Nuevo* 54 (December 1970): 4-16.
Bradfield, Stillman. "Selectivity in Rural-Urban Migration: The Case of Huaylas, Peru." In *Urban Anthropology,* edited by Aidan Southall, pp. 351-372. New York: Oxford University Press, 1973.
Brim, Orville, and Wheeler, Stanton. *Socialization after Childhood.* New York: John Wiley, 1966.
Briones, Guillermo. "La calificación y adaptación de la fuerza de trabajo en las primeras etapas de la industrialización: Un estudio en Lima, Perú." *América Latina* 6, no. 4 (October-December 1963): 13-26.
————. "Movilidad ocupacional y mercado de trabajo en el Perú," *América Latina* 6, no. 3 (July-September 1963): 63-76.
————, and Valera, José Mejía. *El obrero industrial.* Lima: Universidad Nacional Mayor de San Marcos, 1964.
Brislin, Richard W.; Lonner, Walter J.; and Thorndike, Robert M. *Cross-Cultural Research Methods.* New York: John Wiley, 1973.
Brody, Eugene B., ed. *Behavior in New Environments: Adaptation of Migrant Populations.* Beverly Hills, Cal.: Sage Publications, 1969, 1970.
Bromley, Juan, and Barbagelata, José. "La evolución urbana de la ciudad de Lima." Lima: Consejo Provincial de Lima, 1945.

Browning, Harley, and Feindt, Waltraunt. "Selectivity among Migrants to a Metropolis in a Developing Country." *Demography* 6, no. 4 (November 1969): 347-357.

Brunn, Stanley D. *Urbanization in Developing Countries: An International Bibliography.* Michigan State University Latin American Studies Center Research Report No. 8. East Lansing, Mich.: Michigan State University Latin American Studies Center, 1971.

Bryce-Laport, Roy S. "Family Adaptation of Relocated Slum Dwellers in Puerto Rico: Implications for Urban Research and Development." *Journal of Developing Areas* 2, no. 4 (July 1968): 533-540.

Burgess, E. W., and Bogue, Donald J., eds. *Contributions to Urban Sociology.* Chicago: University of Chicago Press, 1964.

Butterworth, Douglas. "A Study of the Urbanization Process among the Mixtec Migrants from Tilantongo in Mexico City." *América Indígena* 22, no. 3 (1962): 257-274.

──────. "Squatters or Suburbanites? The Growth of Shantytowns in Oaxaca, Mexico." In *Latin American Modernization Problems,* edited by Robert Scott, pp. 209-232. Urbana-Champaign: University of Illinois Press, 1973.

──────. "Grass-Roots Political Organization in Cuba: A Case of the Committees for the Defense of the Revolution." In *Anthropological Perspectives on Latin American Urbanization,* edited by Wayne A. Cornelius and Felicity Trueblood, pp. 183-203. Vol. 4 of *Latin American Urban Research.* Beverly Hills, Cal.: Sage Publications, 1974.

Byars, Robert. "Culture, Politics, and the Urban Factory Worker in Brazil: The The Case of Zé Maria." In *Latin American Modernization Problems,* edited by Robert Scott, pp. 26-86. Urbana-Champaign: University of Illinois Press, 1973.

Caiden, Naomi, and Wildavsky, Aaron. *Planning and Budgeting in Poor Countries.* New York: John Wiley, 1974.

Cardona, Ramiro. *Las invasiones de terrenos urbanos.* Bogotá: Tercer Mundo, 1969.

Cardoso, Fernando Enrique. "Associated-Dependent Development: Theoretical, and Practical Implications." In *Authoritarian Brazil: Origins, Policies, and Future,* edited by Alfred Stepan, pp. 142-178. New Haven: Yale University Press, 1973.

──────, and Faletto, Enzo. *Dependencia y desarrollo en América Latina.* Mexico City: Siglo XXI, 1969.

Carmichael, Stokely, and Hamilton, Charles. *Black Power.* New York: Vintage Books, 1967.

Carter, William. "Agrarian Reform in Latin America." In *Changing Latin America: New Interpretations of Its Politics and Society,* edited by D. Chalmers, pp. 1-14. New York: Academy of Political Science, Columbia University, 1972.

Castells, Manuel. "La urbanización dependiente en América Latina." In *Imperialismo y urbanización en América Latina,* edited by Manuel Castells, pp.

7-26. Barcelona, Spain: Ed. Gustavo Gili, 1973.

_____, ed. *Imperialismo y urbanización en América Latina.* Barcelona, Spain: Ed. Gustavo Gili, 1973.

_____. *The Urban Question.* Cambridge, Mass.: M.I.T. Press, 1977.

Castilla Meza, Jorge, et al. *Guía de servicios al ciudadano.* Lima: Oficina de Organización y Métodos, Ministerio de Vivienda, 1971.

Cebrecos Revilla, Rufino. *El empleo y el desempleo en el Perú.* Lima: Pontificia Universidad Católica, CISEPA, 1977.

Centro de Investigaciones Sociales por Muestreo. *Barriadas de Lima: Actitudes de los habitantes respecto a servicios públicos y privados.* Lima: Ministerio de Trabajo y Comunidades, Servicio del Empleo y Recursos Humanos, 1967.

CETIM. *Dependencia y estructura de clase en América Latina.* Geneva: Centre Europe Tiers Monde, 1972.

Chalmers, Douglas A., and Riddle, Donald H. *Urban Leadership in Latin America.* New Brunswick, N.J.: Eagleton Institute of Public Affairs, 1964.

Chaplin, David. *The Peruvian Industrial Labor Force.* Princeton: Princeton University Press, 1967.

_____. ed. *Peruvian Nationalism: A Corporatist Revolution.* New Brunswick, N.J.: Transaction, 1976.

Chenery, Hollis, et al. *Redistribution with Growth.* New York: Oxford University Press, 1974.

Chilcote, Ronald, and Edelstein, Joel, eds. *Latin America: The Struggle with Dependency and Beyond.* Cambridge, Mass.: Schenkman, 1973.

Clark, Terry. "There Is No General Urban Theory." *Comparative Urban Research* 6, no. 2/3 (1978): 9.

Clinard, Marshall B. *Slums and Community Development.* New York: Free Press, 1966.

Clinton, Richard L. "The Modernizing Military: The Case of Peru." *Inter-American Economic Affairs* 24, no. 4 (Spring 1971): 43-66.

Cloward, Richard. "The War on Poverty: Are the Poor Left Out?" *The Nation* 21 (August 1965): 55-60.

Cohen, Benjamin J. *The Question of Imperialism.* New York: Basic Books, 1973.

Cole, John P. *Estudio geográfico de la Gran Lima.* Lima, 1957.

Coleman, James S. "Community Disorganization and Conflict." In *Contemporary Social Problems,* edited by R. K. Merton and R. A. Nisbet, pp. 657-708. New York: Harcourt, Brace and Jovanovich, Inc., 1971.

Collier, David, and Collier, Ruth Berins. "Who Does What, to Whom, and How: Toward a Comparative Analysis of Latin American Corporatism." In *Authoritarianism and Corporatism in Latin America,* edited by James Malloy, pp. 489-512. Pittsburgh: University of Pittsburgh Press, 1977.

Collier, David. *Squatter and Oligarchs.* Baltimore, Md.: Johns Hopkins University Press, 1976.

Collier, David. "Industrial Modernization and Political Change: A Latin
American Perspective." *World Politics* 30, no. 4 (July 1978): 593-614.
_____, ed. *The New Authoritarianism in Latin America.* Princeton, N.J.:
Princeton University Press, 1979.
Consiglieri C., Luis. "Rol del estado peruano en el control del funcionamiento
del mercado de tierras. Estudio del caso: Lima metropolitana 1968-1972."
Revista Interamericana de Planificación IX, 34 (June): 63-73.
Corbett, John, and Linn Hammergren. "Continuity and Change in Public
Policy-Making at the Local Level: A Comparative Study of Mexico and
Peru." Unpublished paper, 1979.
Córdova, Alfredo. *La vivienda en el Perú: Estado actual y evaluación de las
necesidades.* Lima: Comisión para la reforma agraria y la vivienda, 1958.
Cornelius, Wayne. "Urbanization as an Agent in Latin American Political In-
stability: The Case of Mexico." *American Political Science Review* 63, no.
3 (September 1969): 833-857.
_____. "The Political Sociology of Cityward Migration: Toward Empirical
Theory." In *Latin American Urban Research,* vol. 1, edited by Francine
Rabinovitz and Felicity Trueblood, pp. 95-150. Beverly Hills, Cal.: Sage
Publications, 1971.
_____. "A Structural Analysis of Urban Caciquismo in Mexico." *Urban
Anthropology* 1, no. 2 (Fall 1972): 234-261.
_____. "Political Learning among the Migrant Poor: The Impact of Resi-
dential Context." *Comparative Politics Series,* vol. 4 Beverly Hills, Cal.:
Sage Publications, 1973.
_____. "The Impact of Governmental Performance on Political Attitudes
and Behavior: The Case of the Urban Poor in Mexico." In *National-Local
Linkages: The Interrelationship of Urban and National Politics in Latin
America,* edited by Francine Rabinovitz and Felicity Trueblood, pp. 217-
258. Vol. 3 of *Latin American Urban Research.* Beverly Hills, Cal.: Sage
Publications, 1973.
_____. *Politics and the Migrant Poor in Mexico City.* Stanford: Stanford
University Press, 1975.
_____, and Dietz, Henry. "Urbanización, formulación de demandas y sobre-
carga del sistema político." *Revista Latinoamericana de Estudios Urbano
Regionales* (Santiago, Chile) 5, no. 13 (June 1976): 9-46.
_____, and Trueblood, Felicity, eds. *Anthropological Perspectives on Latin
American Urbanization.* Vol. 4 of *Latin American Urban Research.* Beverly
Hills, Cal.: Sage Publications, 1974.
_____, and Trueblood, Felicity, eds. *Urbanization and Inequality: The
Political Economy of Urban and Rural Development in Latin America.* Vol.
5 of *Latin American Urban Research.* Beverly Hills, Cal.: Sage Publications,
1975.
Cotler, Julio. "The Mechanics of Internal Domination and Social Change in
Peru." *Studies in Comparative International Development* 3, no. 12,

series 38 (1968).

Cotler, Julio. "Actuales pautas de cambio en la sociedad rural." In *Dominación y cambios en el Perú rural,* edited by José Matos Mar and William F. Whyte, pp. 60-79. Lima: Instituto de Estudios Peruanos, 1969.

_____. "Political Crisis and Military Populism in Peru." *Studies in Comparative International Development* 6, no. 5 (1970-1971): 95-113.

_____. "Lima." In *Rural-Urban Migrants and Metropolitan Development,* edited by Aprodicio Laquian, pp. 111-133. Toronto: INTERMET, 1971.

_____, and Quijano, Aníbal, eds. *Sociedad y política.* (Lima), various issues, 1972-1973.

_____. "The New Mode of Political Domination in Peru." In *The Peruvian Experiment: Continuity and Change under Military Rule,* edited by Abraham Lowenthal, pp. 44-78. Princeton: Princeton University Press, 1975.

Cutright, Philips. "National Political Development: Measurement and Analysis." *American Sociological Review* 28 (April 1965): 253-264.

Cvejanovich, George J. "Assymetrical Interdependence and Development in Aruba." M.A. thesis, Latin American Studies Institute, Louisiana State University, 1977.

Czudnowski, Moshe. "A Salience Dimension of Politics for the Study of Political Culture." *American Political Science Review* 62, no. 3 (September 1968): 878-888.

_____. *Comparing Political Behavior.* Vol. 28 of *Sage Library of Social Research.* Beverly Hills, Cal.: Sage Publications, 1976.

Dahl, Robert. *Polyarchy.* New Haven, Conn.: Yale University Press, 1971.

Daland, Robert T. "Urbanization Policy and Political Development in Latin America." *American Behavioral Scientist* 12, no. 5 (May-June 1969): 22-33.

Davis, James. "Citizen Participation in a Bureaucratic Society: Some Questions and Skeptical Notes." In *Neighborhood Control in the 1970's: Politics, Administration, and Citizen Participation,* edited by George Frederickson, pp. 59-72. New York: Chandler, 1973.

Deler, Jean Paul. *Lima 1940-1970: Aspectos del crecimiento de la capital peruana.* Lima: Centro de Investigaciones Geográficas, 1975.

Delgado, Carlos. "La Unidad Vecinal No. 3 y Matute: Estudio social y comparativo referido a problemas de planeamiento físico.' Lima: Oficina de nificación Sectoral de Vivienda y Equipamiento Urbano, July 1966.

_____. "Three Proposals Regarding Accelerated Urbanization in Metropolitan Areas: The Lima Case." In *Latin American Urban Policies and the Social Sciences,* edited by John Miller and Ralph Gackenheimer, pp. 269-311. Beverly Hills, Cal.: Sage Publications, 1971.

_____. *El proceso revolucionario peruano: Testimonio de lucha.* Mexico City: Siglo XXI, 1972.

_____. "SINAMOS: La participación popular en la Revolución Peruana."

Participación 2, no. 2 (February 1973): 6-22.

Delgado, Carlos. *Revolución peruana autonomía y deslindes.* Lima: Libros de Contratiempo, 1975.

Departamento de Servicio Social y Vivienda, División de Servicio Social y Vivienda, Sección de Investigaciones Sociales. *Barriadas de Lima Metropolitana.* Lima: Ministerio de Salud Pública y Asistencia Social, Fondo Nacional de Salud y Bienestar Social, 1960.

DESAL. *Marginalidad en América Latina.* Barcelona, Spain: Herder, 1967.

Deutsch, Karl. "Social Mobilization and Political Development." In *Comparative Politics: A Reader,* edited by Harry Eckstein and David Apter, pp. 582-603. New York: Free Press, 1963.

Dietz, Henry. "Urban Squatter Settlements in Peru: A Case Study and Analysis." *Journal of Inter-American Studies* 11, no. 3 (July 1969): 353-370.

————. *Rural-Lima and Intra-Lima Migration to the Pueblos Jóvenes in Lima, Peru.* Cambridge, Mass.: M.I.T., Center for International Studies, Migration and Development Series, 1976.

————. "Metropolitan Lima: Urban Problem-Solving under Military Rule." In *Metropolitan Latin America: The Challenge and the Response,* edited by Wayne Cornelius and Robert van Kemper. Vol. 6 of *Latin American Urban Research.* Beverly Hills, Cal.: Sage Publications, 1978.

————, and David Scott Palmer. "Citizen Participation under Innovative Military Corporatism in Peru." Presented at the Seminar on the Faces of Participation in Latin America, November 12-13, 1976, San Antonio, Texas.

————, and ————. "Citizen Participation under Innovative Military Corporatism in Peru." In *Political Participation in Latin America,* vol. 1, *Citizen and State,* edited by John Booth and Mitchell Seligson, pp. 172-188. New York: Holmes and Meier, 1978.

Dirección Nacional de Estadística y Censos. *Censo nacional de población y ocupación de 1940,* volumes I and V. Lima: DNEC, 1944.

————. *Encuesta de inmigración de Lima metropolitana,* volumes 1, 2, 3. Lima: DNEC, 1966.

————. *Sexto censo nacional de población,* vols. 1, 2, 3. Lima: DNEC, 1966.

Dogan, Mattei, and Rokkan, Stein, eds. *Quantitative Ecological Analysis in the Social Sciences.* Cambridge, Mass.: M.I.T. Press, 1969.

Dongo Denegri, Luis. *Vivienda y urbanismo.* Arequipa: Editorial El Deber, 1962.

Dore, Elizabeth, and Weeks, John. "Class Alliances and Class Struggle in Peru." *Latin American Perspectives* IV, 3, no. 14 (Summer 1977): 4-17.

Dos Santos, Theotonio. "The Structure of Dependence." *American Economic Review* 60, no. 2 (1970): 231-236.

Doughty, Paul. "Behind the Back of the City: 'Provincial' Life in Lima, Peru." In *Peasants in Cities,* edited by William Mangin, pp. 30-46. Boston: Houghton-Mifflin, 1970.

Duncan, Otis Dudley. "Path Analysis: Some Sociological Examples." *American Journal of Sociology* 72 (July 1976): 1-16.

Eames, Edwin, and Goode, Judith Granich. *Urban Poverty in a Cross-Cultural Context.* New York: Free Press, 1973.

Eckstein, Susan. "The Rise and Demise of Research on Latin American Urban Poverty." *Studies in Comparative International Development* 11, no. 2 (Summer 1976): 107-126.

―――. *The Poverty of Revolution: The State and the Urban Poor in Mexico.* Princeton: Princeton University Press, 1977.

Edelman, Murray. *Politics as Symbolic Action.* Chicago: Markham, 1971.

―――. *Political Language: Words That Succeed and Policies That Fail.* New York: Academic Press, 1977.

Einaudi, Luigi. "Revolution from Within? Military Rule in Peru since 1968." In *Studies in Comparative International Development* 8, no. 1 (Spring 1973): 71-87.

―――. "The Military and Government in Peru." In *Development Administration in Latin America,* edited by Clarence Thurber and Lawrence Graham, pp. 294-313. Durham, N.C.: Duke University Press, 1973.

Eisinger, Peter. "The Pattern of Citizen Contacts with Urban Officials." In *People and Politics in Urban Society,* edited by Harlan Hahn, pp. 43-70. Vol. 6 of *Urban Affairs Annual Reviews.* Beverly Hills, Cal.: Sage Publications, 1972.

―――. "The Conditions of Protest Behavior in American Cities." *American Political Science Review* 67, no. 1 (March 1973): 11-28.

―――. *Patterns of Interracial Politics: Conflict and Cooperation in the City.* New York: Academic Press, 1976.

Elder, Glenn H. "On Linking Social Structure and Personality." In *Linking Social Structure and Personality,* edited by Glenn Elder, pp. 7-23. Vol. 12 of *Sage Contemporary Social Science Issues.* Beverly Hills, Cal.: Sage Publications, 1973.

Elegrén, Fernando. "Mirones Bajo." Unpublished manuscript. Lima: Pontificia Universidad Católica, 1971.

Espinoza, Humberto. *Dependencia económica y tecnología.* Lima: Universidad Nacional Federico Villarreal, Centro de Investigaciones Económicas y Sociales, 1971.

Eulau, Heinz. *Micro-Macro Political Analysis: Accents of Inquiry.* Chicago: Aldine, 1969.

Fagen, Richard. "Studying Latin American Politics: Some Implications of a *Dependencia* Approach." *Latin American Research Review* 12, no. 2 (1977): 3-26.

―――, and Tuohy, William S. *Politics and Privilege in a Mexican City.* Stanford: Stanford University Press, 1972.

Faris, Robert E. L. *Chicago Sociology, 1920-1932.* San Francisco: Chandler, 1967.

Figueroa, Adolfo. *Estructura del consumo y distribución de ingresos en Lima metropolitana.* Lima: Pontificia Universidad Católica, CISEPA, 1974.

———. "Impacto de las reformas actuales sobre la distribución del ingreso en el Perú." *Revista de la Sociedad Interamericana de Planificación* 11, no. 26 (July 1973): 41-56.

Fischer, Claude S. "The City and Political Psychology." *American Political Science Review* 69, no. 2 (June 1975): 559-571.

Flinn, William L. "Rural and Intra-Urban Migration in Colombia: Two Case Studies in Bogotá." In *Latin American Urban Research,* vol. 1, edited by Francine Rabinovitz and Felicity Trueblood, pp. 84-94. Beverly Hills, Cal.: Sage Publications, 1971.

Flynn, Peter. "Class, Clientelism, and Coercion: Some Mechanisms of Internal Dependency and Control." *Journal of Commonwealth and Comparative Politics* 12 (July 1974): 133-156.

Forbes, H. Donald, and Tufte, E. R. "A Note of Caution in Causal Modeling." *American Political Science Review* 62 (December 1968): 1258-1264.

Foster, George C. "Peasant Society and the Image of the Limited Good." In *Peasant Society: A Reader,* edited by Jack Potter et al., pp. 300-323. Boston: Little, Brown and Co., 1967.

Fox, Robert. *Urban Population Growth in Peru.* Urban Population Series Report no. 3. Washington, D.C.: Inter-American Development Bank, 1972.

Franco, Carlos. *La revolución participatoria.* Lima: Mosca Azul, 1975.

Frey, Frederick, et al. *Survey Research on Comparative Social Change.* Cambridge, Mass.: M.I.T. Press, 1969.

———. "Cross-Cultural Survey Research in Political Science." In *The Methodology of Comparative Research,* edited by Robert Holt and John Turner, pp. 173-294. New York: Free Press, 1970.

Friedgut, Theodore H. *Political Participation in the USSR.* Princeton: Princeton University Press, 1979.

Frohlich, Norman; Oppenheimer, Joe; and Young, Oran. *Political Leadership and Collective Goods.* Princeton: Princeton University Press, 1971.

Gans, Herbert. *The Urban Villagers.* New York: Free Press, 1962.

———. "Poverty and Culture: Some Basic Questions about Methods of Studying Life-Styles of the Poor." In *The Concept of Poverty,* edited by Peter Townsend, pp. 146-164. New York: American Elsevier, 1970.

García, José. "Military Government in Peru, 1968-1971." Ph.D. dissertation, University of New Mexico, 1973.

Geisse, Guillermo, and Hardoy, Jorge, eds. *Regional and Urban Developmental Policies: A Latin American Perspective.* Vol. 2 of *Latin American Urban Research.* Beverly Hills, Cal.: Sage Publications, 1972.

Gerlach, Allen. "Civil-Military Relations in Peru, 1914-1945." Ph.D. dissertation, University of New Mexico, 1973.

Germani, Gino. "Aspectos teóricos de la marginalidad." *Revista Paraguaya de Sociología,* año 9, no. 23 (January-April 1972): 7-35.

Germani, Gino. *Marginality.* New Brunswick, N.J.: Transaction, 1979.

Gianella, Jaime. *Marginalidad en Lima Metropolitana.* Cuaderno A8. Lima: DESCO, 1970.

Gilbert, Alan, and Ward, Peter. "Housing in Latin American Cities." In *Geography and the Urban Environment,* edited by R. J. Johnston and D. Herbert, ch. 7. New York: John Wiley, 1978.

Giusti, Jorge. "Organizational Characteristics of the Latin American Urban Marginal Settler." *International Journal of Politics* 1, no. 1 (1971): 54-89.

Glaser, Barney G., and Strauss, Anselm. *The Discovery of Grounded Theory.* Chicago: Aldine, 1967.

Goldrich, Daniel. "Toward the Comparative Study of Politicization in Latin America." In *Contemporary Cultures and Civilizations in Latin America,* edited by D. B. Heath and Richard Adams, pp. 361-377. New York: Random House, 1965.

_____. "Political Organization and the Politicization of the Poblador." *Comparative Political Studies* 3, no. 2 (July 1970): 176-202.

_____, et al. The Political Integration of Lower-Class Urban Settlements in Chile and Peru." In *Masses in Latin America,* edited by Irving Louis Horowitz, pp. 175-214. New York: Oxford University Press, 1970.

Gorman, Stephen. "Corporatism with a Human Face? The Revolutionary Ideology of Juan Velasco Alvarado." *Inter-American Economic Affairs* 32, no. 2 (Autumn 1978): 25-37.

Grayson, George W. "Peru's Revolutionary Government." *Current History* 64, no. 378 (February 1973): 61-66.

Greenberg, Stanley B. *Politics and Poverty: Modernization and Response in Five Poor Neighborhoods.* New York: John Wiley, 1974.

Greenstone, J. David, and Peterson, Paul. *Race and Authority in Urban Politics: Community Participation and the War on Poverty.* New York: Russell Sage Basic Books, 1973.

Guerrero de los Rios, Raúl, and Sánchez León, Abelardo. *La trampa urbana: Ideología y problemas urbanos: El caso de Lima.* Lima: DESCO, 1977.

Gunder Frank, Andre. "The Development of Underdevelopment." *Monthly Review* 18 (September 1966): 17-31.

Hammergren, Linn. "Corporatism in Latin American Politics: A Reexamination of the Unique Tradition." *Comparative Politics* 9, no. 4 (July 1977): 443-461.

Handleman, Howard. "The Political Mobilization of Urban Squatter Settlements." *Latin American Research Review* 10, no. 2 (1975): 35-72.

Handlin, Oscar. *The Uprooted.* Boston: Little, Brown and Co., 1951.

Hanna, William; Niculescu, Susan; and Silver, Steven. "A Framework for the Study of Urban Politics and the Quality of Urban Life." In *Power, Paradigms, and Community Research,* edited by Roland J. Liebert and Allen W. Imershein, pp. 153-182. Vol. 9 of *Studies in International Sociology.* Beverly Hills, Cal.: Sage Publications, 1977.

Harnecker, Marta. *Cuba: ¿Dictadura o democracia?* Mexico City: Siglo XXI, 1975.

Harrington, Michael. *The Other America: Poverty in the United States.* New York: Macmillan, 1962.

_____. *The Vast Majority.* New York: Simon and Schuster, 1977.

Harris, Walter D. *The Growth of Latin American Cities.* Athens, Ohio: Ohio University Press, 1971.

_____, and Hosse, Hans. *La vivienda en el Perú.* Washington, D.C.: Panamerican Union, 1963.

Hauser, Philip M., ed. *Urbanization in Latin America.* New York: International Documents Service, 1961.

Henry, Etienne. "El consumo urbano y sus expresiones en los asentamientos urbanos populares." *Revista de la Sociedad Interamericana de Planificación* 10, no. 39 (September 1976): 47-62.

Hirschman, Albert. *Exit, Voice, and Loyalty.* Cambridge, Mass.: Harvard University Press, 1970.

Hobsbawn, Eric. "Peru: The Peculiar Revolution." *New York Review of Books* (December 16, 1971): 19-36.

Hodara B., Josef. *Marginalidad y percepción de cambio cultural en los líderes de las barriadas.* Lima: Universidad Nacional Federico Villarreal, 1965-1966.

Horowitz, Irving Louis. "The Military Elites." In *Elites in Latin America,* edited by Seymour Martin Lipset and Aldo Solari, pp. 146-189. New York: Oxford University Press, 1966.

_____. "Masses in Latin America." In *Masses in Latin America,* edited by Irving Louis Horowitz, pp. 3-27. New York: Oxford University Press, 1970.

_____, and Trimberger, Ellen Kay. "State Power and Military Nationalism in Latin America." *Comparative Politics* 8, no. 2 (January 1976): 223-245.

Huntington, Samuel P. *Political Order in Changing Societies.* New Haven: Yale University Press, 1968.

_____, and Domínguez, Jorge. "Political Development." In *Macropolitical Theory,* edited by Fred Greenstein and Nelson Polsby, pp. 1-114. Vol. 3 of *Handbook of Political Science.* Reading, Mass.: Addison-Wesley, 1975.

_____, and Moore, Clement, eds. *Authoritarian Politics in Modern Society.* New York: Basic Books, 1970.

_____, and Nelson, Joan. *No Easy Choice: Political Participation in Developing Countries.* Cambridge, Mass.: Harvard University Press, 1976.

Inkeles, Alex. "Making Men Modern: On the Causes and Consequences of Individual Change in Six Developing Countries." *American Journal of Sociology* 75, no. 2 (September 1969): 208-225.

_____. "Participant Citizenship in Six Developing Countries." *American Political Science Review* 63, no. 4 (December 1969): 1120-1141.

International Organization 32, no. 1 (Winter 1978).

Jaquette, Jane. *The Politics of Development in Peru.* Latin American Dissertation Series, no. 33. Ithaca: Cornell University Latin American Studies, 1971.

Jaquette, Jane. "Revolution by Fiat: The Context of Policy-Making in Peru." *Western Political Quarterly* 25, no. 4 (December 1972): 648-666.

Jaworski, Helan. "La planificación participante y la planificación de base en el Perú." *Revista Interamericana de Planificación* 9, no. 34 (June 1975): 5-15.

Johnson, Charles W. "Perú: Los militares como un agente de cambio económico." *Revista de la Sociedad Mexicana de Sociología* 34, no. 2 (April-June 1972): 293-316.

Jones, Bryan; Greenberg, Saadia; Kaufman, Clifford; and Drew, Joseph. "Bureaucratic Response to Citizen-Initiated Contacts: Environmental Enforcement in Detroit." *American Political Science Review* 71, no. 1 (March 1977): 148-165.

Jongkind, C. F. "La supuesta funcionalidad de los clubes regionales en Lima, Perú." In *Boletín de los Estudios Latinoamericanos*, pp. 1-12. Amsterdam: CEDELA, University of Amsterdam, 1971.

Jordan, Robert E. "An Evaluation of Public Housing Policy in Peru." Ph.D. dissertation, Department of Economics, University of Texas at Austin, 1979.

Karst, Kenneth L. "Rights in Land and Housing in an Informal Legal System: The *Barrios* of Caracas." *The American Journal of Comparative Law* 19, no. 3 (Summer 1971): 550-573.

_____, and Schwartz, Murray and Audrey. *The Evolution of Law in the Barrios of Caracas.* Los Angeles: UCLA, Latin American Center, 1973.

Katznelson, Ira. "The Crisis of the Capitalist City: Urban Politics and Social Control." In *Theoretical Perspectives on Urban Politics,* edited by Willis D. Hawley, et al., pp. 214-229. Englewood Cliffs, N.J.: Prentice-Hall, 1976.

Kaufman, Clifford. "Latin American Urban Inquiry: Some Substantive and Methodological Commentary." *Urban Affairs Quarterly* 5 (June 1970): 394-411.

Kaufman, Robert. "The Patron-Client Concept and Macro-Politics: Prospects and Problems." *Comparative Studies in Society and History* 16 (June 1974): 284-308.

_____; Chernotsky, Harry; and Gellar, Daniel. "A Preliminary Test of the Theory of Dependency." *Comparative Politics* 7, no. 3 (April 1975): 303-330.

Keller, Suzanne. *The Urban Neighborhood.* New York: Random House, 1968.

Kim, Jae-On; Nie, Norman; and Verba, Sidney. "The Amount and Concentration of Political Participation." *Political Methodology* 1, no. 2 (1974): 105-131.

Kirkpatrick, Jeanne. *Leader and Vanguard in Mass Society: A Study of Peronist Argentina.* Cambridge, Mass.: M.I.T. Press, 1971.

Klitgaard, Robert. "Observations on the Peruvian National Plan of Development." *Inter-American Economic Affairs* 25, no. 3 (Winter 1971): 3-22.

Kuczynski, Pedro-Pablo. *Peruvian Democracy under Economic Stress: An Account of the Belaúnde Administration, 1963-1968.* Princeton: Princeton

University Press, 1977.

Landy, David M. "Resurrection of the Corporatist Model in Latin American Politics." *Studies in Comparative International Development* 12, no. 3 (Fall 1976): 70-83.

Lane, Robert. *Political Life.* New York: Free Press, 1959.

La Porte, Robert, and Petras, James. *Perú: ¿Transformación revolucionaria o modernización?* Buenos Aires: Amorrortu, 1971.

Larson, Magali S., and Bergman, Arlene. *Social Stratification in Peru.* Berkeley: Institute of International Studies, University of California, 1969.

Leacock, Eleanor, ed. *The Culture of Poverty: A Critique.* New York: Simon and Schuster, 1971.

Leeds, Anthony. "The Significant Variables Affecting the Growth of Squatter Settlements." *América Latina* 12 (1969): 44-86.

_____. "The Concept of the 'Culture of Poverty': Conceptual, Logical, and Empirical Problems, with Perspectives from Brazil and Peru." In *The Culture of Poverty: A Critique,* edited by Eleanor B. Leacock, pp. 226-284. New York: Simon and Schuster, 1971.

_____. "Locality Power in Relation to Supralocal Power Institutions." In *Urban Anthropology,* edited by Aidan Southall, pp. 15-42. New York: Oxford University Press, 1973.

_____, and Leeds, Elizabeth. "Brazil and the Myth of Urban Rurality: Urban Experience, Work, and Values in 'Squatments' of Rio de Janeiro and Lima." In *City and Country in the Third World: Issues in the Modernization of Latin America,* edited by Arthur J. Field, pp. 229-285. Cambridge, Mass.: Schenkman, 1970.

_____, and _____. "Accounting for Behavioral Differences: Three Political Systems and the Responses of Squatters in Brazil, Peru, and Chile." In *The City in Comparative Perspective,* edited by John Walton and Louis Masotti, pp. 193-248. New York: Halsted Press, John Wiley, 1976.

Lemarchand, Rene, and Legg, Keith. "Political Clientelism and Development: A Preliminary Analysis." *Comparative Politics* 4, no. 2 (January 1972): 148-165.

Lerner, Daniel. *The Passing of Traditional Society.* New York: Free Press, 1958.

_____. "Comparative Analysis of Processes of Modernization." In *Comparative Research across Cultures and Nations,* edited by Stein Rokkan, pp. 82-92. The Hague: Mouton, 1968.

Levine, Daniel H. "Urbanization in Latin America: Changing Perspectives." *Latin American Research Review* 14, no. 1 (1979): 170-183.

Lewis, Hylan. *Culture, Class, and People.* Washington, D.C.: Cross-Tell, 1967.

Lewis, Oscar. "The Culture of Poverty." *Scientific American* 215 (October 1966): 19-25.

_____. *A Study of Slum Culture: Backgrounds for La Vida.* New York: Random House, 1968.

Lewis, Oscar. "The Culture of Poverty." In *On Understanding Poverty*, edited by Daniel P. Moynihan, pp. 187-200. New York: Basic Books, 1969.

Lewis, Robert A. *Employment, Income, and the Growth of the Barriadas in Lima, Peru.* Latin American Dissertation Series, no. 46. Ithaca, N.Y.: Cornell University Latin American Studies, 1973.

Ligon, Austin. "The Peruvian Revolution: An Analysis." Unpublished manuscript. Department of Government, University of Texas, 1973.

Lindqvist, Sven. *The Shadow: Latin America Faces the Seventies.* Baltimore: Penguin, 1972.

Lineberry, Robert L. "Approaches to the Study of Community Politics." In *Community Politics: A Behavioral Approach*, edited by C. M. Bonjean, T. N. Clark, and R. L. Lineberry, pp. 16-25. New York: Free Press, 1971.

Linz, Juan J. "Ecological Analysis and Survey Research." In *Quantitative Ecological Analysis in the Social Sciences*, edited by Mattei Dogan and Stein Rokkan, pp. 91-132. Cambridge, Mass.: M.I.T. Press, 1969.

_____. "An Authoritarian Regime: Spain." In *Mass Politics*, edited by Stein Rokkan, pp. 251-283. New York: Free Press, 1970.

_____. "Totalitarian and Authoritarian Regimes." In *Macropolitical Theory*, edited by Fred Greenstein and Nelson Polsby, pp. 175-412. Vol. 3 of *Handbook of Political Science*. Reading, Mass.: Addison-Wesley, 1975.

Lipsky, Michael. "Protest as a Political Resource." *American Political Science Review* 62 (December 1968): 1144-1158.

Lipton, Michael. *Why Poor People Stay Poor: Urban Bias in World Development.* Cambridge, Mass.: Harvard University Press, 1977.

Little, D. Richard. "Mass Political Participation in the U.S. and the U.S.S.R.: A Conceptual Analysis." *Comparative Political Studies* 8, no. 4 (January 1976): 437-460.

Llontop, Orlando. *El proceso de urbanización en el Perú.* Lima: Universidad Nacional Mayor de San Marcos, 1970.

Lloyd, Peter. *Slums of Hope? Shanty Towns of the Third World.* Harmondsworth, England: Penguin, 1979.

Lobo, Susan Bloom. "Urban Adaptation among Peruvian Migrants." *Rice University Studies* 62, no. 3 (Summer 1976): 113-130.

Lomnitz, Larissa. *Networks and Marginality: Life in a Mexican Shantytown.* New York: Academic Press, 1977.

Low, Sanford H. "The Social and Spatial Organization of a Peruvian Barriada." Ph.D. dissertation, Harvard University, 1975.

Lowenthal, Abraham, ed. *The Peruvian Experiment: Continuity and Change under Military Rule.* Princeton: Princeton University Press, 1975.

Lutz, Thomas. "Self-Help Neighborhood Organizations, Political Socialization, and the Developing Political Orientations of Urban Squatters in Latin America: Contrasting Patterns from Case Studies in Panama City, Guayaquil, and Lima." Ph.D. dissertation, Georgetown University, 1970.

Maidenburg, H. J. "Chaos Hovers over Latin Lands." *New York Times* (January 26, 1970): 49.

Malloy, James. *Bolivia: The Uncompleted Revolution*. Pittsburgh, Pa.: University of Pittsburgh Press, 1970.

_____. "Dissecting the Peruvian Military: A Review Essay." *Journal of Inter-American and World Affairs* 15, no. 3 (August 1973): 375-382.

_____. "Authoritarianism, Corporatism, and Mobilization in Peru." *The Review of Politics* 36, no. 1 (January 1974): 52-84.

Manaster, Kenneth A. "The Problem of Urban Squatters in Developing Countries: Peru." *Wisconsin Law Review*, Volume 1968: 23, no. 1, pp. 23-61.

Mangin, William. "The Role of Regional Associations in the Adaptation of Rural Migrants to Cities in Peru." In *Contemporary Cultures and Societies of Latin America*, edited by D. B. Heath and Richard Adams, pp. 311-323. New York: Random House, 1965.

_____. "Latin American Squatter Settlements: A Problem and a Solution." *Latin American Research Review* 2, no. 3 (Summer 1967): 65-97.

_____. "Squatter Settlements." *Scientific American* 217, no. 4 (October 1967): 21-29.

_____. "Sociological, Cultural, and Political Characteristics of Some Urban Migrants in Peru." In *Urban Anthropology*, edited by Aidan Southall, pp. 315-350. New York: Oxford University Press, 1973.

_____. "Introduction." In *Peasants in Cities*, edited by William Mangin, pp. viii-xxxix. Boston: Houghton Mifflin, 1970.

Mariátegui, Javier, et al. *Epidemología psiquiátrica de un distrito urbano de Lima*. Lima: Revista Neuro-Psiquiatria, 1969.

Marshall, Dale Rogers. *The Politics of Participation in Poverty*. Berkeley: University of California Press, 1970.

Martínez, Héctor. *Las migraciones internas en el Perú*. Caracas: Monte Avila Editores, 1968.

_____, et al. *Bibliografía indígena andina peruana, 1900-1967*. Lima: Centro de Estudios de Población y Desarrollo, 1969.

_____. "Relatos de barriadas." *Mundo Nuevo* 51-52 (September-October, 1970): 19-28.

_____. *El éxodo rural en el Perú*. Lima: Centro de Estudios de Población y Desarrollo, June 1973.

Maruska, Donald L. "Government Policy and Neighborhood Organizations in the Squatter Settlements of Lima." Honors thesis, Harvard University, 1972.

Matos Mar, José. *Estudio de las barriadas limeñas*. Lima: Universidad Nacional Mayor de San Marcos, 1966.

_____. *Urbanización y barriadas en América del Sur*. Lima: Instituto de Estudios Peruanos, 1968.

_____. *Bibliografía peruana de ciencias sociales* (1957-1969). Lima: Instituto de Estudios Peruanos, 1971.

McCrone, D. J., and Cnudde, D. F. "Toward a Communication Theory of Democratic Political Development: A Causal Model." *American Political Science Review* 63 (1967): 72-79.

McDonough, Peter. "Representation and Authoritarianism: Notes on Elite-Mass Studies." Durham, N.H.: Workshop on Modern Portugal, University of New Hampshire, 10-14 October, 1973.

McGee, T. G. *The Urbanization Process in the Third World.* London: G. Bell and Sons, 1971.

McNicoll, Robert E. *Peru's Institutional Revolution.* Pensacola: University of West Florida, 1973.

Michl, Sara. "Urban Squatter Organization as a National Government Tool: The Case of Lima, Peru." In *Latin American Urban Research,* vol. 3, edited by Francine Rabinovitz and Felicity Trueblood, pp. 155-178. Beverly Hills, Cal.: Sage Publications, 1973.

Middlebrook, Kevin, and Palmer, David Scott. *Military Government and Political Development: Lessons from Peru.* Vol. 5 of *Sage Professional Papers in Comarative Politics.* Beverly Hills, Cal.: Sage Publications, 1975.

Milbrath, Lester. *Political Participation.* Chicago: Rand McNally, 1965.

————, and Goel, M. L. *Political Participation: How and Why Do People Get Hooked in Politics?* 2nd. ed. Chicago: Rand McNally, 1977.

Millones, Luis. *Tugurios: La cultura de los marginados.* Lima: Instituto Nacional de Cultura, 1978.

Ministerio de Vivienda. Dirección General de Edificaciones, Dirección de Renovación e Integración Urbana. *La población de "El Porvenir" y la renovación urbana: Consideraciones sociológicas y económicas.* Lima: n.p., 1973.

Mollenkopf, John H. "On the Causes and Consequences of Neighborhood and Political Mobilization." Presented at the 1973 meeting of the American Political Science Association, New Orleans, September 4-8, 1973.

Moncloa, Francisco. *Perú: Qué Pasó (1968-1976).* Lima: Editorial Horizonte, 1977.

Montaño, Jorge. *Los pobres de la ciudad en los asentamientos espontáneos.* Mexico Mexico City: Siglo XXI, 1976.

Montoya Rojas, Rodrigo. "La migración interna en el Perú." *América Latina* 10)October-December 1967): 83-108.

Moore, Richard J. T. "Assimilation and Political Participation among the Urban Poor in Guayaquil, Ecuador." Ph.D. dissertation, Department of Government, University of Texas at Austin, 1977.

————. "The Urban Poor in Guayaquil, Ecuador: Modes, Correlates, and Context of Political Participation." In *Political Participation in Latin America,* vol. 2, *Politics and the Poor,* edited by John Booth and Martin Seligson, pp. 198-218. New York: Holmes and Meier, 1979.

Moreira, Neiva. *Modelo peruano.* Buenos Aires: La Línea, 1974.

Morse, Richard. "Recent Research on Latin American Urbanization: A Selective Survey with Commentary." *Latin American Research Review* 1, no. 1 (Fall 1965): 35-74.

Morse, Richard. "Trends and Issues in Latin American Urban Research, 1965-1970 Parts I and II." *Latin American Research Review* 6, no. 1 (Spring 1971): 3-52; 6, no. 2 (Summer 1971): 19-75.

Moynihan, Daniel Patrick. *Maximum Feasible Misunderstanding.* New York: Macmillan-Free Press, 1969.

_____, and Glazer, Nathan. *Beyond the Melting Pot.* Cambridge, Mass.: M.I.T. Press, 1963.

Musgrove, Philip, and Ferber, Robert. "Identifying the Urban Poor: Characteristics of Poverty Households in Bogotá, Medellín, and Lima." *Latin American Research Review* 14, no. 2 (1979): 25-53.

Nelson, Barbara J. "Hat in Hand: The Invisible Politics of Authoritarian Help-Seeking." Presented at the 1976 meeting of the American Political Science Association, Chicago, September 2-5, 1976.

Nelson, Joan. *Migrants, Urban Poverty, and Instability in Developing Nations.* Cambridge, Mass.: Harvard University, Center for International Affairs, 1969.

_____. "The Urban Poor: Disruption of Political Integration in Third World Cities." *World Politics* 22, no. 3 (April 1971): 393-414.

_____. *Access to Power: Politics and the Urban Poor in Developing Nations.* Princeton: Princeton University Press, 1979.

Newton, Ronald. "On 'Functional Groups,' 'Fragmentation,' and 'Pluralism' in Spanish American Political Society." *Hispanic American Historical Review* 50 (1970): 1-29.

_____. "Natural Corporatism and the Passing of Populism in Spanish America." *Review of Politics* 36, no. 1 (January 1974): 34-51.

Nie, Norman H.; Powell, G. Bingham; and Prewitt, Kenneth. "Social Structure and Political Participation: Developmental Relationships, Parts I and II." In *Cross-National Micro-Analysis,* edited by John C. Pierce and Richard A. Pride, pp. 135-197. Beverly Hills, Cal.: Sage Publications, 1972.

Nordlinger, Eric. "Soldiers in Mufti: The Impact of Military Rule upon Economic and Social Change in the Non-Western States." *American Political Science Review* 64, no. 4 (December 1970): 1131-1148.

_____. *Soldiers and Politics.* Englewood Cliffs, N.J.: Prentice-Hall, 1977.

Nun, José. "La marginalidad en América Latina." *Revista Latinoamericana de Sociología* 5, no. 2 (July 1969): (Special issue; Nun was issue editor.)

Nunn, Frederick. "Professional Militarism in Twentieth-Century Peru: Historical and Theoretical Background to the *Golpe de Estado* of 1968." *Hispanic American Historical Review* 59, no. 3 (August 1979): 391-417.

Nygreen, G. T. "Interactive Path Analysis." *American Sociological Review* 6 (February 1971): 37-43.

O'Brien, Philip J. "A Critique of Latin American Theories of Dependency." In *Beyond the Sociology of Development: Economy and Society in Latin America and Africa,* edited by Ivan Oxaal, Tony Barnett, and David Booth. London: Routledge and Kegan Paul, 1970.

O'Donnell, Guillermo A. *Modernization and Bureaucratic-Authoritarianism.*
Berkeley: Institute of International Studies, University of California, 1973.
_____. "Corporatism and the Question of the State." In *Authoritarianism and Corporatism in Latin America,* edited by James Malloy, pp. 47-88.
Pittsburgh: University of Pittsburgh Press, 1977.
ONDEPJOV (Oficina Nacional de Desarrollo de los Pueblos Jóvenes). *Boletines.*
Nos. 1, 2, 3, 4, 5. Lima: ONDEPJOV, 1969-1970.
_____. *Guía para la organización de los pueblos jóvenes.* Folleto de Divulgación no. 1. Lima: ONDEPJOV, 1970.
_____. *Catálogo de instituciones de servicio a la comunidad: Trujillo, Chimbote, Lima y Arequipa.* Lima: ONDEPJOV, 1971.
_____. *Informe preliminar del censo, 1970.* Lima: Centro de Estudios de Población y Desarrollo, 1971.
ONEC (Oficina Nacional de Estadística y Censos). *Contribución al estudio de la concentración urbana en el Perú: 1940-1972.* Lima: Oficina Nacional de Estadística y Censos, 1974.
_____. *Los pueblos jóvenes en el Perú.* Boletín de Análisis Demográfico no. 13. Lima: Oficina Nacional de Estadística y Censos, 1972.
ONPU (Oficina Nacional de Planeamiento y Urbanismo). *Esquema director, 1967-1980.* Lima: Oficina Nacional de Planeamiento y Urbanismo, 1967.
_____. *Estudio de Tugurios en los distritos de Jesús María y La Victoria.* Cuaderno Violeta no. 2. Lima: Oficina Nacional de Planeamiento y Urbanismo, n.d.
_____. *Lima metropolitana: Algunos aspectos de su expediente urbano y soluciones parciales varias.* Lima: Oficina Nacional de Planeamiento y Urbanismo, 1954.
Olson, Mancur. *The Logic of Collective Action.* Cambridge, Mass.: Harvard University Press, 1965.
Orbell, John M. "The Impact of Metropolitan Residence on Social and Political Orientations." *Social Science Quarterly* 51, no. 3 (December 1970): 634-648.
_____, and Uno, Toru. "A Theory of Neighborhood Problem-Solving: Political Action vs. Residential Mobility." *American Political Science Review* 67, no. 3 (June 1972): 471-489.
Orum, Anthony, and Wilson, Kenneth. "Toward a Theoretical Model of Participation in Political Movements." Paper presented at the Southwestern Sociological Assocaition Meeting at Dallas, March 1974.
Ozbudun, Ergun. *Social Change and Political Participation in Turkey.* Princeton: Princeton University Press, 1976.
Palmer, David Scott. *Revolution from Above: Military Government and Popular Participation in Peru, 1968-1972.* Latin American Dissertation Series, no. 47. Ithaca, N.Y.: Cornell University, 1973.
_____, and Rodríguez Beruff, Jorge. "The Peruvian Military Government: The Problems of Popular Participation." *Bulletin of the Institute of Development*

Studies 4, no. 4 (University of Sussex, 1972).

Palumbo, Dennis. "Comparative Analysis: Quasi Methodology or New Science?" *Comparative Urban Research* 4 (Winter 1973-1974): 37-53.

Paredes, Marcia Koth de. "Análisis ecológico del área metropolitana." In *Plan de desarrollo metropolitano Lima-Callao a 1980*, vol. 3. Lima: Ministerio de Vivienda, Dirección General de Desarrollo Urbano, 1971.

_____. "Urban Community Organization in Lima, Peru." Ph.D. dissertation, Massachusetts Institute of Technology, Department of Political Science, 1973.

Parenti, Michael. "Power and Pluralism: A View from the Bottom." *Journal of Politics* 32, no. 3 (August 1970): 501-530.

Park, Robert E. "Human Migration and the Marginal Man." *American Journal of Sociology* 33 (May 1928): 881-893.

Pásara, Luís, et al. *Dinámico de la comunidad industrial.* Lima: DESCO, 1974.

Patch, Richard. "Life in a Callejón." *American Universities Field Staff Reports,* West Coast South America, VIII, 6 (June 1961).

_____. "La Parada, Lima's Market, Parts I, II, III." *American Universities Field Staff Reports,* West Coast South America, XIV, 1, 2, 3 (1967).

Payne, Arnold. *The Peruvian Coup d'Etat of 1962.* Washington, D.C.: Institute for the Comparative Study of Political Systems, 1968.

Payne, James L. *Labor and Politics in Peru: The System of Political Bargaining.* New Haven: Yale University Press, 1967.

Paz Soldán, Carlos Enrique. *Lima y sus suburbios.* Lima: Universidad Nacional Mayor de San Marcos, Biblioteca de Cultura Sanitaria, Instituto de Medicina Social, 1957.

Pease García, Henry. *El ocaso del poder oligárquico.* Lima: DESCO, 1977.

Peattie, Lisa. *The View from the Barrio.* Ann Arbor: University of Michigan Press, 1968.

Pennock, J. Roland. "Political Development, Political Systems, and Political Goods." *World Politics* 18, no. 3 (April): 415-434.

Perlman, Janice. *The Myth of Marginality: Urban Poverty and Politics in Rio de Janeiro.* Berkeley: University of California Press, 1975.

Petras, James F. "Chile: Nationalization, Socioeconomic Change, and Popular Participation." Paper presented at the 1972 meetings of American Political Science Association, Washington, D.C.

Philip, George D. E. *The Rise and Fall of the Peruvian Military Radicals, 1968-1976.* London: Athlone Press, 1978.

Pike, Frederick. *The Modern History of Peru.* New York: Praeger, 1967.

_____. "Religion, Collectivism, and Intrahistory: The Peruvian Ideal of Dependence." *Journal of Latin American Studies* 10, no. 2 (November 1978): 239-263.

Pinelo, Adalberto. *The Multi-National Corporation as a Force in Latin American Politics: A Case Study of the International Petroleum Company in Peru.* New York: Praeger, 1973.

Piven, Frances Fox, and Cloward, Richard A. *Regulating the Poor: The Functions of Public Welfare.* New York: Vintage Books, 1971.

Piven, Frances Fox, and Cloward, Richard A. *Poor People's Movements: Why They Succeed, How They Fail.* New York: Pantheon Books, 1977.

Plotnick, Robert D. "The Effect of Macroeconomic Conditions on the Poor." In *Progress against Poverty,* edited by Robert D. Plotnick and Felicity Skidmore, pp. 109-134. New York: Academic Press, 1975.

Poitras, Guy. "Inter-American Clientelism: Perspectives on the Latin American Military in United States-Latin American Relations." *Proceedings of the Pacific Coast Council on Latin American Studies* 3 (1974): 123-139.

Popkin, Samuel L. *The Rational Peasant: The Political Economy of Rural Society in Vietnam.* Berkeley: University of California Press, 1979.

Portes, Alejandro. "Urbanization and Politics in Latin America." *Social Science Quarterly* 53, no. 2 (December 1971): 697-720.

_____. "Rationality in the Slum: An Essay on Interpretive Sociology." *Comparative Studies in Society and History* 14, no. 3 (June 1972): 268-286.

_____. "Housing Policy, Urban Poverty, and the State: The *Favelas* of Rio de Janeiro, 1972-1976." *Latin American Research Review* 14, no. 2 (1979): 3-24.

_____, and Ferguson, D. Frances. "Comparative Ideologies of Poverty and Equity: Latin America and the United States." In *Equity, Income, and Policy,* edited by I. L. Horowitz, pp. 70-105. New York: Praeger, 1977.

_____, and Ross, Adreain. "A Model for the Prediction of Leftist Radicalism." *Journal of Political and Military Sociology* 2, no. 1 (Spring 1974): 33-56.

_____, and Walton, John. *Urban Latin America: The Political Condition from Above and Below.* Austin: University of Texas Press, 1976.

Powell, John D. "Peasant Society and Clientelist Politics." *American Political Science Review* 64, no. 2 (June 1970): 411-425.

Powell, Sandra. "Political Participation in the Barriadas: A Case Study." *Comparative Political Studies* 2, no. 2 (July 1969): 195-215.

Pratt, Raymond. "Community Political Organization and Lower-Class Politicization in Two Latin American Cities." *Journal of the Developing Areas* 5, no. 1 (July 1971): 523-542.

_____. "Parties, Neighborhood Associations, and the Politicization of the Urban Poor in Latin America." *Midwest Journal of Political Science* 15 (August 1971): 495-524.

Prysby, Charles. "Neighborhood Class Composition and Individual Partisan Choice: A Test with Chilean Data." *Social Science Quarterly* 56, no. 2 (September 1975): 225-238.

Purcell, Susan Kaufman. "Authoritarianism." *Comparative Politics* 5, no. 2 (January 1973): 301-312.

_____. "Decision-Making in an Authoritarian Regime: Theoretical Implications from a Mexican Case Study." *World Politics* 26, 1 (October 1973): 28-54.

Quinto Congreso Interamericano de Vivienda. *Abaratamiento de Vivienda.*
Lima: Quinto Congreso Interamericano de Vivienda, 1975.
_____. *Políticas y acciones de renovación, rehabilitación, y conservación
urbanas.* Lima: Quinto Congreso Interamericano de Vivienda, 1975.
Quijano, Anibal. *Nationalism and Capitalism in Peru.* New York: Monthly
Review, 1971.
_____. "La formación de un universo marginal en las ciudades de América
Latina." In *Imperialismo y urbanización en América Latina,* edited by
Manuel Castells, pp. 141-166. Barcelona, Spain: Ed. Gustavo Gili.
_____. "The Urbanization of Latin American Society." In *Urbanization in
Latin America,* edited by Jorge Hardoy, pp. 109-156. Garden City, N.Y.:
Anchor Doubleday, 1975.
Rabinovitz, Francine, and Trueblood, Felicity, eds. *Latin American Urban
Research,* vol. 1. Beverly Hills, Cal.: Sage Publications, 1971.
_____, and _____, eds. *National-Local Linkages: The Interrelationship
of Urban and National Politics in Latin America.* Vol. 3 of *Latin American
Urban Research.* Beverly Hills, Cal.: Sage Publications, 1973.
Ray, David. "The Dependency Model of Latin American Underdevelopment:
Three Basic Fallacies." *Journal of Inter-American and World Affairs* 15, no.
1 (February 1973): 4-20.
Ray, Talton F. *The Politics of the Barrios of Venezuela.* Berkeley, Cal.: Uni-
versity of California Press, 1969.
Redfield, Robert. "The Folk Society." *American Journal of Sociology* 52:
293-308.
_____. *Peasant Society and Culture.* Chicago: University of Chicago Press,
1961.
Republic of Peru. *Plan nacional de desarrollo para 1971-1975, Volumen I:
Plan Global.* Lima: Oficina de la Presidencia de la República, 1971.
Riggs, Fred. *Administration in Developing Countries.* Boston: Houghton
Mifflin, 1964.
Riofrio, Gustavo. *Se busca terreno para próxima barriada.* Lima: DESCO, 1978.
Roberts, Bryan R. *Organizing Strangers: Poor Families in Guatemala City.*
Austin: University of Texas Press, 1973.
_____. *Cities of Peasants.* London: Edward Arnold, 1978.
Robin, John P., and Terzo, Frederick C. *Urbanization in Peru.* New York:
Ford Foundation, International Urbanization Survey, 1973.
Robles, Diego. "Development Alternatives for the Peruvian Barriadas." In
Latin American Urban Research, vol. 2, edited by Guillermo Geisse and
Jorge Hardoy, pp. 229-240. Beverly Hills, Cal.: Sage Publications, 1972.
Rodríguez, Alfredo. *Segregación residencial y desmobilización política: El
caso de Lima.* Buenos Aires: Ediciones SIAP, 1973.
_____, et al. *Aportes a la comprensión de un fenómeno urbano: La barriada.*
Cuaderno A2. Lima: DESCO, 1969.
_____; Riofrio, Gustavo; and Welsh, Eileen. *De invasores a invadidos.*

Lima: DESCO, 1973.

Rofman, Alejandro B. "Influencia del proceso histórico en la dependencia externa y en la estructuración de las redes regiones y urbana actuales." In *El proceso de urbanización en América desde sus orígenes hasta nuestros días*, pp. 133-155. Vol. 2 of *Actas y Memorias del XXXIX Congreso Internacional de Americanistas*, Lima: Instituto de Estudios Peruanos, 1972.

Rogler, Lloyd. "Slum Neighborhoods in Latin America." *Journal of Inter-American Studies* 9, no. 4 (October 1967): 507-528.

_____. *Migrant in the City*. New York: Basic Books, 1972.

Rogowski, Ronald. *Political Legitimacy: A Theory of Political Support*. Princeton: Princeton University Press, 1974.

_____, and Wasserspring, Lois. *Does Political Development Exist? Corporatism in Old and New Societies*. Vol. 2, no. 01-024 of *Comparative Politics Series*. Beverly Hills, Cal.: Sage Publications, 1971.

Rokkan, Stein. *Citizens, Elections, Parties*. New York: David McKay, 1970.

Ross, Marc Howard. "Community Formation in an Urban Squatter Settlement." *Comparative Political Studies* 6, no. 3 (October 1973): 296-328.

Roth, Guenther. "Personal Rulership, Patrimonialism, and Empire-Building in the New States." *World Politics* 20, no. 2 (January 1968): 194-206.

Rothenberg, Jerome. *On the Microeconomics of Internal Migration*. Publication C/76-17. Cambridge, Mass.: Migration and Development Study Group, M.I.T.

Rotondo, Humberto, et al. *Estudios de psiquiatría social en el Perú*. Lima: Ediciones del Sol, 1963.

Rozman, Stephen L. "The Evolution of the Political Role of the Peruvian Military." *Journal of Inter-American Studies* 12, no. 4 (October 1970): 539-654.

Rudofsky, Bernard. *Architecture Without Architects*. Garden City, N.Y.: Doubleday, 1964.

Rusk, Jerold G. "Political Participation in America: A Review Essay." *American Political Science Review* 70, no. 2 (June 1976): 583-591.

Salamon, Lester M., and van Evera, Steven. "Fear, Apathy, and Discrimination: A Test of Three Explanations of Political Participation." *American Political Science Review* 67, no. 4 (December 1973): 1288-1306.

Salazar Larraín, Arturo. *Lima: Teoría y práctica de la ciudad*. Lima: Campadonico, 1968.

Samuels, Richard J. "Extralocal Linkages and the Comparative Study of Local Politics." *Comparative Urban Research* 5, nos. 2-3 (1978): 25-43.

Sánchez, Gregorio Rueda, ed. *Barrios Marginales en el Perú: Ley Orgánica de Barrios Marginales No. 13517*. Lima: Editorial Thesis, 1965.

Sánchez León, Abelardo, and Guerrero de los Rios, Raúl. *Tugurización en Lima metropolitana*. Lima: DESCO, 1979.

Sandbrook, Richard. "The Working Class in the Future of the Third World." *World Politics* 25, no. 3 (April 1973): 448-478.

Santos, Milton. "The Periphery at the Pole." In *The Social Economy of Cities*, edited by G. Gappert and H. M. Rose, pp. 335-360. Vol. 9 of *Urban Affairs Annual Review*. Beverly Hills, Cal.: Sage Publications.

Saravia, Alfredo. *El gobierno metropolitano y Limatrópoli*. Lima: Consejo Provincial y la Cámara de Comercio, 1968.

Scheuch, Erwin K. "The Cross-Cultural Use of Sample Surveys: Problems of Comparability." In *Comparative Research across Cultures and Nations*, edited by Stein Rokkan, pp. 176-209. The Hague: Mouton, 1968.

————. "Social Context and Individual Behavior." In *Quantitative Ecological Analysis in the Social Sciences*, edited by Mattei Dogan and Stein Rokkan, pp. 133-156. Cambridge, Mass.: M.I.T. Press, 1969.

Schmidt, Steffan. *Friends, Followers, and Factions*. Berkeley: University of California Press, 1977.

Schmitter, Philippe. "Still the Century of Corporatism?" *The Review of Politics* 36, no. 1 (January 1974): 85-131.

Schoultz, Lars. "Urbanization and Changing Voting Patterns: Colombia, 1946-1970." *Political Science Quarterly* 87, no. 1 (March 1972).

————. "The Socio-Economic Determinants of Popular-Authoritarian Electoral Behavior: The Case of Peronism." *American Political Science Review* 71, no. 4 (December 1977): 1423-1446.

Scoble, Harry M. "Access to Politics." *International Encyclopedia of the Social Sciences*, I, 10-14.

Scott, James. "Corruption, Machine Politics, and Political Change." *American Political Science Review* 63, no. 4 (December 1969): 1142-1158.

Scott, Robert E., ed. *Latin American Modernization Problems*. Urbana-Champaign: University of Illinois Press, 1973.

Scurrah, Martin J. *Neither Capitalist nor Communist: Authoritarianism and Participation in Peru*. Lima: Escuela de Administración de Negocios para Graduados, 1974.

————, and Montalvo, Abner. *Social Bases of Support for Peru's Revolutionary Military Government*. Lima: Escuela de Administración de Negocios para Graduados, 1975.

Selznick, Philip. *TVA and the Grass Roots: A Study in the Sociology of Formal Organization*. New York: Harper Torch Books, 1966.

Shannon, Lyle W., and Shannon, Magdaline. ' The Assimilation of Migrants to Cities." In *Social Science and the City*, edited by Leo F. Schnore, pp. 49-75. New York: Praeger, 1968.

Shively, W. Philips. "'Ecological' Influence: The Use of Aggregate Data to Study Individuals." *American Political Science Review* 63,mo. 4 (December 1969): 1183-1197.

Simmons, Ozzie G. "El uso de los conceptos de aculturación y asimilación en el estudio del cambio cultural en el Perú." *Perú Indígena* 2 (1952): 40 ff.

Singer, Paul. "Migraciones internas en América Latina: Consideraciones teóricas sobre su estudio." In *Imperialismo y urbanización en América Latina*, edited by Manuel Castells, pp. 27-56. Barcelona, Spain: Ed. Gustavo Gili, 1973.

Sloan, John W. "Dependency Theory and Latin American Development: Another Key Fails to Open the Door." *Inter-American Economic Affairs* 31, no. 3 (Winter 1977): 21-40.

Smelser, Neil J. "The Methodology of Comparative Analysis." In *Comparative Research Methods,* edited by Donald Warwick and Samuel Osherson, pp. 42-86. Englewood Cliffs, N.J.: Prentice-Hall, 1973.

Smith, Peter H. "The Social Base of Peronism." *Hispanic American Historical Review* 52 (February 1972): 55-73.

Solow, Anatole A. "Housing in Latin America: The Problem of the Urban Low Income Families." *Town Planning Review* 38 (June 1967): 83-102.

Southall, Aidan, ed. *Urban Anthropology.* New York: Oxford University Press, 1973.

Stein, Steve. *Populism and the Politics of Social Control in Peru.* Madison, Wis.: University of Wisconsin Press, 1980.

Stepan, Alfred. *The State and Society: Peru in Comparative Perspective.* Princeton: Princeton University Press, 1978.

Stokes, Charles. "A Theory of Slums." *Land Economics* 38, no. 3 (August (1962): 187-197.

Strauss, Anselm, and Glaser, Barney G. *The Discovery of Grounded Theory: Strategies for Qualitative Research.* Chicago: Aldine, 1967.

Suárez, M. D. "Militares y oligarquía en el Perú." *Mundo Nuevo* 43 (January 1970): 19-24.

Sulmont, Denis. *El movimiento obrero en el Perú.* Lima: Universidad Católica, 1975.

Sunkel, Osvaldo. "Desarrollo, subdesarrollo, dependencia, marginación y desigualdades espaciales: Hacia un enfoque totalizante." In *Desarrollo urbano y regional en América Latina,* edited by Luis Unikel and Andrés Necochea, pp. 179-236. Mexico City: Fondo de Cultura Económica, 1975.

Torres, Jorge. *Análisis de la estructura económica de la economía peruana.* Série Documento de Trabajo no. 17. Lima: CISEPA, Universidad Católica, 1974.

Townsend, James. *Political Participation in Communist China.* Berkeley: University of California Press, 1967.

Turner, John. "Lima's *Barriadas* Today." *Architectural Design* 33, no. 8 (1963): 369-380, 389-393.

_____. "Lima's *Barriadas* and *Corralones." Ekistics* 19, no. 112 (1965): 152-156.

_____. "Uncontrolled Urban Settlements: Problems and Policies." *International Social Development Review* 1, no. 1 (1968): 107-130.

_____, et at. *Nueva visión del deficit de vivienda.* Lima: DESCO, Cuaderno A1, 1969.

_____, et al. *Urban Dwelling Environments.* Cambridge, Mass.: M.I.T. Press, 1969.

_____. "Barriers and Channels for Housing Development in Modernizing

274   Bibliography

Countries." In *Peasants in Cities,* edited by William Mangin, pp. 1-19. Boston: Houghton Mifflin, 1970

Turner, John. *The Squatter Revolution: Autonomous Urban Settlement and Social Change in Transitional Economies.* Unpublished manuscript.

Tussing, A. Dale. *Poverty in a Dual Economy.* New York: St. Martin's Press, 1975.

Tyson, Brady. "The Emerging Role of the Military as National Modernizers and Managers in Latin America: The Case of Brazil and Peru." In *Latin American Prospects for the 1970's: What Kinds of Revolution?,* edited by David H. Pollock and Arch R. M. Ritter, pp. 107-130. New York: Praeger, 1973.

Uchuya Reyes, Héctor E., ed. *Normas legales de pueblos jóvenes.* Lima: Ediciones HEUR, 1971.

Ugalde, Antonio. *Power and Conflict in a Mexican Community.* Albuquerque: University of New Mexico Press, 1970.

———, et al. *The Urbanization Process of a Poor Mexican Neighborhood.* Austin: Institute of Latin American Studies, University of Texas, 1973.

Upshaw, Harry. "Attitude Measurement." In *Methodology in Social Research,* edited by Hubert and Anne Blalock, pp. 60-149. New York: McGraw-Hill, 1968.

Usandizaga, Elas, and Havens, A. Eugene. *Tres barrios de invasión.* Bogotá: Tercer Mundo, 1966.

Uzzell, John Douglas. "Bound for Places I'm Not Known to: Adaptation of Migrants and Residence in Four Irregular Settlements in Lima, Peru." Ph.D. dissertation, University of Texas, 1972.

———. "Cholos and Bureaus in Lima: Case History and Analysis." In *Class and Ethnicity in Peru,* edited by Pierre van den Berghe, pp. 23-30. Leiden: E. J. Brill, 1974a.

———. "A Strategic Analysis of Social Structure in Lima, Peru, Using the Concept of 'Plays.'" *Urban Anthropology* 3, no. 1 (Spring 1974b): 34-46.

Valdez Pallete, Luis. "Antecedents of the New Orientation of the Armed Forces in Peru." *International Journal of Politics* 1, nos. 2-3 (Summer-Fall 1971): 212-237.

Valdivia Ponce, Oscar. *Migración interna a la Metropoli.* Lima: Universidad Nacional Mayor de San Marcos, 1970.

Valentine, Charles A. *Culture and Poverty.* Chicago: University of Chicago Press, 1968.

Valkonen, Tapani. "Individual and Structural Effects in Ecological Research." In *Quantitative Ecological Analysis in the Social Sciences,* edited by Mattei Dogan and Stein Rokkan, pp. 53-68. Cambridge, Mass.: M.I.T. Press, 1969.

Vandendries, René. "Internal Migration and Economic Development in Peru." In *Latin American Modernization Problems,* edited by Robert Scott, pp. 193-208. Urbana-Champaign: University of Illinois Press, 1973.

Van Til, Jon. "Becoming Participants: Dynamics of Access among the Welfare Poor." *Social Science Quarterly* 54, no. 2 (September 1973): 345-358.

Vanderschueren, Franz. "Political Significance of Neighborhood Committees in the Settlements of Santiago." In *The Chilean Road to Socialism*, edited by Dale L. Johnson, pp. 256-283. Garden City, N.Y.: Doubleday-Anchor, 1973.

Vázquez, Mario, and Dobyns, Henry, eds. *Migración e integración en el Perú.* Lima: Instituto de Estudios Andinos, 1963.

Vedlitz, Arnold. "Neighborhood Estrangement and Political Participation among Blacks in a Southern City." Presented at 1974 meeting of Southwestern Political Science Association, Dallas, March 28-30.

Velasco Alvarado, Juan. *La revolución peruana.* Buenos Aires: Universitaria, 1973.

Verba, Sidney. "Some Dilemmas in Comparative Politics." *World Politics* 20, no. 1 (October 1967): 111-127.

_____. "The Uses of Survey Research in the Study of Comparative Politics." In *Comparative Survey Analysis: A Trend Report and Bibliography*, edited by Stein Rokkan et al., pp. 56-106. The Hague: Mouton, 1969.

_____. "Cross-National Survey Research: The Problem of Credibility." In *Comparative Methods in Sociology*, edited by Ivan Vallier, pp. 309-356. Berkeley: University of California Press, 1971.

_____, and Nie, Norman H. *Participation in America.* New York: Harper and Row, 1972.

_____; Nie, Norman H.; and Kim, Jae-On. *The Modes of Democratic Participation: A Cross-National Comparison.* Vol. 2 of *Comparative Politics Series.* Beverly Hills, Cal.: Sage Publications, 1971.

_____, et al. "The Modes of Participation: Continuities in Research." *Compara-Comparative Political Studies* 6, no. 2 (July 1973): 235-250.

Vermunt, Kornelius, et al. *Opiniones y actitudes frente a la procreación en el estrato bajo de Lima metropolitana.* Lima: CISEPA, Universidad Católica, 1971.

Villanueva, Víctor. *¿Nueva mentalidad militar en el Perú?* Lima: Mejía Vaca, 1969.

_____. *El CAEM y la revolución de la fuerza armada.* Lima: Instituto de Estudios Peruanos, 1972.

_____. *Ejército peruano: Del caudillaje anárquico al militarismo reformista.* Lima: Mejía Vaca, 1973.

Villar, Olga Mercado; Puente Lafoy, Patricio de la; and Uribe-Echevarría, Francisco. *La marginalidad urbana: Orígen, proceso y modo.* Buenos Aires: Ediciones Troquel, 1970.

Violich, Francis. *Cities in Latin America.* New York: Holt, Rinehart, 1944.

Walton, John. "Standardized Case Comparison: Observations on Method in Comparative Sociology." In *Comparative Social Research: Methodological Problems and Strategies*, edited by Michael Armer and Allen D. Grimshaw, pp. 173-188. New York: John Wiley, 1973.

_____. *Elites and Economic Development: Comparative Studies on the Political Economy of Latin American Cities.* Austin: Institute of Latin American Studies, The University of Texas at Austin, 1977.

_____. "From Cities to Systems: Recent Research on Latin American Urbanization." *Latin American Research Review* 14, no. 1 (1979): 159-169.

_____. "Urban Political Economy: A New Paradigm." *Comparative Urban Research* 7, no. 1 (1979): 5-17.

Warren, R. L.; Rose, S. M.; and Bergunder, A. F. *The Structure of Urban Reform.* Lexington, Mass.: Heath, 1974.

Warwick, Donald, and Osherson, Samuel, eds. *Comparative Research Methods.* Englewood Cliffs, N.J.: Prentice-Hall, 1973.

Webb, Richard. *The Distribution of Income in Peru.* Princeton: Princeton University, Woodrow Wilson School, Research Program in Economic Development, Discussion Paper No. 26, September 1972.

_____. *Government Policy and the Distribution of Income in Peru, 1963-1973.* Cambridge, Mass.: Harvard University Press, 1977.

_____, and Figueroa, Adolfo. *Distribución del ingreso en el Perú.* Vol. 14 of *Perú Problema.* Lima: Instituto de Estudios Peruanos, 1975.

Weiner, Myron. "Political Participation: Crisis of the Political Process." In *Crises and Sequences in Political Development,* edited by Leonard Binder et al., pp. 159-204. Princeton: Princeton University Press, 1971.

Weingrod, Alex. "Patrons, Patronage, and Political Parties." *Comparative Studies in Society and History* 10 (1968): 376-400.

Weisslitz, Jacqueline. "Migración rural e integración urbana en el Perú." In *Imperialismo y urbanización en América Latina,* edited by Manuel Castells, pp. 27-56. Barcelona: Ed. Gustavo Gili, 1973.

Welch, Claude E., and Smith, Arthur K. *Military Role and Rule: Perspectives in Civil-Military Relations.* North Scituate, Mass.: Duxbury Press, 1971.

Wellhofer, E. Spencer. "The Mobilization of the Periphery: Perón's 1946 Triumph." *Comparative Political Studies* 7 (July 1974): 239-251.

Welsh, Eileen. *Bibliografía sobre el crecimiento dinámico de Lima, referente al proceso de urbanización en el Perú.* Cuaderno A5. Lima: DESCO, 1970.

White, Allen L. "The Impact of Metropolitan Fiscal Consolidation on the Distribution of Real Income: The Case of Lima, Peru." Ph.D. dissertation, Ohio State University, Department of Geography, 1976.

White, James W. *Political Implications of Cityward Migration: Japan as an Exploratory Test Case.* Vol. 4, no. 01-038 of *Comparative Politics Series.* Beverly Hills, Cal.: Sage Publications, 1973.

White, Morton and Lucia. *The Intellectual versus the City.* New York: Mentor Books, 1962.

Whyte, William F. "Peruvian Paradox: Military Rule and Popular Participation." In *Chile and Peru: Two Paths to Social Justice,* edited by Lila Bradfield, pp. 17-44. Kalamazoo, Mich.: Western Michigan University, Institute of

International and Area Studies, 1974.

Whyte, William F., and Alberti, Giorgio. *Power, Politics, and Progress.* New York: Elsevier, 1976.

Wiarda, Howard J. "Toward a Framework for the Study of Political Change in the Iberic-Latin American Tradition: The Corporative Model." *World Politics* 25 (January 1973): 206-236.

_____. "Corporatism in Iberian and Latin American Political Analysis: Criticisms, Qualifications, and the Context and 'Whys.'" *Comparative Politics* 10, no. 1 (January 1978): 307-312.

Wilker, Harry R., and Milbrath, Lester. "Political Belief Systems and Political Behavior." *Social Science Quarterly* 51, no. 3 (December 1970): 477-493.

Wilson, James Q. "Planning and Politics: Citizen Participation in Urban Renewal." *Journal of the American Institute of Planners* 29, no. 4 (November 1963).

Wilson, Patricia. "From Mode of Production to Spatial Formation: The Regional Consequences of Dependent Industrialization in Peru." Ph.D. dissertation, Cornell University, Department of City and Regional Planning, 1975.

Wolf, Eric. "Kinship, Friendship, and Patron-Client Relations in Complex Societies." In *The Social Anthropology of Complex Societies,* edited by Michael Banton, pp. 1-21. New York: Barnes and Noble, 1966.

World Development 6, no. 9/10 (September-October 1978).

Woy-Hazelton, Sandra. "Political Participation in Peru: A Military Model for Mobilization." Ph.D. dissertation, University of Virginia, 1978.

_____. "Political Participation in a Non-Electoral System." Paper presented at International Studies Association, Toronto, Canada, March 1979.

Index

Printed and bound by CPI Group (UK) Ltd, Croydon, CR0 4YY

09/06/2025

14685840-0004